My Happy Life

Darius Milhaud

My Happy Life

Translated from the French by
Donald Evans, George Hall
and Christopher Palmer

With an introductory essay by
Christopher Palmer

Marion Boyars
London • New York

Published in Great Britain and the United States
in 1995 by Marion Boyars Publishers
24 Lacy Road, London SW15 1NL
237 East 39th Street, New York NY 10016

Distributed in Australia and New Zealand by Peribo Pty Ltd
58 Beaumont Road, Mount Kuring-gai, NSW 2080

Originally published in 1987 by Editions Belfond under the title of *Ma Vie Heureuse*
© Editions Belfond 1987
© This translation Marion Boyars Publishers 1995

British Library Cataloguing in Publication Data
Milhaud, Darius
    My Happy Life   I. Title   II. Evans, Donald   III. Palmer,
    Christopher
    780.92

Library of Congress Cataloging in Publication
Milhaud, Darius, 1892–1974.
    [Ma vie heureuse. English]
    My happy life/Darius Milhaud; translated from the French by
Donald Evans and Christopher Palmer; with an introductory essay by
Christopher Palmer.
    Includes bibliographical references.
    1. Milhaud, Darius, 1892–1974.   2. Composers—France—Biography.
I. Title.
ML410.M674A3   1994
780'.92—dc20
[B]   94–9018

ISBN 0–7145–2957–5 Original paperback

Laserset in 11/13pt Times and Bookman by
Ann Buchan (Typesetters), Middlesex
Printed and bound in Great Britain by
Biddles Ltd, Guildford and King's Lynn

Contents

A Note on the Text

Milhaud's autobiography was originally called *Notes sans Musique* and was first published in 1949 in Paris by René Julliard; it took us up to the end of Chapter 34, with the Milhauds eagerly looking forward to their return to France after the war. Donald Evans' English translation, called *Notes without Music*, came out in 1952 and forms the basis of the present English edition. The complete text in French, re-titled *Ma Vie Heureuse*, was published in Paris by Belfond in 1974, the same year as Milhaud's death in Geneva in June 22. Those who are interested in a full, detailed listing of Milhaud's music are referred to the English edition of Paul Collaer's *Darius Milhaud* (San Francisco, 1988). The translator, Jane Hohfeld Galante, has established a definitive catalogue of works in association with Madeleine Milhaud, the composer's widow.   *C.P.*

Introduction

DARIUS MILHAUD: POET OF PROVENCE
by Christopher Palmer

Darius Milhaud once described in a radio interview an incident which took place at Mills College, a girls' college in Oakland, California where he taught during World War II and many years subsequently. It seems that one day, as Milhaud was sitting having lunch in the canteen with his students, one of them approached him, clearly in a state of some perturbation. There ensued the following conversation, or something like it:

STUDENT   Something you said yesterday disquieted me so much I could scarcely sleep for thinking and worrying about it.
MILHAUD   *(raising his eyebrows)* Oh? What? Why?
STUDENT   You said you had had a happy life. But how *can* a composer have a happy life? Surely he must fight with his wife, fall into debt, endure many difficulties and disappointments. Doesn't he need those conditions to produce great art?
MILHAUD   *(shrugging his shoulders in that placid manner of his)* Well, I manage otherwise.

This benighted girl had clearly been heavily influenced by an excess of Thomas Mann (probably *Tonio Kröger*) or Wagner, which amounts to much the same thing. Moreover, even as this student was berating him for having presumed to enjoy his 'happy' life, Milhaud would almost certainly have been sitting in the wheelchair to which he was confined for most of the latter part of his life.

'Happiness' is, of course, a quality of mind, an inborn state which has little or nothing to do with material circumstances, and everything to do with a sense of humour: the ability to see the world in a proper perspective. Those who are born without it tend to make life difficult both for themselves and for everybody else. Milhaud did not belong in that category. Madeleine Milhaud has described her husband as being an extremely easy man to live with; they were married for almost 50 years without ever exchanging a cross word. He was at ease with people in all walks of life. He genuinely *liked* people, loved to be surrounded by them and was genuinely interested in other composers and their music. Wherever they were, in Europe or America, the Milhauds kept open house and constantly made new friends without losing the old ones. Small wonder that Milhaud's pupil, the American composer and musicologist Everett Helm, described him as one of the finest examples of *homo sapiens* imaginable.

The key to this affable personality lies surely in the enormously strong racial and family security which enveloped Milhaud from birth. He sprang from one of the oldest Southern-French Jewish families. It could trace its roots back as far as the tenth century; and the outline of the strong, rugged Provençal hills was engraved on his subconscious from time immemorial. The result is that much, if not all, of his music is shaped and coloured by the physical characteristics of Aix and its environs, just as the novels of Jean Giono, such as *Le Chant du Monde* and *Que ma joie demeure* (read them, if you never have), and the paintings of Cézanne have made the Provençal landscape familiar to those who have never seen it. Peter Mayle's delightful *A Year in Provence* set out to tell us what it's really like to live in Provence. *He* needed a whole book; Milhaud requires only a few bars of music, if one is in the mood and lets the imagination rove. Garlic and olive-oil; village gardens and vineyards; intense heat and sharp, blinding light; damp, green, steamy and sensual summers: once we have experienced these characteristics of the real Provence we can never listen to Milhaud's earthy, chunky, robust music the same way again. Milhaud's lifelong friend and standard-bearer, Paul Collaer, has memorably described the 'vast unfolding landscape' which had so pervasive an influence on the young composer, just as it did on Bizet and Van Gogh:

It is both wild and orderly, like the landscape of Tuscany but more glowing; for along with grapevines and almond trees, the red, charred soil is overlaid with the wind-shifted gray or silver haze of olive orchards . . . . Around a bend in the road, all of a sudden, in a hollow, is 'yellow' Aix, or rather, 'russet' Aix, basking in the sunlight. It seems as though its rays penetrate the very heart of the stones, baking them thoroughly . . . . The abrasive sunlight, more than the Mistral, has eaten away the trimming on balconies and cornices. What an ode to summer the spectacle of this town is, glowing in the sun and dust, framed by yellow vegetation and ruddy earth: what an affirmation! Many other delights await the person who searches further into the byways of the city and discovers the secrets of life that emanate from them. Above all, he will be aware of contrasts: though Aix may be a symphony composed to the glory of the sun, there is also, beneath its plane trees, the deepest possible shade ... the splashing water from mossy fountains, located at every stree-corner, murmurs unceasingly. As shadow complements the brilliance of sunlight, so water satisfies this thirsty earth: where can this special equilibirum, this balance of contrasting passions, be better observed?[1]

I have dwelt at some length on the character of Provence as I feel it is impossible to appreciate Milhaud's music fully without some knowledge of it, even at second-hand. His music grows out of the landscape and is an integral part of it. Milhaud himself had no choice in the matter. He heard, saw and felt; and *wrote* what he heard, saw and felt. Armand Lunel, Milhaud's lifelong friend and librettist for many of his stage works, even suggests that the taste of Provençal almonds can be enjoyed in some of his works. Milhaud, it seems, habitually munched almonds from the first moment he was able to munch anything

The result is that Aix, in one form or another, is rarely absent from Milhaud's music. There are, of course, many works, often suites of shortish movements, which make their intentions clear in their titles: the *Suite provençale* (probably Milhaud's best-known work), the *Suite française*, the *Suite Campagnarde*, the *Cueillette des citrons* (*Intermède provençale*), the *Ouverture mediterranéen*, the *Carnaval d'Aix*, the *Symphonie Rurale* and others. We can be equally sure that the many works with the word '*printemps*' in their titles will also bring Provence to the mind's eye: there are two volumes of piano pieces so named, likewise the First Chamber Symphony, and the Concertino de Printemps for solo violin and small orchestra, one of Milhaud's most beautifully-made shorter works. The same is true in the case of the 'Pastorale' (the Second Chamber Symphony), the third movement of the Second Symphonic Suite (*'Protée'*), the *Fantaisie pastorale* for piano and orchestra, and so on. There is also much concern for 'old' music, following Stravinsky's lead in *Pulcinella*, where he showed how the seventeenth century could be updated to the twentieth without loss of dignity to the original; hence, in Milhaud's case, the *Suite provençale*, the *Suite d'après Corrette*, *L'Apothéose de Molière*, *Le Carnaval de Londres*, *La Cheminée du roi René* and others.

Now, all this might suggest that Milhaud was a mere sender of picture-postcards, or a skilful time-traveller. Nothing could be further from the truth. The same characteristics, mostly derived from folk-songs, nursery ditties and traditional tunes (for example the 'Lydian' sharp fourth, a C sharp in the scale of G major, a familiar modal connotation of freshness and innocence, turns up again and again) are unmistakable features of the Milhaud landscape, whether specifically designated as such or not. Take the

---

[1] *Darius Milhaud* by Paul Collaer, translated and edited by Jane Hohfeld Galante, San Francisco, 1988, pp. 2–4.

case of the First Symphony, Milhaud's first full-dress 'symphonic' symphony, not *Le Printemps*, which was his first *chamber* symphony. Milhaud
describes in *My Happy Life* how he first heard from his sickbed the news of
the invasion of Poland:

> Bedridden and incapable of working, I listened to the radio night and day.
> When I think back to that time now, it seems like some interminable period of
> waiting, in which the predominant feeling was one of impotence and frightful
> anguish ... yet I had to deliver a work for the Chicago Orchestra. The idea that
> it would be the only French work on the programme helped me shake off my
> torpor, and I made a start on my First Symphony. . . .

Milhaud reveals no more than that, but if we listen to this work, one of his
best, it is not difficult at all to hear the Provençal spring in the pastoral first
movement; the anguished turmoil of war in the second; deep sorrowing in
the third; and a finale in which a noble, proud, austere chorale is gradually
overrun by a lively crop of Provençal dance-tunes. We may also note the
recurrence of a characteristic type of drum-ensemble in Milhaud's symphonic scores: whether they have any specific Provençal connection or no,
the 'tambour provençal', a kind of deep tenor drum without snares, is a
regular member of this ensemble. Similarly in the *Fête de la lumière*, a half-
hour score composed for the 1937 Universal Exhibition in Paris (see *My
Happy Life*, p. 189) the flavour of Provence is noticeably stronger than that
of Paris, even though the music was designed to accompany light-shows
and firework displays along the banks of the Seine. And nothing can stop the
coda of *La Création du monde*, Milhaud's masterly stylization of a Harlem
jam session, from dissolving at the end, via oboe and sweetly sorrowing alto
saxophone, into the fresh mists of a Provençal spring.

Milhaud was fond of remarking that, for him, 'Provence' began in
Constantinople, passed via Aix and ended up in Rio de Janeiro; but it can be
argued that the great revelatory experience of Milhaud's life had nothing
immediately to do with Provence or with Provençal music.In 1916 the poet-
diplomat Paul Claudel, with whom Milhaud had already collaborated on a
number of stage-works including *Agamemnon*, *Protée* and *Les Choëphores,*
invited him to Rio de Janeiro as his secretary. Such an opportunity would
probably never come the young composer's way again, and he seized it
eagerly. It does seem there are young composers who need to be banished
from their familiar surroundings for a period: thereafter returning to them as
'new' people; that is, as men not boys. Delius and Britten are notable
examples. Delius, supposedly minding a grapefruit plantation in Florida
which his father had been talked into buying for him, encountered the
indigenous black music of the area — primarily spirituals treated vocally
with a wholly spontaneous, instinctive, non-European harmonic and rhythmic freedom — which haunted and possessed him for the rest of his life.

Britten endured his *saison en enfer* in North America and returned home a wiser man and a more mature composer. Milhaud himself describes so vividly the impact of the Latin American landscape and music on him that there is no need to rehearse it here: except to point out that it kindled in him a deep delight in popular traditional music wherever he might happen to find it: England, for instance, in his quodlibet on tunes from Gay's *Beggar's Opera* (*Le Carnaval de Londres*); North America (*Kentuckiana*, based on no fewer than 20 Kentuckian folk-tunes) and France herself in the *Suite française* for concert band (an orchestral version also exists, but is less effective). Percy Grainger paid a charming impromptu tribute to this last piece which probably never came to Milhaud's notice. Ten days after a 1948 concert at the Carnegie Hall in which Grainger conducted the Goldman Band in his own *Power of Rome and The Christian Heart*, he wrote in a round-letter to friends, after deriding his own piece, '. . . what I got from the Goldman Band Tone-show was PURE JOY in hearing Milhaud's *Suite française*, written straight for wind-band. What a bewitching work! What enthralling she-like little tunes darting about, what mastery of form and tone colour, what manly power in the use of 7-tone scales. . . .'[2]

The first musical fruits of Milhaud's Brazilian sojourn were the *Saudades do Brasil* for piano, later orchestrated. Let me quote from one of Leonard Bernstein's 1974 Harvard Lectures, *The Unanswered Question*, whose theme is the development of early twentieth-century music:

It wasn't only the Russian vernacular that attracted [Stravinsky] but *all* vernaculars, old and new — an international street language, so to speak, which ultimately included jazz, café music, and salon music, with all their attendant waltzes, polkas, foxtrots, tangos, and rags. Here was yet another department of fresheners for tonality, letting some fresh air into a stuffy post-Victorian room — a totally different air, chemically different from that other-planetary air, that '*Luft vom anderen Planeten*' that Schoenberg was breathing at the same time. But on Stravinsky's planet people now spoke in the vernacular; post-World War I aesthetic life could be relaxed, facile, and fun. This new aesthetic relaxation caught on like wildfire, so attractive was the sheer relief of it. It was to produce pieces like this delectable *Saudade do Brasil* by Darius Milhaud; and the point to note is not only that it is bitonal, the left hand in G and the right hand in D, but that is a Parisian speaking the Brazilian vernacular. Do you see how charming and relaxed bitonality can be?

'Fun', yes; although there's more to the *Saudades* than just 'fun'. *Le Boeuf sur le toit* is more consistently 'funny'. At the beginning, the strings are playing in C major; the flute pipes up in E flat major, only to be answered by the flute in F sharp major. That is certainly Milhaud at his 'funniest' in a fantasy on popular Brazilian themes — see *My Happy Life* pp. 86–88 —

[2] Quoted in J. Bird, *Percy Grainger*, London 1976, p. 225

designed solely for entertainment and amusement: sexy rhythms, charming tunes and instrumental effects, and the purest Milhaud from first to last. Counterpoint is scaffolding, pressed ineluctably into the service of one of those lovely Bach-like muddles. Incidentally, doesn't this piece brand Milhaud as one of the first 'cross-over' composers to produce music of lasting merit? Music-hall, jazz, circus, bal musette: all were grist to the Milhaudian mill; and the fact that both *Le Boeuf* and *La Création du monde* are among his most recorded works bears witness to his skill in making these transitions. Other composers who attempted them are for the most part forgotten.

There is, however, another vitally important dimension to Milhaud's multi-tonal experiments. A remark made to Collaer is astonishingly revealing. Milhaud claimed that when he was in the country at night, 'I would feel rays and tremors converging on me from all points in the sky and from below ground, simultaneous musics rushing towards me from all directions.' In other words, Milhaud had a quite special vision of how nature-mysticism, nature-worship, might be articulated. He was, however, not altogether original in creating this musical language. As we know, Stravinsky (*Petrushka* and *Le Sacre du printemps*) is generally reckoned to be the father of modern bitonality and polychordality. Although we cannot dispute the influence of Stravinsky's *Soldier's Tale* and *Mavra* on Milhaud's own chamber-operas (e.g. *Les Malheurs d'Orphée*) and we have also mentioned *Pulcinella* in relation to the *Suite provençale, L'Apothéose de Molière* and other 'new-old' music, it would be quite wrong to attribute Milhaud's innovations in the sphere of pitchless percussion to *Les Noces*. The latter came out in its definitive version (the earlier ones were never published) only in 1923; *Les Choëphores* was completed some eight years before, in 1915. Furthermore, there was another, quieter voice whose explorations into this particular area of *terra incognita* were no less thorough-going for receiving less than their share of réclame. This was Charles Koechlin.

Koechlin is one of the great unknowns of twentieth-century French music. His opus-tally cannot lag that far behind Milhaud's, although, unlike Milhaud's, very little of it has been published or even performed. Like Milhaud, he was taught by André Gédalge, from whom they both claimed to have learned everything of value relating to the technical composition of music. Both Koechlin and Milhaud idolized Debussy. Koechlin was also much attracted to Fauré, and to the music of the early Renaissance and the Middle Ages; from these he evolved non-metrical rhythms, polymodal lines and polyharmonic textures. He often dispenses with key signatures and time signatures in a further quest of that quasi-improvisational freedom which was Debussy's ideal and Milhaud's. And, like Milhaud, Koechlin's technical experimentation was generally a means to an end rather than an end in itself; that 'end' being to penetrate Nature in her complexity and profundity.

Koechlin's early reading of Jules Verne instilled in him a love of the night sky, ocean depths, the primeval forest, effects of light — all long-time favourite Impressionist attractions — but both Koechlin and Milhaud wanted to take these further. The very titles of Koechlin's symphonic works are indicative enough — *La Forêt Paienne* (ballet), *La Forêt* (symphonic poem in two parts), *En Mer, La Nuit, L'Automne, Soleil et Danse dans la Forêt, Vers la plage lointaine*, a pair of symphonic poems (*Le Printemps* and *L'Hiver*), a matching pair entitled *L'Été* ('Nuit de juin' and 'Midi en août'), *Suite legendaire* (among whose movements are '*l'ame de Mélisande revient la nuit, dans la forêt*'), *Vers la voute etoilée, Sur les flots lointains* — and a vast cycle of symphonic poems after Kipling, one of which (*Les Bandar-Log*) was the first of Koechlin's larger works to become generally known, thanks to a recording released in the late 1960s with Antal Dorati conducting. Many of these larger orchestral scores were composed contemporaneously with Milhaud's as the century wore on. What Milhaud came to know and be influenced by in his formative years would have been the early songs, the piano and chamber music. Milhaud was in fact the dedicatee of the consistently polytonal Sonata for viola and piano (1906–15) and gave its first performance. Moreover, Milhaud may well have derived his love and aptitude for counterpoint not only from Gédalge but also from Koechlin, a fanatical admirer of J.S. Bach. In 1947, Milhaud had to listen to the first European performance of his Second Symphony from his sickbed in Aix; but the aged Koechlin was present and wrote him an appreciative letter, particularly with regard to the fugal finale, 'Alleluia', which was clearly inspired by thoughts of the liberation of Paris, dating from 1944. Milhaud remained a loyal friend and supporter of Koechlin to the end of the latter's life. This is hardly to be wondered at, since if we had to isolate one particular figure as mentor and guide for Milhaud in the years when he was still developing a musical speech of his own, it would have to be Koechlin. This has been a longish digression in his favour but, I believe, a worthwhile one; and I am sure Milhaud would have approved.

Koechlin would certainly have approved of an extraordinary work in which many of his ideas are exploited to the full, namely *L'Homme et son désir*, a musical poem of South American jungle and rain-forest. Milhaud and Claudel, the librettist, have left between them such a full account of the work that little needs to be added except to remark that *L'Homme et son désir* has striking affinities with Ives's *Central Park in the Dark* and many works by Percy Grainger[3] which aspire to the ideal of freedom from bar-

[3] There is an interesting link between Koechlin and Grainger in that they were both powerfully motivated by Kipling: particularly by the *Jungle Book*, whose evocations of boyhood in a physically and metaphysically remote India are legendary. Most are rites of passage and myths of rebirth — exactly what Milhaud's *L'Homme et son désir* is, although *his* jungle was for real. As I write, Koechlin's complete *Jungle Book* has just been issued on CD for the first time.

lines and key-monopolies. This is all in the interest of emulating Nature, exploring the complexities of man's *relationship* with Nature, penetrating the deeper mysteries of Nature herself, recording for all to hear at least one night in the life of our vanished Eden. The music ranges unselfconsciously from euphony to cacophony; but since cacophony is not synonymous with atonality, and since tonality is an acoustical fact of Nature, it is an acoustical fact of Milhaud's music too, however uncompromisingly dissonant it may sound. And for those with tuned-in hearing, fresh-toned memories of Provence rarely hide from view, however thick the surrounding tangle of undergrowth.

The two books of *Saudades do Brasil* (for piano or orchestra) are based on the music of Ernesto Nazareth and also use bitonality in their much simpler way, more as a matter of colour and to enhance the evocative and atmospheric power of the music. The effect is, as Leonard Bernstein says, magical. *L'Enfant prodigue* (cantata after Gide) was an early experiment in which, as Milhaud says, 'I recaptured the sounds I had dreamed of as a child, when I closed my eyes for sleep and seemed to hear music I thought I should never be able to express.' Another work (or rather a *pair* of works) in which I'm sure Milhaud consciously aspired to this ideal is the String Quartet No. 14 coupled with No. 15. In an astonishing feat of contrapuntal virtuosity, Milhaud composed them in such a way that they can be performed either individually or simultaneously as an Octet. Milhaud makes a point of describing how moved he was upon hearing these two quartets finally played together shortly after they were completed, between 1948 and 1949. This was surely because, ultimately and definitively, he was hearing 'the sounds he had dreamed of as a child which I thought I should never be able to express.'

Around the time of *L'Homme et son désir*, the *Saudades* and *L'Enfant prodigue* Milhaud also wrote the first of his 'Little' or 'Chamber' symphonies; the first three ('Le Printemps', 'Pastorale' and 'Serenade'), being nature-music, naturally lead the composer to apply bitonal procedures; too late, now, to rely on Debussy. The result of these contrivances of euphonious dissonance is wholly successful. No South American ingredients are left in this mix, but Milhaud never saw any reason to eliminate them wholly from his system. The 'Souvenir de Rio' in *Le Carnaval d'Aix* is a charming cameo; the two-piano suites *Scaramouche*, *La Libertadore*, *Le Bal martiniquais*, *Les Songes* and *Carnaval à la Nouvelle-Orléans* are all full-scale dance-pieces with strong Latin American elements. *Le Bal martiniquais* dates from the time of the liberation of Paris, with Milhaud recalling the scenes of joy and triumph with which the 1918 Armistice was greeted. After Milhaud returned home he composed *Paris* in 1948, for not two but *four* pianos; that is, eight hands. Most of these suites exist in orchestral format (why do we never hear them?) yet the multiple piano medium is excitingly well-attuned to Milhaud's idiom. Those clangourous, chunky polychords — great fistfuls of them, often — make a clearer, cleaner impact, with the occasional salutary blow to the listener's solar plexus, than when we hear them mixed, and therefore blurred, in with the orchestra. A strong Latin-American input is, not surprisingly, also present in the great Central-American operatic trilogy of the 1930s and 1940s, *Maximilien*, *Bolivar* and, what is probably Milhaud's outstanding masterpiece in the genre, *Christophe Colomb*. The American Marc Blitztein, composer of *The Cradle Will Rock*, told Wilfrid Mellers he considered *Christophe Colomb* to be one of the great operas of the century.

Milhaud described himself as a Mediterranean composer first and last. His mother was Italian[4], and right from the start he was a dedicated Germanophobe, at least as far as music was concerned. In later years he found more concrete reasons to be anti-German, as the note appended to the score of his *Suite française* makes clear:

> The five parts of this Suite are named after French Provinces, the very ones in which the American and Allied armies fought, together with the French Underground, for the liberation of my country: Normandy, Brittany, the Île de France (of which Paris is the centre), Alsace Lorraine and Provence.
> I used some folk-tunes of these provinces. I wanted the young Americans to hear the popular melodies of those parts of France where their fathers and brothers fought to defeat the German invaders, who in less than seventy years have brought war, destruction, cruelty, torture and murder three times to the peaceful and democratic people of France.

Yet Milhaud conducted many an early performance of Schoenberg's *Pierrot Lunaire*, and it was in Berlin, in 1930, that he scored one of the great triumphs of his career, namely the premiere of *Christophe Colomb*. To appreciate the motive force of Milhaud's operas, we need to assimilate what Collaer says *à propos* the Provençal artist's deep inner need 'to be cast in the same mould of wisdom that has shaped the Mediterranean mind from time immemorial, shaped it and given it its deep religious conviction . . . the Mediterranean spirit consists of a lyric quality based on eternal truths and commonly shared by all the inhabitants of the littoral. This is the spirit of the *Odyssey*, of Greek tragedy, Hebrew scriptures, the Bible, Horace and Virgil.' No wonder Milhaud's Jewish heritage inspired many of his most powerful and beautiful works: the *Poèmes juifs*, the *Six Chants populaires hébraïques*, the *Service Sacré* (Sabbath Morning Service), the opera *David* and the cantata *Le Chateau du feu* (a short but harrowing piece in which Milhaud confronts the actuality of the concentration camps). It cannot be by accident that so many of the subjects of his operas are rooted in myth and

---

[4] Her maiden name was Allantini. *Allantinis* may be bought in your local delicatessen: they are a biscuit-like confection subtly flavoured with orange and chocolate.

legend and explore, in his own highly original manner, the immemorial priorities of human rights and responsibilities. This was a concept that first encouraged Milhaud to experiment with polychords and non-musical sonorities in which the former are used as an enhanced means of expression in the *piano* and *forte*, that is, in the wider, richer subtleties of both sweetness and violence; and the latter are a kind of stylized recreation of how humans would have communicated with each other before speech, then in heightened speech and song, out of which the lyrical quality has evolved. It is a fascinating topic and one which I have not really the space to treat adequately here. Let us at least note, however, the seemingly inevitable way in which Milhaud's music gradually gained pre-eminence as Claudel's Aeschylean triptych took shape. *Agamemnon*, the first of the three tragedies, has very little music. *Les Choëphores*, on the other hand, has a fairly substantial score and has been recorded several times, in whole or in parts. Ironically, although *Les Euménides*, the third part of the triptych, is a through-composed no holds barred opera, no actual recording of it has been made since Louis de Vocht's 78s of the finale, produced in the 1920s. This is no doubt on account both of its excessive difficulty and the demands it makes in terms of numbers of performers. The critic Ronald Crichton had some revealing comments to make on *Les Euménides* in *Opera* magazine:

> Sometimes in the ensembles Milhaud lays on polytonality almost as a colour wash. In *Les Euménides*, when the crowd swarms on the Acropolis for the trail of Orestes and the goddess Athena, who has saved him with her casting vote, ordains the formation of a great procession, it is almost impossible to follow the individual lines and blocks of sound yet the accumulated reverberations are tremendous [the vocal-piano score needs six staves — i.e. 3 players — to accommodate all the notes]. At the long-delayed premiere of *Les Euménides* (Belgian Radio, Brussels, 1949) I was suddenly reminded of a morning a few months previously on the deck of a steamer in Piraeus harbour, when I was spellbound by the wonderful mixture of sounds from the crowd on the quay below bangs, crashes, shuntings, snatches of song, competing cries of vendors, violent disputes. There, one realized, was a real Greek chorus. At the party afterwards I rather nervously mentioned this to Milhaud. 'That is exactly what I wanted,' he replied, 'I had a similar experience in the Piraeus many years ago.'

Look now at the later operas: *Les Malheurs d'Orphée*, *Le Pauvre Matelot*, the three *opéras-minute* (*L'Enlèvement d'Europe*, *L'Abandon d'Ariane*, *La délivrance de Thésée*), *Esther de Carpentras*, *Médée* and *David*. All have their backgrounds in myth or folk-tale. The theme of *Christophe Colomb*, *Maximilien* and *Bolivar* is, in each case, the rights of man. Milhaud treats these ideas of human justice in grandly-conceived historical tableaux whose elaboration and complexity inevitably place obstacles in the way of their being produced today. This is particularly regrettable in the case of *Christophe Colomb*, an opera conceived on the grandest scale. Part symbolic, part expressionist, its structure refers to Greek tragedy and its all-important chorus to the medieval mystery-play and to the Wagnerian leitmotif. Milhaud's vision calls for a small army of executants, including 45 vocal soloists, an offstage orchestra, non-singing actors and a huge chorus; plus filmed sequences to be inserted as backdrops at strategic points. All facets of Milhaud's polymorphous musical personality are represented in this tremendous work, whose impact registers and reverberates unforgettably even on record.

My use of the word 'polymorphous' just now was, I must admit, an unconscious reference on my part to Milhaud's *Protée,* a work which, when I first heard it as a student, on Monteux's old San Francisco recording, turned me into a Milhaud fan for life. It is, however, a key work in relation to Milhaud's own personality, which changes by the minute; *Christophe Colomb*, for example, with all its mountainous dramaturgical paraphernalia, was written in 1928, the year following the three *opéras-minutes*. 'Contradictory' and 'paradoxical' are other epithets which apply; their thematic relationship to 'polymorphous' scarcely needs much pointing out. Milhaud indeed is a mass of contradictions or paradoxes: miraculously they all gel and with no trace, except in his student years, of eclecticism. A statesman and spokesman for Provence, who is one of twentieth-century music's great cosmopolitans; a composer whose expressive range encompasses both the tremulously tender and the volcanically violent; who can carve on a cherry-stone one minute and fill the largest, gaudiest canvas the next. And despite his renunciation of Wagner and Wagnerism, Milhaud came closer to realizing Wagner's ideal of the *Gesamtkunstwerk* in his mixed-media conception of *Christophe Colomb* than Wagner himself ever did. Whatever kind of twentieth-century music it is we like, we can probably find it in Milhaud if we look diligently enough.

Why, one wonders, has Milhaud never quite achieved the popular success of his contemporaries, Poulenc and Honegger? Of the other members of Les Six, Auric ceased to be a vital force quite early, and Durey and Tailleferre have long disappeared into the footnotes of history books. For a start, there is the sheer intimidating bulk of Milhaud's output. He finally closed his account at Op. 443, and, apart from the faithful Collaer, it is doubtful if any living person can claim familiarity, either through study or live performance or records, of *every* Milhaud score. Inevitably, of course, the output is variable. In my experience, however, I have yet to encounter a work by Milhaud which doesn't have *something* good in it. Mostly there are many good things. But what do we make of this immense productivity, of this ceaseless outpouring of music in all genres and for all media? Let us also not forget that there is far more to producing a work than merely producing the work. There are proofs to be read, often two or three sets; vocal or piano scores to be prepared of ballets or operas; individual parts of orchestral works to be checked. Then, of course, there is the routine of rehearsal, performance and maybe recording, and the bigger the work, the more time it consumes. Much of Milhaud's fecundity as a composer must have been promoted by his accomplishments as a performer. He was a fine pianist who wrote piano concerti and other works for himself to play with the orchestra (for example Piano Concerto No. 2, *Le Carnaval d'Aix*, *Ballade* and *Pastorale*). As a violinist he premiered his Second Violin Sonata, Sonata for Two Violins and Piano, and as a member of the Soëtans Quartet, String Quartets Nos. 1 and 2. He was also sufficiently well thought-of to be invited by the publisher Durand to participate in the world premiere of Debussy's Sonata for Flute, Viola and Harp in December 1915. He began to conduct from an early age. In later years this was the only performing activity he could undertake, and until quite late in life he made many guest appearances, albeit seated. He was also present at many recordings of his own works. Clearly, all these commitments made inroads into Milhaud's composing time; but he once explained that, like Mozart and Malcolm Arnold, he finished every detail of a composition in his mind before putting pen to paper.This latter process was simply a mechanical process which could be carried out with the greatest dispatch; nor did he ever revise anything. There are stories of Milhaud discussing a commissioned work with the artist at dinner one night and appearing at breakfast the following morning with a completed score under his arm. These stories may or may not be true; I don't want to give any more particulars for fear of disseminating disinformation!

As I said earlier, the girl-student who challenged Milhaud on the artistic validity of his 'happy life' was apparently oblivious of the wheelchair. This had been in increasing use since the 1930s, and from the 1950s onwards, Milhaud was more or less permanently confined either to it or to his bed, a victim of rheumatoid arthritis. He had suffered from poor health since childhood. Madeleine is of the opinion that an increasingly sedentary lifestyle, in which he was writing those reams and reams of music, did nothing to help. Whatever the reason, the fact remains that Darius became less and less mobile as time went on. Often the severity of a bout of ill health seemed to be directly induced by any great emotional and psychological stress, as when the Nazis were over-running Europe and hammering at the gates of *la douce France* itself . Milhaud knew that, as one of the most prominent representatives of Jewish culture, he would be one of the first to be arrested; the Nazi authorities would have already noted his popularity and many successes in pre-Nazi Germany (particularly with *Christophe Colomb*) and the fact that many of his works had been issued by Universal-Edition, an Austrian publisher. Madeleine said to her husband, 'My dear, I can do many things for you, but I cannot put you on my shoulders and carry you to a place of safety.' When they returned after the cessation of hostilities it was to find their homes looted and a Wagner score ensconced on the piano in the Boulevard de Clichy apartment. Most of the Milhauds' possessions in the latter had been stolen by their concierge, but they managed to retrieve many of them. Worst of all for his health, however, was the time in 1947 when Milhaud finally made his way back to Aix. Then it was that the full horror of what had taken place finally hit him. He knew that from then on Aix was his *Paradis Perdu*, to which he could never return. Mills College and, eventually, Geneva, came ultimately to replace it.

There are several important, indeed amazing, points to be made about this life-long history of physical adversity. Firstly, in spite of everything, Milhaud always retained his serenity. Those who knew him and saw him close-to speak of fine-cut features of the greatest delicacy and refinement, countermanding the overall impression of physical bulk. Secondly, Milhaud rarely permitted his incapacity to interfere with his passion for travel — and it really *was* a passion, as all readers of *My Happy Life* will appreciate. Madeleine recalls that, even at the very end of his life, when a heart condition and the fitting of a pace-maker restricted his mobility further still, she might announce that she was going shopping, and Milhaud would say simply: 'I will come with you.' If he were working at the time he would bring writing implements and paper with him and continue in the car. In other words, he was determined at all times to be living a full life in every feasible particular. This brings me to my third point: it is arguable that Milhaud's increasingly enforced immobility actually stimulated his productivity. He claimed that he inherited the discipline of regular work from his mother, and this stood him in good stead all his life; but we also know that, quite often, the deterioration of one faculty is counterbalanced by enhanced activity in another. So it seems likely that, increasingly traumatized by pain and physical infirmity, Milhaud's creativity may have been stimulated and enhanced. It would certainly be in keeping with what we know of his personality, which was strong and determined and irradiated optimism: 'whatever the day bringeth thee, set it down as gain.' Had that poor student — and I've probably been castigating her quite unduly — learned the wisdom of that maxim from her distinguished mentor, his *vie heureuse*, his 'happy life' would surely have been hers for the asking. Milhaud's sturdy optimism and generosity of spirit strongly echo the words spoken by the blind and paralyzed Delius to his amanuensis Eric Fenby, around 1930: 'Not being able to see does not trouble me. I have seen the best of the earth and done everything that was worth doing. I am content. I have had a wonderful life.'

Christopher Palmer
London — Blackheath, 1994

Preface to the Original Edition

How many times have I been told: 'You ought to write your memoirs!' 'Impossible — I have such a bad memory.' 'That doesn't matter; you've known so many artists and musicians and been everywhere . . . .' 'Yes, but so many others have described all these things better than I could. Besides, except for the catalogue of my works which might help me to supply a few exact dates, I don't possess a single letter or document . . . .' 'Well then, talk about yourself.' It is true there is so much misunderstanding between the public, the critics, and myself that I should be quite pleased to clear some of it away. That decided me.

It was August 25, 1944. Paris had just been liberated, and, for the first time, after four dramatic years during which our despondency contrasted with the hospitality and comfort we enjoyed in the United States, it was possible at last to foresee final victory. After being ill for seven months I was obliged to rest and recuperate at the Stanford Hospital at San Francisco, and had time to look back over the half-century which had been my life.

I am going to conjure up memories of my friends and of my travels. I am going to try to describe the course of my musical development without going into technicalities, and without any literary pretensions. This book, jotted down in fits and starts, will perhaps help to throw light upon certain aspects of musical history during the last thirty years in the form of 'notes' — but this time, without music.

Chapter One

Origins

I am a Frenchman from Provence, and, by religion, a Jew.

The establishment of the Jews in the South of France dates back to remote antiquity. Six hundred years before Christ, when the city of Marseilles was founded, the Phocaeans, the Greeks and the Jews set up their counting-houses on the shores of the Mediterranean in France, and so came there not as emigrants, but as traders. There are tombstones showing that there were Jews in the Rhône valley before the Christian era. At that time the Jewish religion was the only one that was monotheistic, and conversions among the Gauls were very numerous. After the second destruction of the Temple the Jews emigrated from Palestine to Italy, Spain and Provence. In Provence they amalgamated with the Jewish colony which was living there under comparatively peaceful conditions . . . Nevertheless, early in the twelfth century King René, Count of Provence, threatened them with exile unless they all became converted to Christianity. According to the archives of the Museum of Old Aix, two noble families of Aix, who pride themselves that they have never allowed a Jew to cross the threshold of their house, would seem to be, by a charming irony of fate, the descendants of Jews who were forced to embrace the Christian faith . . . And yet a large number of Israelites refused to forswear their faith, and preferred exile at Avignon or elsewhere in the County ('Comtat') of Venaissin.

The 'County' belonged to the Popes after 1274, and the Jews, under their jurisdiction, were extremely well treated. They were, indeed, so well aware of their good fortune that they were afraid of losing it, and it was for this reason that they refused hospitality to the wandering tribes of Askenazi

Jews (Russians, Poles or Germans fleeing from persecution) whose manners and customs differed from their own. The Library at Carpentras possesses a request presented to the Cardinal Bishop for 'four sergeants to guard the gates of their "quarry" [the popular name for the Jewish quarter] so as to prevent the vagabonds from entering there'. Their request was granted in return for a few sacks of saffron.

The Jews used to speak a jargon consisting of a mixture of Hebrew and Provençal. A little Jewish-Provençal dictionary containing a fairly complete list of these expressions, which are still used in the South of France by a few persons respectful of tradition, was published about the year 1860 in a Hebrew Almanack in Paris. Armand Lunel found several folklore texts written in Hebrew-Provençal dialect, very humorous and outspoken in style — carols in the form of dialogues, with one strophe in Provençal favouring the conversion of the Jews, and another in Hebrew refuting the arguments of the Christians; some *Pioutims* (circumcision songs); a little eighteenth-century comedy describing a visit paid by the Jews Arcanoth and Barcanoth to the Bishop; and a 'Tragedy of Queen Esther'.

Like most of their co-religionists, the Mediterranean Jews bore the names of towns: Lunel, Milhaud, Bédarrides, Monteux, Valabrègue etc . . . The 'County' was the only place where their names were entered in the official archives, and their genealogy can be traced down to the Middle Ages. The Library at Carpentras and the Calvet Museum at Avignon possess some interesting documents of this kind. I have seen there a sixteenth-century picture representing a view of Carpentras, with its ramparts, belfries and low-built houses, and its 'quarry' where the houses sometimes were fifteen storeys high because there was not enough space for the growing population. Each tenant in the 'quarry' became the owner of the floor he lived on, looked upon the Pope as the Head of the State, and hung his portrait on the wall opposite the traditional print representing 'Moses and the Tables of the Law'. Prayers were also said for the Pope in the synagogues.

The Provençal rite resembles, in its pronunciation of liturgical Hebrew, that of the Sephardims, or Latin Jews; but the services are slightly different. There are only two synagogues in France which date from before the Revolution: one at Cavaillon, in Louis XV style, and the other at Carpentras whose foundations, as well as the women's ritual bathing pool, date from the Middle Ages. This one was rebuilt under Louis XVI, and is decorated with finely-worked wood panelling and enchanting chandeliers more suggestive of an elegant *salon* than of a sacred edifice. Thanks to the generosity of Madame Fernand Halphen and the Fine Arts Administration these two temples have been restored and classified as 'historical monuments'. The Temple at Aix-en-Provence was founded in 1840. The speech at the inauguration was delivered by my great-grandfather, at that time President of the Consistory and Administrator of the Temple, who was succeeded in this position by his sons and grandsons. I intended to celebrate with my father the centenary of this little synagogue, and composed a Cantata, *Couronne de gloire*, on three texts by Gabirol, a Jewish Renaissance poet, and on three taken from the 'Comtadin' (Provençal) liturgy translated by Armand Lunel: *Prière pour le pape, Prière pour les ames des persécutés*, and *Chant pour le jour de la réclusion*. Unfortunately the sad events of 1940 prevented us from carrying out our project.[1]

My paternal ancestors came from the Venaissin 'Comtat'. I found among the family archives some old papers stamped with the pontifical arms dating from the fifteenth century where mention is made of a Milhaud from Carpentras in connection with some lawsuit. I have also been told that when Mirabeau needed four thousand pounds to go to Paris he asked my great-great-grandfather, Benestruc Milhaud, for the money, promising in exchange 'to make a man of him'. He kept his word, since the Jews acquired their citizenship rights after the Revolution. My great-grandfather, Joseph Milhaud, was born in the reign of Louis XV, and as he lived to a great age he witnessed all the different régimes that followed the Revolution, and died as the Third Republic was born. Of a profoundly religious nature, he wrote works of religious exegesis, including a study of the Pentateuch and the book of Deuteronomy, and a life of Jethro. He was made responsible for establishing a census of all the Israelites who returned to France after the Revolution. I have unearthed some of these lists; many of the names are followed by a note: 'Naturalized French after the restoration of the Venaissin "Comtat".' My grandmother, Précile Valabrègue, came from a large family living in Carpentras. One of her brothers was in the madder-dyeing business — the colour that was used for French soldiers' trousers but which fell into disuse after the invention of chemical dyes.

My mother, Sophie Allatini, was born at Marseilles. Her parents, who came from Modena, were descendants of the Sephardim Jews who have been established in Italy for centuries, and one of her ancestors in the fifteenth century was medical adviser to the Pope. Her family was very numerous and had vast business interests all over the world. Her grandfather owned the tobacco monopoly in Austria, a bank at Marseilles, mines in Serbia and flour-mills at Salonica which were run by French engineers on the model of those at Corbeil. My mother had spent a year in Turkey when she was a child and had a fund of stories and memories of her stay there which she used to tell me when I was small. She described the customs of the Jews who had been at Salonica ever since their expulsion from Spain in

[1] This work was a sequel to *Prières Journalières à l'usage des Juifs du Comtat Venaissin* composed in 1929, and to *Trois chants de Rosch Haschanna (Liturgie Comtadine)*, authentic liturgical melodies which I harmonized freely.

the fifteenth century and still spoke the language as it used to be spoken then.[2]

My mother used to tell me stories about the adventures and misdeeds of the brigands who lived in caves in the mountains, and of how the brigand chief once called on my grandfather to ask him for one of his estates which he coveted, in return for which he promised his protection, not only for him, but for all his family. And as my grandfather was on such friendly terms with the brigand chief he was often able to help those who were captured and arrange for them to be ransomed. My mother used to speak of going riding on horseback with her father; sometimes they would be rudely disturbed by herds of wild buffalo. She recalled, too, the visits paid them by Pashas, to whom, according to oriental custom, you had to offer anything to which they took a fancy, and the 'Khavas', armed to the teeth, who stood sentinel outside the dors. But what I liked best to dream about, being a spoilt and greedy child, were the rose-flavoured syrups which the Turkish servants used to bring to my mother, on silver trays, after the siesta.

[2] In Paris there is a little Temple, in the Rue Saint-Lazare, still frequented by the Salonica Jews. There I have heard, at the Feast of Purim, the *Story of Esther* sung in old Spanish. It is a fine language, rather harsh and primitive, but very impressive.

Chapter Two

My Childhood

After their marriage my parents settled at Le Bras d'Or in Aix-en-Provence. It was in this old house that my childhood was spent. When I was still very young I was already sensitive to my surroundings and to familiar noises. Le Bras d'Or was in the centre of the town, on a little square which was the terminus of both the Avignon road and the Cours Sextius. From my window I could see the whole length of the Cours Sextius as far as the Hydro, which on market days especially was very entertaining. It was thronged with farm-carts and mules and provisions of every kind; and, just as you see them in a picture by Cézanne, there were blue-bloused peasants drinking and playing cards in the cafés.

The 'south room', opposite my bedroom, was kept specially for me; it was, in turn, play-room, school-room and music-room. How often did I linger there, watching the distant trees which lined the road to Marseilles and the soft curve of the hills on the horizon outlined in the setting sun. . . .

But what attracted and intrigued me most was 'the station' — a goods depot situated behind our house which was nearly always deserted and only used when the main station was too congested. It was at its best during military manoeuvres, when it was crowded with soldiers in their red and blue uniforms, guns, lorries, ambulances and horses. An officer would shout out orders and the train would — sometimes — steam out. But more often than not there was no engine attached during these entrainment exercises.

We occupied the whole of the first floor of Le Bras d'Or. My father, who was the director of a firm exporting almonds (founded by his grandfather in 1806), had his offices on the ground floor. In the mornings, still half asleep,

I could hear the women pushing their trolleys laden with sacks, the conversation of the men loading and unloading the drays, the noise of the latter being driven off drawn by a couple of powerful horses and, dominating everything else, the exclamations of the drivers swearing in Provençal!

The sounds I heard from the south room were quite different: the hum of conversation and scraps of song that floated up to me were mingled with the soft sound of fruit falling into the baskets and the monotonous and soothing drone of the machines for sorting the almonds: the *flots*, the *béraudes*, the *cassées* and the *avolas*. Sometimes in the evenings, too, the same sounds could be heard again, and I would lie listening to echoing voices, distant singing and the rumble of drays until I fell asleep.

I was a well-behaved but rather neurotic child, continually subject to nervous attacks which would be brought on by the slightest thing — a fright, a noise in the dark, a shadow. I shall always remember the shadow cast by the huge alabaster vase which stood on the mantelpiece in my parents' room, magnified in the wavering light of my bedside lamp. And how many times, when we were travelling, did I force them to change our hotel bedroom because I could not take my eyes from the flowers on the wallpaper intertwined with geometrical figures at which I would gaze unceasingly until overcome with terror. And nothing could relieve my anguish until my mother appeared to give me a dose of bromide.

The three daughters of my uncle David Milhaud, who was my father's partner, were like sisters to me, especially the eldest, Rosine. She was almost the same age as I was, and we used to go out together every day. She was vivacious and charming, and led me into all kinds of mischief which I would never have thought of alone. My grandmother, Précile Milhaud, lived opposite us in the same house as my cousins. She was sensitive, reserved and shy; she did not like going out very much, and we used to lunch with her every Saturday. At Passover the family circle was almost complete; our uncles and aunts used to come from Lyons for the holidays and joined us at the traditional dinner during which my father read prayers in Hebrew while we ate *coudoles* (the local name for the unleavened bread which the Jews eat at Passover). These *coudoles* came from Carpentras and were of many different kinds. My uncle, Michel Milhaud, who was a solicitor in Paris, used to come with his wife and two children, Etienne and Madeleine. The latter, who was ten years my junior, had a mischievous little face framed in golden curls. Ever since she was quite small she used to amuse us by imitating Sarah Bernhardt and reciting the fables of La Fontaine.

My uncle Michel had very definite ideas about hygiene, and Rosine and I were always very amused by the row of gloves which they used for their toilet hanging out to dry on the balcony; for the 'Parisians' changed them every day and used a different pair for each part of their bodies. Their luxurious ways, their elegance and their little foibles excited in my cousins and myself a feeling of inferiority mixed with a touch of irony.

Every summer my parents left their house, and we went to stay with grandmother Précile on the outskirts of the town on an estate which had belonged to my great-grandfather. I always liked going there, and it is one of the places where I have done my best work. L'Enclos, built level with the earth without any basement, like most Provençal houses in the country, was deliciously cool and fresh inside in summer if one were careful to keep all the doors and windows shut. There was a big garden, divided in two by a path lined with chestnut trees, and a terrace where my parents liked to sit in the shade of four huge plane-trees. In certain years it became a rendezvous for sparrows; there they indulged in their mysterious games and made the air thrum with the flutter of their wings. Little paths fringed with spindle-trees, laurel, Abraham's balm, Japanese medlar and arbutus, wound in and out among these trees, and this was my chosen domain, where I would read and work under an arbour of honeysuckle, looking out over the kitchen-gardens and the vines that clambered over the trellis round the tennis court. A little row of quince-trees and hazel, above which towered a tall cypress, a pine and two cedars, ran alongside the Vauvenargues road as far as the little entrance to our grounds. Every day I used to perch in the topmost branch of one of the cedars and watch for the carriage in which my father would drive home to lunch. His punctuality was so proverbial that many people used to set their watches when they saw Monsieur Milhaud drive along the Cours Mirabeau. The garden at L'Enclos seemed huge to me, and this was not the only favourite corner of mine that it contained; there was a little paddock with a pretty fountain and all kinds of trees, magnolias, acacias, lime-trees of the kind known as muscat, and a crape myrtle whose slightly draped foliage bowed beneath the weight of pink, almost purple, flowers. As a precaution against drought, my grandfather had built an enormous orna-mental pond quite out of proportion to the size of our garden, and here I loved to lie and watch the swallows lured there by its waters, or to clamber up on its stone parapet to catch a glimpse of the surrounding countryside.

The meadow abutting on one of the boundary walls of L'Enclos was owned by the municipal authorities of Gardanne, whose townsfolk pastured their flocks there during the *transhumance*. At the beginning of summer, all the inhabitants of the villages in the district sent their sheep to the mountains. In a noisy mass, the flocks pushed along the road to the Alps, and the familiar sounds of L'Enclos were submerged in a flood of continu-ous baa-ing. At night the long modulated notes of the nightingales thrilled me with anguish, until they were resolved in a short deliciously careless trill. A little later, a regular, full-throated chorus of frogs would strike up. Sometimes a sharp sound rather like a sudden click of shears rang through the night air. Was it an insect or a bird? I have never been able to find out. . . . Even as I lay in bed I could see a tiny grey owl in one of the tall cedars, and hear its plaintive hoot. Dawn was an explosion of cockcrows that mingled with the shrilling of the cicalas and the sound of bells, for we were surrounded on all sides by convents.

I could hear the Angelus from the convent of St Thomas chiming out in triple time a major sixth, which hung in the air nearly as long as the note whose harmonic it was. Far off, like an echo, the bells of the Cathedral church of St Saviour and of St Mary Magdalen faintly answered; but how near the tocsin from the Mairie, hammering out like a feverish pulse its warning note that announced a hillside afire or a house ablaze!

These were the sights and sounds that awaited me each year at L'Enclos.

One by one, the carefree summers flowed peacefully by. When the weather was too hot, we would go off to the mountains for a few weeks. It was coming back from one such stay that I first showed signs of my musical vocation. Mother told me that she heard someone playing 'Funiculi, funicula' on the old piano in the drawing-room. She thought it was my grandmother, who occasionally amused herself by picking out old tunes, but she could not understand where she had learnt that particular melody, nor why she was playing it so hesitantly. So she went into the drawing-room to clear up the mystery, and found me all alone perched on a stool and absorbed in groping after the tune I had heard some little Italians singing under our window a few weeks before. When my father came home from the office, I played him 'my tune', to which, to my delight, he immediately hummed an accompaniment. Thereafter he helped me to remember tags of melody I had heard, and encouraged me to play duets with him, which awakened my sense of rhythm. He was a born musician, endowed with a very sure musical instinct; he was the pillar of the Musical Society of Aix and accompanied all their vocalists. My mother had a powerful contralto voice, and up to the time I was born had studied in Paris under Duprez, who taught her to render operatic arias. Thus music was already a familiar friend in our house.

Léo Bruguier, son of an old dancing teacher who accompanied his pupils on a *pochette* or pocket violin, was a delightful musician. A former pupil of Massart, and a laureate of the Conservatoire, he devoted his life to giving violin lessons in Aix, where with the help of his wife he organized chamber music recitals. His marriage to one of his pupils had scandalized some of the inhabitants of Aix, and led to a permanent breach with the Fabri family. Yet this marriage between 'an artist' and a 'young lady of society' was an extremely happy one, and for many years the Bruguiers were a living symbol of marital bliss. When it came to Bruguier's ears that 'Gabriel Milhaud's son was playing duets with his father although he was not yet four!' he offered to give me lessons. My parents were willing, but so many doctors had recommended complete rest and tranquillity for me — one of them, the famous Dr Grasset, had even specifically said: 'No music!' — that they thought it wise to wait a few years.

I had started to learn the violin when I was seven. Bruguier's method might well serve as an example for all teachers. When he had taught me the elementary principles of the instrument, he made me read and play easy little pieces. He had realized from the outset that he would get nothing out of me by forcing me to do exercises that were too dull. He wished to avoid rubbing me the wrong way and inspiring in me a dislike for the violin; he wanted to make a musician of me, not a virtuoso. Thanks to his teaching, I made rapid progress, and could soon play sonatas with my father, and transcriptions of classical symphonies.

Until I went to the lycée at the age of ten, I had been having private lessons. Afterwards, mother made me submit to a system of regular discipline, which turned me into a model pupil of the sort that wins all the prizes year after year. No sooner had I started school than she began to supervise my homework and see that I learnt my lessons, which she read over to me next morning at breakfast. To avoid all danger of overstrain, she made me revise all my work long before the dates prescribed for writing essays. If I had a few pages of verbs to write out, she wrote them for me, imitating my handwriting. Thanks to her care, and to Bruguier's, I was able to go on with my studies and still put in a few hours' daily practice on my violin. Already I could play virtuoso pieces, but what I liked best of all was to play music with my father when he came home from the office. As he could read music with ease, he used to accompany me during my sight-reading lesson on Sundays. Every Thursday I went to Bruguier's on my own, and played to him in his drawing-room littered with trinkets and rare violins. In the summer, he would come to L'Enclos, for he owned a charming house near ours. He was one of the first in our part of the country to have a car, one of those vehicles standing as high as a wardrobe, and fiendishly difficult to start. After my lesson, we used to go and take leave of him before going home to lunch, and often we would find him on the pavement, brandishing a starting-handle and cranking desperately.

In 1904, Bruguier asked me to take part in a string quartet, consisting of himself, Monsieur Pourcel, a professional cellist and teacher at the Conservatoire of Aix, and a local carpenter, Ségalas, who was an accomplished viola player. As I had to go to school, he arranged the rehearsals for Wednesdays and Saturdays so as to give me a chance to recuperate by resting next morning. We played chiefly classical quartets, but my teacher also took an interest in contemporary works: he used to play Franck at a time when provincial opinion still found that composer's work 'too noisy' and thought that 'the angels in heaven ought to play more sweetly — and more quietly too!' In 1905 we studied Debussy's Quartet, which was such a revelation for me that I hastened to buy the score of *Pelléas*. Opportunities for hearing symphony concerts were few and far between. There were, of course, the concerts conducted by Gabriel Marie at Marseilles, but my parents did not approve of my going on long journeys, and only took me when there was some good chamber recital such as those given by the Cortot-Thibaud-Casals Trio, or else when a virtuoso was going to play one of the concertos I had been studying. I remember hearing in this way Pablo de Sarasate, that truly great violinist, give dazzling interpretations of the Saint-Saëns concerto and of a few of his own entertaining compositions; Eugène Ysaye, the prince of violinists, whose playing held both depth and sobriety; Jacques Thibaud, sensitive and elegant; Jan Kubelik, a brilliantly dexterous virtuoso. Music was becoming a more and more imperious necessity for me, as my parents now realized. They thought I might become a virtuoso, and though they would assuredly have preferred me to go into my father's business, they put no obstacles in the way of my aspirations; throughout my childhood and thereafter, they gave me support, both material and moral.

Some cousins of my father, Annette Naquet Laroque and Esther Bloch-Laroque, often came to spend their holidays in Aix. At Passover, they would come back to their house in the Cours Mirabeau. They loved to revisit the scenes of their youth, and their drawing-room was always full of people: their old friends and relations were always dropping in, to join in animated conversation only interrupted at about four o'clock when a herd of goats would stop before the outer door. My cousins would buy a little milk and drink it, having added a few drops of black coffee. Gabrielle, Esther Bloch-Laroque's daughter, had married the philosopher, Xavier Léon, who edited the *Revue de Métaphysique et de Morale*, and was writing a book on Fichte. Both of them loved music and never failed to ask me to play. They insisted, as did Bruguier, that my parents should send me to the Conservatoire, saying that what I needed was to feel the spur of emulation. My parents agreed, but said that I should first take my baccalaureate. From that time on, however, they got into the habit of taking short holidays in order to accompany me to Paris and give me the opportunity of having a few lessons with Alfred Brun, the teacher in the elementary classes at the Conservatoire. His severity made me all the more appreciative of my own teacher's gentleness and patience. I also studied under Firmin Touche during a brief stay with the Xavier Léons at Dieppe in the summer of 1905. This was the first time I had ever stayed by the sea, and it filled me with delight, as did the lovely Normandy countryside whose contours seemed so soft after the harsh outlines of our Provençal hills.

In spite of my tender years, I held very pronounced musical opinions. The Concerts Symphoniques of Dieppe, conducted by Monteux, filled me with enthusiasm, but I could not stand the blare of the Casino Orchestra. I also made my dear parents walk out of the concert hall at Dieppe in the middle of the first Act of *Samson et Dalila*. They willingly fell in with my wishes, although they had been looking forward to this opera as a great treat.

A few days after we got back to Aix, I went through the Bar Mitzvah, or initiation into the Jewish religion. What a great day that was! I had been getting ready for it for the previous two years, and knew just enough Hebrew to say my prayers. I have always regretted not having learnt to read Hebrew fluently. As 'godmother', my grandmother gave me the traditional watch, and although too weak to attend the religious ceremony, she was able to sit at her bedroom window and from there take part in the family party held in the grounds of L'Enclos. Three days later, like a lamp whose oil was all used up, she passed peacefully away, without suffering.

In October, Bruguier advised me to start to study harmony. In the whole of Aix, there was only Lieutenant Hambourg, the conductor of the band of the 61st Regiment, who was qualified to teach me. He was a splendid teacher, but dreadfully impatient, and as I could not always understand Reber and Dubois's excellent treatise on harmony, he often had occasion to be angry with me, so much so that mother was afraid his irritation might upset me, and pulled frightful faces at me behind his back. This would set me off into fits of untimely laughter, which I had much trouble concealing. I finished the study of chords as best I could and attempted a few exercises in writing on a bass, or developing set themes, but these bored me more than anything I had ever had to do before. I had started composing, turning out with great facility rather clumsy works, one of which was a sonata in E minor for piano and violin. I was quite unable to grasp the connection between the study of harmony and the music I wrote, for in the latter I made use of harmonic sequences absolutely different from those I was making such efforts to learn.

The Laroques and the Xavier Léons, who stayed in the vicinity of Aix for a few weeks every summer, would often send word that they were coming to see us. At once we would send out for a goat and shut up our dogs, which always terrified the two elderly cousins. The Léons were very hospitable, and had many friends from Paris to stay with them, so they would often bring them along too. In this way, there stepped down one day from the carriage that drove smartly up, Chartier, better known as the philosopher Alain. He asked to hear my music, and I played him a few settings I had composed for poems by Heine. I had been learning a little German that summer, and had tried to set the original words to music. Alain seemed to like my songs, and all that afternoon kept humming the refrain: 'Röslein, Röslein rot, Röslein auf der Heiden.' Xavier Léon suggested that he should show my music to Rabaud, then conductor of the Opéra, whom he knew very well. Rabaud did exactly what I now do myself whenever young composers submit their works to me; while recognizing that I had talent, he advised me to begin by learning my trade, offering to follow my efforts with interest. This was no vain promise.

According to Bruguier, it was high time I had a better violin. He let me have a divinely-proportioned Ruggieri he had picked up in Florence: we called it 'Florentin'. The back of the instrument was remarkable for the sumptuous glitter of the varnish; it was not a very powerful instrument, but at least it had an exquisite fullness and sweetness of tone. When Bruguier brought me my violin, I was playing with a diabolo and at once put down my toy to try the instrument, but as soon as my teacher had gone, took it up again and threw it so clumsily that it fell on the violin. In despair, I screamed: 'Maman! maman! I've broken Florentin!' We rushed off to Bruguier, who said he thought the crack was harmless, and advised us to have it repaired by the instrument-maker Deroux at Paris. My parents had just paid 1500 francs for my violin, which might now have been damaged beyond repair, but they did not punish me, and once again showed only indulgence towards me. They were not weak, however, and while my father, whom I saw less often owing to his work, seldom scolded me, my mother was firm, even strict, as far as work was concerned, and I owe to her all the habits of discipline that have stood me in good stead all my life.

Chapter Three

Leo and Armand

My adolescence was lit by the glow of two wonderful friendships.

Four generations of doctors had handed on a practice from father-in-law to son-in-law in our doctor's family. Dr Latil, who had become a widower shortly after the birth of his sixth child, now lived with his sister, who devoted herself to bringing up her nephews in their splended Louis XVI *hôtel* with its monumental doorway. Their profound religious faith enabled them to bear with equanimity the manifold blows of fate. Léo, the fourth son, attended the Catholic school and also studied music under Bruguier. We became firm friends. He worshipped music and admired my early efforts with passionate conviction: he made me share his admiration for Maurice de Guérin, and we loved to discover contemporary poets together. I think Léo would probably have become a country priest. The infinite tenderness in his gaze betrayed a tendency to melancholy, and a tormented sense of anxiety. He kept a diary which was one long lamentation in which spiritual weariness and painfully intense religious feeling, dominated ever by a deep spirit of sacrifice and absolute resignation, were interwoven with a passionate love of nature, of flowers and of the exquisite blue lines of the horizon at Aix. He was a dreamer, in love with solitary brooding, but he accepted my presence. We often went for walks together; he would always take the same direction, towards the Etang de Berre, west of the town, where the softly curving hills merge into the immensity of the plain, on the edge of which stood Cézanne's property, Jas de Bouffan, with its famous row of poplars gently suffused with the colours of the setting sun. We never wearied of walking past the fields of wheat, blue-green in spring, bordered with almond-trees in bloom, dwarf oaks and pines, through exquisite landscapes, some of which, like the Château de l'Horloge, evoked historical memories: according to Chateaubriand, it was in this solid, roomy farm-house that Napoleon spent the night on his return from Elba. Sometimes we went as far as Malvalat, the Latils' estate near Granettes, a village which took its name from the painter Granet who lived there. One of his pictures, representing the death of his wife, hangs on a wall of the little chapel.

It was on the other side of Aix, towards the Mont Sainte-Victoire and the wild plateau of the Colline des Pauvres, made famous by Cézanne's paintings, that my other friend, Armand Lunel loved to go. Like Léo, he had a passionate love for the countryside around Aix, the *muscade* country as he called it, in honour of its rare qualities. Fearless of the burning sun, we strode across the scorched, arid, wizened hills, a scene to which a touch of solemnity was added by two cypress trees; climbed rocks where the cicalas noisily shrill beneath the torrid pines; clambered up to the lofty eyries of the glorious villages looking down upon the valley of the Durance, that dried-up stream whose stony bed divides the Bouches-du-Rhône from the Basses-Alpes. I had known Armand for a long time, but his extreme shyness had kept us apart. I was in the 'Seconde' (Fifth Form) when I heard that the age limit for entry to the Conservatoire was fixed at eighteen. As it was wiser to take the examination a year in advance, I decided to get my *bachot* out of the way as soon as possible; during the long vacation of 1908 I worked at the syllabus, and took my Classics baccalaureate in October. That meant I now joined the Philosophy set, where I met Armand Lunel again, and he overcame his shyness and his love of solitude to befriend me. He wanted to be a writer. His brilliant brain and intellectual curiosity would not let him neglect the minutest detail of the subjects in which he was interested; he loved to browse in archives, and devoted hours to the study of all sorts of historical documents. We discovered Maeterlinck's plays, the *Serres chaudes*; we loved the poet's rather morbid, dream-bound imagination, and as I was still strongly under the influence of Debussy, his *Pelléas* was then my favourite spiritual nourishment, it was under these signs that, while we were still at school, our collaboration began. Armand wrote vague, excessively lyrical and slightly extravagant prose poems, which I endeavoured to set to music. Whenever he came to see me, he would roar out his poems, while I thumped out on the piano sequences of chords I tried to make as wild as I could.

At night before I fell asleep I would shut my eyes and imagine I heard music so amazingly untrammelled I could never have transcribed it. How shall I put it? To me it was a tremendous mystery in which my soul delighted, as in a refuge wherein, deep down in the recesses of my subconscious mind, my musical language was slowly taking form.

Chapter Four

Paris 1909–1912

As soon as we had taken our *Philosophie*, Armand and I set out for Paris. Monsieur and Madame Lunel and my parents tearfully accompanied us as far as the station at Marseilles, whence an express train was about to carry us off towards our new destinies: Armand was to try and get into the Ecole Normale Supérieure in order to win the material position which would enable him to become a writer, while I was to attempt the competitive examination for entry to the Conservatoire.

I went to live with a delightful family at No. 2 Boulevard des Italiens. I have always loved movement, and noise has never disturbed me, indeed quite the contrary: so it was a real joy for me to gaze down from my window at the crowded boulevard, and the tangled mass of cabs whose drivers wore shiny top hats of waxed cloth, and the horse-drawn double-decker buses.

Bruguier had advised me to continue my violin studies with Berthelier who, like himself, attached as much importance to an expressive and sober style as to technical dexterity. He was totally blind, and only the untiring devotion of his wife, who went with him everywhere, enabled him to go on teaching. She sat through all his classes and played the piano accompaniment to the concertos executed by his pupils. Her musical talent and rare kindness endeared her to us all.

Having been cut off from concerts all through my childhood, I now made up for lost time, and became an assiduous concert-goer. I heard Beethoven's sonatas played by Ysaye and Pugno; Povla Frish interpreting with an ineffable lightness of touch the Lieder of Schubert; Olénine d'Alheim, accompanied by Cortot, singing songs by Mussorgsky with her head thrown back in an impressively grandiose and austere style. This music moved me so deeply that I rushed off and bought the score of *Boris Godunov*. I also went to the concerts at the Salon d'Automne at which Ravel's *Gaspard de la Nuit* was given its first performance, and the concerts of the Schola Cantorum when new works by Déodat de Séverac, Vincent d'Indy and Charles Bordes were given, usually interpreted by Blanche Selva.

As a protest against the ultra-conservative policy of the Société Nationale, which had just turned down the *Poèmes hindous* by Maurice Delage, a disciple of Maurice Ravel, the latter founded, in association with Florent Schmitt, Charles Koechlin, Louis Aubert, Roger Ducasse, Inghelbrecht and Léon Moreau, a new concert society, the S.M.I., with Gabriel Fauré as president. Their programmes consisted almost exclusively of first perform-ances of works characteristic of trends in European music at that date. I was a regular listener. I had developed the habit of spending Sunday evenings with my cousins the Naquet Laroques, whose daughter Cécile was a very gifted musician. After dinner my fellow students at the Conservatoire, the cellist Félix Delgrange and my cousin Eric Allatini, who played the viola and the violin as an amateur, would drop in for the evening, and we would play together. I also tried to form a string quartet from among my colleagues in the violin classes; but as they were more anxious to develop their techniques than to extend their musical culture, I had to approach the students in the harmony class, Louis Fourestier, Victor Larbey and Sauveplane, in order to realize my project. We used to meet at my lodgings every Tuesday.

When it was announced that *The Ring* was to be played in its entirety at the Opéra under the direction of Weingartner, I took a subscription for the whole cycle. On this occasion, I, who always went up into the 'gods', took an orchestra stall in order to enjoy the spectacle properly. I had already heard fragments of Wagner at Marseilles: I was intrigued by his lyricism and tumultuous orchestration, and his reputation as a revolutionary both dis-turbed me and made me feel closer to him. I shall never forget those four performances: the audience rapt in the music, silent and attentive as if in a church, suddenly bursting into wildly enthusiastic applause at the end of each Act, and I myself bored to tears. . . . Unable as I was to share in the general emotion, I felt lonely, as if abandoned by the wayside. My cousin Eric Allatini, a fervent Wagnerian, took me to hear *Tristan*; I never dared tell him how deadly boring I found that 'sonorous love-philtre.' When the Bayreuth copyright expired, and *Parsifal* was given at the Opéra, I went to hear it: this work, which everyone had been impatiently waiting to hear, sickened me by its pretentious vulgarity. I did not realize that what I felt was merely the reaction of a Latin mind, unable to swallow the philosophico-musical jargon and the shoddy mixture of harmony and mysticism in what was an essentially pompous art. I felt that even the *leitmotif* was a childish device, like so many thematic Baedekers, flattering the audience's self-esteem by the feeling that they always 'knew where they were.' I also deplored the influence of this music on ours. Yet I was not so foolish as to underestimate its importance, and when Wagner's operas were published by Durand at five francs a copy, I bought them all; I do not remember ever having been tempted to play them. But *Pelléas* and *Boris Godunov* always stood by my bedside.

When I first saw a performance of the Ballets Russes, who had just made their début in Paris, I was carried away with enthusiasm. At one bound, Diaghilev leapt into the role of innovator which was to be his until the end of his career; he was not content to put on classical ballets like *Les Sylphides* or *Le Spectre de la rose* to show off the exceptional talents of some of his dancers, Nijinsky and Karsavina, or specifically Russian ballets such as the *Prince Igor Suite, Sheherazade*, or *Cleopatra*, which seemed so vivid, savage and new to us; he also had the merit of discovering and revealing the work of the greatest musician of the century, Igor Stravinsky.

I lived very close to the Opéra-Comique, but I only went there when there was something good to see, in other words, very seldom. Once I had been invited to go to see *Werther*, and I had squirmed in my seat to the end of the performance, not daring to leave the theatre for fear of offending my hosts. But when they played Bloch's *Macbeth* (libretto by Fleg), whose virile qualities I found particularly pleasing, I went to all six performances. I also attended the dress rehearsal of Ravel's *L'Heure espagnole*. . . . I found the subtle elegance of this music seductive, but felt some regret at not finding the same depth of feeling in Ravel as in Debussy. From that time on, therefore, I was hostile to Ravel, and so I have remained, although I freely confess my attitude was not always justified.

Every Thursday I went to call on Armand Lunel at the Lycée Henri IV. He was doing his 'Rhétorique Supérieure', under Alain. On Sundays he would come and spend part of the day with me in my room on the Boulevard des Italiens. He always arrived early. Sometimes he would amuse himself by writing a poem, which I would set to music, and my landlady, Madame Montel, who had a charming voice, would sing it at sight. Armand and I assiduously visited all the current exhibitions of paintings. At Bernheim's, Félix Fénéon, Mallarmé's friend, showed amateurs the latest canvasses by Bonnard, Rousseau, Van Dongen, Signac, etc. One day we went to Vollard's, and he gave us a very cold reception until he realized we were from Aix; at once he became very amiable, and showed us all his Cézannes, which he kept upstairs. Most of them represented some scene closely associated with the memory of one of our walks.

Aix kept breaking through into our Parisian existence; my mother wrote me every day, relating all that was going on around her; father wrote less often, more briefly but no less affectionately. Léo poured forth his soul in his letters as in his Diary. He was studying for his *Licences* in Letters and in Law, and was following with passionate interest the lectures by Blondel, who was crippled by neuritis and lectured at home, mastering his incessant pain in order to carry his pupils with him into the pure empyrean of metaphysical speculation. Ever a lover of solitude, Léo shunned the company of his fellow students, whom he nicknamed the 'Bandar Log', after the name given by Kipling to the troops of monkeys in *The Jungle Book*.

Armand and I spent all our holidays in Aix and I saw as much of Léo as I could. We had a mutual friend, whom we visited often, in Céline Lagouarde, a photographer and most brilliant pianist. How many times did we play together Lekeu's Sonata, which filled us with such enthusiasm in those days! She had some acquaintance with Francis Jammes, of whom she had made some superb portraits; she showed us some of his poems, which I set to music. During the summer, Léo and I loved to go to Les Saintes-Maries de la Mer, a little village in the Camargue, with low lime-washed cottages; it had a fine romanesque church, a fortified building erected by soldier-monks, with the yellow stonework all crumbling away under the combined effect of the sun and the mistral. We loved to scramble up into the belfry and look out over the surrounding plain, with its spacious horizons where the mirage often made the eye confound solid land with marsh. We even spent one night there; dawn was so steeped in mystery that it seemed to be heralding the birth of Creation. We took Armand up into our tower, but he was more active than us, and had no desire to indulge in endless contemplation: he preferred to drag us off in a horse and trap to Aigues-Mortes, a beautiful little town whose encircling walls gave it an austere grandeur. The road wound through marshes where only *enganes* and red behen and a few rare trees with gnarled trunks contrived to grow.

Every day during my stay in Aix I was composing. Not having enough experience yet to elaborate purely musical work, I sought inspiration in literary ideas. In this way I wrote *Pièces pour quatuor*, inspired by a passage from St Thérèse; a quintet called *Le Pauvre Pêcheur*; a trio which bore an epigraph of two lines by Francis Jammes; a ballet based on *Les Malheurs de Sophie*, and an opera on a libretto by Eric Allatini, *Les Saintes-Maries de la Mer*. The first two acts related the story of the village stranded between sky and sea, where St Martha, St Mary-Jacobé, and St Mary-Salomé, together with their servant Sarah, landed after crossing the sea in a frail barque. The two Maries became the patron saints of the village. Their relics are enshrined, high up in a little chapel under the roof of the church. The gypsies adopted Sarah as their saint, although she was never canonized by the Church. The third and last act of my opera evoked the festival of May 25, when the gypsies of Catalonia, Piedmont and Provence go on pilgrimage to Les Saintes-Maries. I have several times witnessed this festival, when the gypsies encumber the village and all the roads leading to it with their caravans; they spend the night in prayer before a casket containing the relics of Sarah in the crypt under the church, which was built on the site of an altar to the ancient pagan deity Mithras. On the following day, the Archbishop of Aix, who is also bishop of Arles and Embrun, heads a procession bearing the shrines and statues of the saints to the sea; he blesses the sea, and the procession winds its way back to the church, chanting a very ancient canticle which is repeated over and over again. I used this melody in my score. I did the orchestration for the whole opera, which meant more than six hundred pages of music, but I burned them together with all my youthful compositions when, some time later, I started to compose music which, as my teacher Gédalge put it, was 'neither literature nor painting'. From this holocaust, the only thing I rescued was the *Cantique de Camargue*, of which I was especially fond and which I used again in my *Poème* for piano and orchestra. I have not destroyed this piece, but it will never be published by me. . . .

During the summer of 1911, I composed a Sonata for violin and piano, my first work worthy of being preserved. That same year I passed my violin examination, and then had to attend classes in chamber music and orchestral playing. There I made the acquaintance of Yvonne Giraud, a charming and very gifted violinist who had a very extensive musical culture; like me, she dreaded the chamber music classes, in which only works we already knew from A to Z were studied. We shared the same desk in the orchestral class; our teacher, Paul Dukas, was a bad conductor and incapable of directing a rehearsal. None of the students respected him, but Yvonne and I had such an admiration for his work that we overlooked his clumsiness. We were shocked by the behaviour of the hooligans. Paul Dukas was very surprised when I asked him to autograph my copy of his *Ariane*; this is what he wrote: 'To Darius Milhaud, with best wishes for his future, Paul Dukas, Paris, 1911.' I always sent him copies of my printed music, and he invariably took the trouble of answering by letter, with very apt criticism. Ever since my arrival, I had been assiduously attending Xavier Leroux's harmony classes; often his place was taken by Raymond Pech, a former *Prix de Rome*. In spite of the kindness of both my instructors, the subject bored me just as much as at Aix, and I made no progress. My classmates knew how to insert little harmonic refinements, 6/4 chords, in the 'appropriate places', but I was quite incapable of doing so. The themes to which I was required to supply a bass, or a harmonic development, often seemed deadly dull to me, and I thought the exercises themselves anti-musical. Yet I went on composing and was making some progress. I decided to ask Xavier Leroux to grant me an interview, to show him my sonata. I shall never forget the expression of consternation on his face: how could I, who was so weak in harmony, ever dream of composing? What on earth could such a poor harmonist produce? Xavier Leroux refused to see me, offering all his many activities, including the rehearsals for his opera *Théodora*, in which his wife Madame Héglon the rehearsals for his opera *Théodora*, in which his wife Madame Héglon was to create the principal role, as an excuse. A few days later I renewed my request, and he let me play my sonata after the end of a class. At the very first bars, his face lighted up; then he started to sing and play the violin part at the top of the keyboard. At the end of the first movement he said to me: 'What are you doing here? You are trying to learn a conventional musical language, when you already have one of your own. Leave the class! Resign!' This appeared to me to be such a drastic step that I asked Pech for his opinion. After seeing my music, he confirmed Leroux's words, with even greater vehemence. Nevertheless, before resigning from the harmony class, I went to see Rabaud, who fully corroborated what both my teachers had said, and advised me to go to Gédalge. He gave me a letter of introduction, which I sent off straight away. The reply was frightening: 'Monsieur, I will expect you at noon on Thursday, to see what you know.' I knew nothing. . . . On the Thursday, with a racing heart, and carrying a brief-case bulging with manuscripts under my arm, I went to see him. Wearing a beret, and with a serviette round his neck, he was eating a chop: 'Play me something!' said he, without interrupting his eating. I played the first movement of my sonata. 'Why have you used D sharp seventeen times on the first page? You don't know how to construct a melody. What do you want to do, learn your trade, or win prizes?' 'To know my trade,' said I, without a moment's hesitation. 'Right! Then I'll take you in my counter-point class.' Gédalge disapproved of the type of exercise adopted by the authorities at the Conservatoire: the development of a theme, a hybrid exercise which looked like a fugue and yet was not one and had very little to do with counterpoint. This was Caussade's forte, and his mass-trained pupils carried off all the prizes. My work was now corrected by Gédalge's assistants, Eugène Cools and Alice Pelliot. I did my counterpoint and all the studies on Bach's chorales, exercises which combine counterpoint and harmony and, once the pupil is able to produce extended chorales, carry over into the sphere of composition. I made friends with some charming young men attending Gédalge's classes: Jacques Ibert, Henri Cliquet, who set Laforgue's poems to music and could read anything we asked him to, Arthur Honegger, who came up from Le Havre three times a week to study the violin with Capet, and Jean Wiéner, whom I had met at Aix. The latter proposed we should take composition lessons with Gédalge, which were extraordinarily interesting. Then our master organized, for us and one or two classmates, an orchestration class which he made enthrallingly interest-ing and for which he refused all payment on the grounds that he had enjoyed himself too much. . . .

In December 1910 I received an enthusiastic letter from Léo concerning *La Brebis egarée*, a play by Francis Jammes which had just been published in the *Revue hebdomadaire*; I obtained a copy and immediately conceived the idea of turning it into an opera. I asked Céline Lagouarde to get Jammes's permission and no sooner had it been granted than I set to work. A few months later, in Aix, Céline told us of the last time she had seen Jammes, and of how he had talked much of Claudel and of the latter's conversion. She showed us *Le Connaissance de l'Est*, which Jammes had brought to the station for her when she left. Every poem in it was a veritable miniature drama, charged with lyrical emotion. I borrowed the book and started to write settings for one or two of the poems it contained; Claudel's prose added something strong and passionate to my nature.

As my musicianly talent developed, I found the study of the violin increasingly tedious; it was as if I was being robbed of time which otherwise I could have devoted to composition. I was awarded no prize at the *Concours* of 1912 and the idea of spending a third year on the study of the violin now seemed unbearable. This worried my mother, for she loved success, and wanted me to begin by going through with whatever I had undertaken. I countered her arguments and, very tactfully but firmly, announced my intention of abandoning my career as a violinist in order to be a composer. My father, realizing my choice was irrevocable, gave me complete freedom to do what I wished; my cousins, the Xavier Léons, with whom we were staying for a few days after that unfortunate contest, sided with me. That year at L'Enclos I finished my first string quartet. When I played it over with the Bruguier Quartet, only my beloved teacher understood what I was trying to say. His wife could not help blurting out: 'It sounds just like Arab music!' and Ségalas, the carpenter-violinist declared with his heavy Marseilles accent: 'My word! This is hot stuff!'

Chapter Five

The Visit to Francis Jammes

I wanted to show Jammes the first Act, which I had now completed, of *La Brebis egaréee*; Léo also wanted to show him a poem he had written. We planned to go and see him together, and as Act II of my opera was laid in Burgos, we decided to visit Spain on our way, in order that I might steep myself in the atmosphere of that austere and passionate land before going on with my work.

We stopped first at Barcelona; we were enchanted by the tree-shaded walks of La Rambla, thronged day and night by noisy and excited crowds; the peacefulness of the neighbouring quarters was all the more impressive by contrast. Within these peaceful precincts stands the Cathedral, familiarly set down among the old houses as if for their protection, and its cloister in which we saw three geese under a catalpa tree. We saw a bull-fight at Saragossa; a grand sight, the crowd, clad only in the darkest colours, silently participating in the spectacle as in some ritual whose every move was known in advance. While Léo meditated in the church of Our Lady of Pilar, I talked to a few old men sitting outside their doors. They told me the siege of their city by Napoleon's troops had been related to them so often that they had conceived the liveliest dislike for the French. We were disappointed by Madrid, which we christened 'Old Ugly', but not by the pictures in the Prado, through which the soul of Spain was revealed to us. Léo and I were great admirers of Barrès, not only because of his lofty ideas but also because some of his books dealt with scenes we loved, La Camargue or Spain, so we were looking forward to visiting Toledo. We were not disappointed. On a moonlit night swept with great black clouds as in some engraving by Doré, we sped across the bridge over the Tagus in a coach driven by four mules, and so galloped into Toledo. Next morning at daybreak we were awakened by the sounds in the street — the hooves of mules and donkeys laden with milk, vegetables or earthenware pots, the queer guttural cries with which the peasants addressed their animals. This visit was sheer delight for us; everywhere we found the living presence of El Greco, at the museum, in the church, or in the countryside, on the other side of the Tagus, looking back at this matchless city clasped in the yellow meanders of its river.

We travelled third class, in the company of worthy, warmhearted peasants who never failed to offer us some of their meal of *tortilla*, a kind of cold omelette. The carriages were constantly surveyed by the eagle eye of one of the *carabineros*, who with their rifles slung from their shoulders and wearing shiny leather hats, were continually on the move from one compartment to another. It was stiflingly hot as we crossed the orange-tinted uplands of Aragon, absolutely devoid of vegetation. Dust penetrated thickly into the train. At Burgos we found the atmosphere we had come in search of, the very same as that described by Jammes in his second Act. We also noticed immediately how his sharp eye had recorded the most insignificant details to transmute them into poetry. As I strolled along the Plaza del Espolon under the acacias whose foliage was lit from below by electric bulbs, I was able to watch the crowd listening to the military band, see the little coffins for children hanging at the grocer's next to some dried cod, gaze at the little chapel of the Carthusian monastery of Miraflores where a monk was tending daisies that grew so thickly that it was as if he were walking on a sky full of stars.

Before going on to Orthez, we stopped off in the Basque country to see Céline Lagouarde who was spending her holidays in Cambo with one of her friends, Madame Inchauspé, a young widow with two magnificent little girls: Mimi, a dark child whose hair was cut short in a Joan of Arc crop, and Chopé, who had long golden curls and an amazingly solemn expression in the depth of her dark blue eyes. Léo loved children, and throughout a ride which we made together in a landau, he held little Chopé on his knees, a huddled silent little figure utterly indifferent to the scenes through which we were passing: the quaint little Basque villages with their neat, clean cottages, and the ritual wall for the game of *pelota* on every village square. Twenty years later, I found myself once more in Bayonne, and went on as far as Cambo to see Madame Inchauspé, but was unable to find her house again. I had heard that little Chopé had died a year or two before. I laid some flowers on her grave, in memory of that lovely drive, and in memory of Léo.

Finally we reached our destination: Orthez. We arrived late in the afternoon. It was market-day; the peasants in their Béarn berets were driving homewards, sometimes with little calves in the back of their trap, just as in dear Jammes's poems. How glad and proud we were to find a note from the poet awaiting us at the Belle Hôtesse hotel, inviting us to spend the evening with him! He lived in an old house set in the midst of a garden, and gave us a very warm welcome. He introduced us to his aged mother, who had china-blue eyes and a cracked sing-song voice, and his wife Ginette, who had the rather emphatic speaking tones of people from Picardy. She was a musician and sang for us, in a clear, unpretentious voice, settings which Raymond Bonheur had made of Jammes's early poems. I played the ones I had written for *La Connaissance de l'Est*. Jammes was surprised to hear I had tackled such a formidable task — the text being so rich in meaning — and asked me to tell him all about it. Then he asked Léo to read some of his verse. Léo sat down near an occasional table. Dimly in the lamplight we could discern on the walls local landscapes painted by Jammes's boyhood friend Lacoste, a Brazilian Morpho butterfly in a little glass case, and a small Louis XVI clock in the form of a black boy, a wedding-present from Gide, on the mantelpiece. In his muted, melodious voice whose charm lay in both its sensitivity and its lassitude, Léo read his poem, which was an utterly faithful expression of his innermost nature with its two constant themes of tenderness and sadness. Jammes was deeply moved by this sweet lament and promised Léo he would help to get it published in the *Cahiers de l'amitié de la France*, a little review of which we were all very fond and in which Jammes grouped round him a number of young Catholic writers: Mauriac, Vallery-Radot, André Lafond, Eusèbe de Brémond d'Ars, etc. We had got into the way of referring to these young men as 'the chicks', while we called those gravitating around Claudel, Gide and Jammes 'the syndicate'.

During the next few days we walked and rode. We went as far afield as Lagor, and the banks of the torrent. Jammes explained to us the art of fishing, and made us marvel at his knowledge of botany. When we got back to the house, he would carry us off to his tiny study and read us his verse – – those poems which had so profoundly influenced our youth — in his resonant voice with its strong Pyrenean accent rolling the final syllables over his tongue and drawing out the resonance of each individual word.

When Jammes asked to hear my music, I refused to play it on his piano, which was practically unusable; so he begged his aged Huguenot cousins, the Lajuzan ladies, to offer us their hospitality. They had an upright piano, also very old, but in better condition than his. They very graciously consented to receive us and offered us warm tea and very dry *petits fours* in an 1830 drawing-room cluttered up with bookcases, little tables covered with English doileys with blue ribbons, curtains of heavy lace-net, armchairs covered in Utrecht velvet and the inevitable aspidistra. The piano, on which stood a bronze ornament and two Gallet vases, was covered in heavy draperies. With nineteen-year-old enthusiasm I played the whole of the first act of *La Brebis egarée* without stopping — it lasts one hour and twenty minutes! I sang all the parts at the top of my voice and thumped with all my might on the old ladies' piano. They, being unfamiliar with the kind of music a student at the Conservatoire might be expected to write, probably thought they were at the mercy of a lunatic. Jammes was not at all disappointed by this hurricane of sound, nor was his wife. I believe they grasped the general lines of my work, the lovely words of which had echoed so deeply in my young musician's soul.

Next day we set out for home. On our way to the station, Jammes bought us in the market a masterpiece of popular toymaking: dark violet paper vases with handles of cardboard that could be folded at will. We also carried away with us copies of his poems and an autographed photograph each. On Léo's, he had written: 'To the friend of my friend, Darius Milhaud', and on mine: 'To the friend of my friend, Léo Latil'.

Chapter Six

No 5 Rue Gaillard

Before leaving Paris in July 1912, I persuaded my parents to allow me to set up in a little flat of my own. We found an ideal spot, No. 5 Rue Gaillard. Although it was right in the centre of the city, not far from the Church of the Trinité, this street was purely provincial in character. Hardly a carriage passed along it, pigeons fluttered up and down, and there were even hens strutting around in it; electricity had not yet reached there. It was a heavenly little flat. I had it papered green, and put divans covered in green velvet in the drawing-room and dining-room for when my father and mother came to Paris. As for myself, I contented myself for the moment with a big iron bed and a kitchen table and chairs, for I meant to get rid of this makeshift furniture and gradually replace it with carefully chosen antiques. Armand Lunel and I were crazy about antiques; everywhere we went we gave free rein to our passion. 'Antique hunting' for us had a genuine poetic exaltation about it. At Aix not a day passed without us waiting for some dealer to return from an expedition, and we ourselves visited private individuals in quest of some treasure. We used to buy Second Empire at a time when this was still looked down upon by amateurs who thought Charles X and Louis-Philippe too modern. In Paris, every Sunday saw us at the Marché aux Puces at Saint-Ouen. There we would have a lunch of mussels and chips; then we would pile up all our finds in a cab and bring them to my place. In this way, my little flat was soon adorned with Directoire furniture and coloured prints of the First Empire.

We also collected rare books, but I confined my attention to Claudel, Jammes and Gide, my three favourite authors. I sold all my Victor Hugo to buy Claudel's *Cinq Grandes Odes*, published at forty francs in a limited edition by the Bibliothèque de l'Occident. The bookshop called *L'Art Indépendant* still existed at that time, at the rear of a courtyard in the Rue

Saint-Lazare, but the old bookseller was now only interested in theosophy. He had in his stock rare books which were fetching high prices in the trade but he let me have them at the ordinary prices and in this way I acquired *La Ville* and *Paludes*. I also got a second-hand copy of *Les Cahiers d'André Walter* with the following queer dedication: 'To Rodolphe Darzens, Poet of intimate worship and gloomy piety.'

This book, like *La Porte étroite*, influenced me profoundly. I set to music some of the extracts from Alissa's diary, letters and snatches of dialogue, and fashioned them into a sort of long intimate song-cycle. Armand, Yvonne and I had adopted a 'paludian' manner of speech; Gide entered into our everyday lives. Armand and I wrote 'paludian' letters to one another, and Yvonne and I kept up a correspondence steeped in the character of Angèle. We also had a great admiration for Claudel, and in a fine frenzy Armand would declaim whole passages of him to me.

Armand was always light-hearted and at ease with me, but although he was not unhappy at the Ecole Normale, his timidity gave him the reputation of being stand-offish among his comrades. The prospect of the Annual Ball filled him with dismay: 'You can't even go to bed,' he told me, 'They use the dormitories as cloak-rooms!' To avoid this dreaded function, he proposed that we should go off on various little expeditions. We went to Chartres, to Rouen, and in the third year even as far as Holland. We reached Amsterdam on a Saturday morning, and the lovely old city enchanted us. We had time to visit the harbour with its shop signs written in every language under the sun, including Chinese; the Jewish quarter near the station; the beautiful Synagogue attended by the descendants of the old refugees from Spain and Portugal, belonging to the Sephardim sect; the canals with their dark waters. . . . Next day we visited the museums of Harlem — only the later Franz Hals found favour in our sight — and in the evening caught the train from The Hague just in time to get back to our work. Armand wrote a short account of our little journey and called it *La Géographie des Pays-Bas*. In it his compact style and personality were expressed more fully than ever before.

During my stay at Orthez, Jammes had pressed me to go and see his old friend Lacoste and he had written to him to say that I would call. He looked rather like Jammes himself; he had a long beard and lively eyes, but his smile was much gentler. He showed me his pictures with great affability and kindness. They nearly all depicted the scene from the windows of his apartment: the Lycée Pasteur and the Boulevard Pasteur in the snow, or steeped in summer sunlight, or toned down by the golden leaves of autumn. Yet through all his paintings one could sense the longing for the light of his native Béarn. His wife Jeanne was a charming person; we soon became friends. She was a great reader, and introduced me to Saint-Léger Léger's *Eloges* and Valéry's *Soirée avec Monsieur Teste*, both of which she loved.

She was an excellent musician, a professional even, and often sang my songs, accompanied by one of her friends, a composer and pupil of Gabriel Fauré. She introduced me to this friend, Jeanne Herscher, who immediately invited me to her house in Passy. She lived on the top floor of a new building erected by her architect husband which contained a very large concert hall. On my way there I often visited the cemetery of Passy to pause a moment before the curious tomb of Marie Bashkirtseff, 'Our Lady of the sleeping-car' as Barrès called her. Léo had sent me her *Journal*. I always gazed in astonishment at this 'ever unsatisfied girl's' tomb, in which her whole studio had been faithfully reproduced down to the pouf cushions, hanging draperies, writing-desk and even her easel.

On his own initiative, Jammes had written to Claudel about me. I received a letter from Frankfurt-am-Main, where he was consul, to say he would be coming to see me soon. This was a bombshell. At the idea that the writer I revered more than any other was coming to visit me, I was beside myself with excitement. Perhaps I was unconsciously aware that this meeting would decide what my life's work was going to be! I knew very little about him, except from Jammes, who had said he was highly-strung, as restless as a force of nature, wore a Chinese robe with a consul-general's hat, hated the scent of vanilla, and was always prepared to pack up for some post in far distant lands. 'He's like a ship with steam up,' concluded Jammes.

Between Claudel and myself, understanding was immediate, our mutual confidence absolute. We did not waste a single moment! I sang *Sept Poèmes de la Connaissance de l'Est* for which I had endeavoured to find music as virile as I could make it. 'How manly that is!' he cried, and at once started to speak of the translation of the *Oresteia* which he had begun in China to assist Rosario's widow in her tragic loneliness: she had contracted leprosy, and he procured a printing-press for her. He had entrusted to her the limited edition of his *Agamemnon*: that was the reason why the first edition appeared in Fuchow. He talked of *Les Choëphores* on which he was then engaged and concerning which he held very decided opinions as to the kind of musical accompaniment required. He described scenes to me in which the text became so intensely lyrical that it called for musical expression; others in which only words could convey the fierce exaltation of the characters. I found his notions perfectly clear and wholly consonant with what I wanted to do myself. What a happy day that was! Not only did it mark the first step in a faithful collaboration, but in a precious friendship too.

Chapter Seven

The Syndicate

During the winter of 1913, Jammes came to spend a few days in Paris. He never liked to stay for long, despite the efforts of his friends to induce him to remain, and despite the many receptions held in his honour. He was so kind as to get me an invitation to most of them; there was an air of a family party about them all, for whether at Madame Ernest Chausson's or Madame Alphonse Daudet's, or in the house of any other of Jammes's friends, it was always the same faces one saw, all eager to see him again. During these receptions Jammes would read his own poems, and Madame Lacoste sang some of my songs while I accompanied them. Jammes used to stay with the Arthur Fontaines, and it was there that I met one of their old friends, Saint- Léger Léger. While still at a boarding school in the south-west of France, Jammes often invited him to spend the holidays at his home in Orthez. It was not only their poetic gifts that they had in common, for Jammes's ancestors too had inhabited the West Indies, as the Creole echoes so frequently heard in his verse attest. That same week, Léo's poem appeared in the *Cahiers de l'amitié de la France*. I wrote to him at once: 'Now you are one of the chicks!', to which he replied: 'You are getting into the "Syndicate"!'

Céline Lagouarde was exhibiting some photographs in the Cercle de la Photographie, Rue Volney; she took advantage of the opportunity this offered to come to Paris. She was slightly acquainted with Ravel, and took me to see him. The great kindness he showed me throughout his life was made manifest at that very first meeting; no sooner had he heard my violin sonata than he suggested I should submit it to the S.M.I. Léon Moreau, whom I met at dinner at my cousins', the Bloch-Laroques, told me the news that my work had been accepted, and that all I had to do now was to choose two performers. After dinner he took me to his publisher, Costallat's, where Jane Bathori was rehearsing his new opera *Myrialde*, before creating the role at its first performance in the provinces. I had admired her a few weeks previously singing the *Chansons de Bilitis* to her own accompaniment at the piano. I was unaware, however, that she was capable of reading any manuscript at sight, and when at her request I showed her my music, I committed the *faux pas* of singing it myself. She did not bear any malice, and when I met her again a few years later said to me: 'I'm sure you must have improved, come and see me!' This time *she* sang: ever after that, she was for me an exceptionally good interpreter and friend.

I do not think that Gide liked *Alissa* (the suite I had based on his *La Porte étroite*) very much. After hearing it, he said to me in his sing-song voice: 'Thank you for making me feel my prose was so beautiful!' The appreciation was for his prose, not my music. Eighteen years later, in 1931, I re-wrote *Alissa* completely. I was very much attached to my old style, although I had now left it far behind. The first version lasted more than an hour, so I cut it down by a half; I re-wrote the music without altering the prosody, merely making the vocal line more melodic; I only varied the harmonies to avoid certain sequences which had dated badly, and emphasized the lines of the piano part by the addition of a little more counterpoint. It was of this version of *Alissa* that Bathori so often gave a characteristically sensitive and intelligent rendering. Indeed, for twenty years she was its *sole* interpreter.

I asked Yvonne Giraud and Georgette Guller to play my Sonata at the S.M.I. Madame Berthelier had recommended Georgette to me. She was one of Philipp's pupils and had a depth of tone and brilliance of execution that occasionally reached the sublime. My two interpreters would come to my flat for rehearsals, and then we would go on to a concert together. Before escorting them back to their *pension* in the Avenue de Villiers, we would go for a ride in a cab in the Bois de Boulogne. They liked these little excursions so much that they invited some of their fellow-boarders to accompany us. As the rules in their *pension* were very strict, and the girls were not allowed out alone with young men, I used to hide in the back of the cab when I brought them home. I would only drive off after I had heard them call to me as they passed the concierge's lodge: 'Good night, Madame, and thank you.'

A few months after the performance of my Sonata, I received a *pneumatique* from the Selection Committee of the S.M.I. to say that owing to a cancellation, my First Quartet would be given in the next programme. I played in it, with Robert Soëtens, Robert Siohan, and Félix Delgrance. After the concert at the Salle Pleyel, while I was putting my instrument away and gazing at the old programmes adorning the walls of the foyer, bearing witness to so many glorious performances and famous visits — one of them even referred to a concert given by Chopin and Mendelssohn — I was jerked out of my reverie by a gentleman with a white moustache and goatee who said to me: 'I am Jacques Durand, I would like to publish your quartet. Come and see me tomorrow.' Next day I signed my first contract.

My cousins the Xavier Léons entertained philosophers twice a month, all the philosophers in Paris, and foreign visitors too. I tried to persuade Armand Lunel to come along, but without much success, so great was his dislike of anything remotely resembling a social function, although he was very fond of Xavier and Gabrielle, more for their love of antiques, for the possession of which they had competed with Armand during their stays in Aix, than for the *Revue de Métaphysique et de Morale*. It was at their place that I met Jacques Emile Blanche. He had a very keen taste for music, and often played pianoforte duets with his sister-in-law Yoyo and Catherine Lemoine. He asked me to play my works at his house for Princess-Edmond de Polignac. I brought along Yvonne for the Sonata. The princess turned the pages. From that time on, she often invited me to the musical evenings she gave at her house. I was very fond of Jacques Emile Blanche and his wife Rose. I liked his studio because 'everybody that was somebody' had had his or her portrait done there. You saw Barrès and Debussy next to Bergson or Nijinsky: no sooner had anyone made a name for himself in Paris than Blanche got to know him and painted his portrait. He had an amazing memory and could relate the most wonderfully scathing anecdotes. His intellectual curiosity was aroused by all the latest developments in music, painting and literature, and his powers of understanding were usually most acute.

That winter there was a revival of *Pelléas*; I went to nearly all the performances; I also heard Debussy's *Les Rondes de printemps* conducted by the composer himself at one of the concerts organized by Durand to introduce some of the orchestral works stocked by him. I witnessed a very interesting dance recital given by a Russian dancer Trouhanowa, at which Florent Schmitt conducted *La Tragédie de Salome*, Vincent d'Indy *Istar*, Paul Dukas the first performance of *La Péri*, and Ravel *Valses nobles et sentimentales*, under the title, for choreographic purposes, of *Adélaïde, ou le langage des fleurs*. Louis Aubert had played these same waltzes a week or two before under very curious circumstances: the selection committee of the S.M.I. had decided to mystify the audience by not giving any composer's names on the programmes. Everyone was handed a programme and a pencil, and was asked to identify the composer of each piece. What a dangerous game that was. The results were wildly out. Some of Ravel's friends and admirers, who were really very familiar with his music, did not recognize his style, and mercilessly ridiculed *Valses nobles et sentimentales*. During one of Léo's flying visits to Paris, we went to see a performance of Wilde's *Salomé*; the decors by Bakst, and the unusual interpretation and strange accents of de Max and Ida Rubinstein made it a most vivid spectacle, and were perfectly suited to Wilde's prose and his aesthetic ideas.

A few days later I read in the *Figaro* that Lugné Poe had announced a performance of *La Brebis egarée*, with my music. Indignantly I rushed off to demand an explanation of him. Jammes had spoken of my music to him and he had thought I would extract from it some incidental music and interludes for his performance of the play. I objected vehemently. The idea of chopping up my music into separate pieces seemed a betrayal of all it meant to me. Moreover, even if I had been willing to accept such a proposal, I should have demanded a full orchestra. This incident tickled Jammes, who said to one of his friends: 'What could you expect Milhaud to do? He wanted an orchestra, and Lugné offered him a fife and drum!' On the other hand, I had produced a Symphonic Suite from my opera, and had orchestrated it in class. It consisted of an overture, the former overture of *La Brebis* which I had suppressed and replaced by a prelude, a slow movement based on the sombre themes of Act II, and a finale made up of rapid extracts from the scene in which Paul evokes the memories of his schooldays.

The pianist Robert Schmitz, with the help of his wife who dealt with all the business arrangements, had formed a choir and orchestra for presenting contemporary works, a task he performed with great enthusiasm. He provided me with the opportunity of hearing myself conduct my own orchestral work in the shape of this symphonic suite. I had no unpleasant surprise, but was reassured at the very first rehearsal: my orchestra sounded exactly as I had wanted it to sound. Roussel's *Evocations* were included in the same programme, and I was able to see for myself the modesty and youthful spirit of that composer. I was enchanted by his work, which tended to move away from the impressionism which, since Debussy, had led French music into an impasse. What interested me most at this time was the music of Magnard, which seemed to me to have harsh and rustic qualities, a sort of harmonic sobriety, providing an antidote against these impressionistic tendencies. At the Opéra-Comique I had heard *Bérénice* which, in spite of its lack of refinement in the instrumentation, or perhaps for that very reason, I had found impressive. I loved the deep feeling in the music, and those long expressive melodies which Magnard gives to the piccolo. Nevertheless, I failed to understand why he had written in the preface to *Bérénice*: '. . . while not having the genius required for a dramatic style properly so-called, he had adopted the Wagnerian leitmotif.' Magnard seemed to me to be such worlds apart from Wagner! I also liked his four symphonies because of their straightforward character; their forthright scherzos are genuine French homespun. The character of the man himself pleased me, for he was independent enough to dispense with a publisher, and had his works produced by an incorporated guild of printers.

It was at this period that I got to know Georges Auric, whom I met sometimes in the corridors of the Conservatoire. He made me marvel at the extent of his culture and his extraordinarily penetrating intelligence and uninhibited ease of composition. Whenever he came to see me, he would pull out of his brief-case manuscripts in which freshness and precocity were combined with a voluntary maturity already firmly under control, without however, impairing the free play of a sensibility which was both carefree and humorous. These are the qualities which have gone into the making of his personality, in which tenderness unites with the piercing lucidity that characterizes the brilliant and striaghtforward works he has continued to produce. About 1910 or 1911 we would often be joined by Honegger when Auric was playing *Chandelles Romaines* or *Gaspard et Zoé* on the piano at the Rue Gaillard.

Honegger and I had started studying fugue in Widor's composition class. That charming teacher, a most brilliant conversationalist, would utter cries of alarm at every dissonance he came across in my works; as he listened he would exclaim: 'The worst of it is that you get used to them!' How far away seemed the justifiably severe criticisms that Gédalge used to make! When the latter heard that I had passed in fugue, he ironically asked me how I had managed it. Wiéner and I were still taking private lessons with him, and I brought him my *Poème* for piano and orchestra (based on the theme of the canticle of Camargue) which I had just completed. No sooner had he run through it than he sat down and wrote two letters which he asked me to post; one was to Gabriel Pierné, suggesting that he should conduct my work, and the other to Lazare Lévy asking him to play it. This instance will serve to illustrate my master's outstanding generosity and devotion. Gabriel Pierné and Lazare Lévy both consented, and my *Poème* was given in 1915 at the Concerts Colonne-Lamoureux.

I saw Claudel again during the rehearsals for *L'Otage* which was being produced by Lugné Poe at the Théatre de l'Oeuvre. He enthusiastically described to me the experimental work being done at the Theatre of Helierau, and persuaded me to go there in September for the performances of *L'Annonce faite à Marie*. He also talked of a satirical drama on which he was working and for which he would require a musical score: 'But you are too serious-minded,' he said to me, suddenly taking his leave.

Chapter Eight

Hellerau

I followed Claudel's advice, and went to Hellerau. I proceeded by easy stages. At Geneva, I called on Ernest Bloch, who played me his *Poèmes juifs* which have a powerful Biblical sweep about them. Jammes had written: 'I have told Henri Duparc you will call on him. Do try and do so.' He was moving house the very day on which I was passing through Montreux, but he was kind enough to invite me to have tea with him in a little pastry-shop. He introduced me to Ernest Ansermet, a young conductor who had just given up his post as a teacher of mathematics in order to devote himself wholly to music.

I made a brief halt at Munich, with its parks and green lawns, and blue-painted trams. I had always been impressed by what Barrès had to say about Venice during its decadence, and about Tiepolo in particular, but I had never had the opportunity of seeing several of his paintings at once. As I strolled through the streets of Munich I came across, in one particular gallery, a retrospective exhibition of his works which thrilled me. On the other hand I could not stomach the paintings of Böcklin, who represented modern German art at that time, and had no inkling that they would have such influence on the young painters of 1930. . . . I loathed Nuremberg, which reminded me too much of paste-board sets for *Die Meistersinger*. Hellerau was six miles from Dresden. To get there you travelled in a tram across a great plain dotted with a few clumps of pines, a sandy plain where tiny little wild pansies grew.

It was quite an ordinary village, only important for its experimental theatre, which also provided a centre for the activities of Jacques Dalcroze. The theatre had been built by Wolf Dohrn, an architect of Polish origin; the highly stylized scenery consisted of huge architectural cubes covered in blue cloth which could be built up in steps and arranged in tiers of varying height, so that performances could proceed on several planes at once. Strips of blue cloth hung from the ceiling, which, according to whether they were placed nearer together or further apart, represented trees, houses, a wall, etc. . . . The lighting came from perpendicular rows of lamps on either side of the stage, which threw the light so that it appeared to come from the actual substance of the walls of the theatre. In the hall the walls consisted of a series of screens that could be opened or closed at will, altering the acoustics according to their position. Salzman, a Russian producer, operated all the complicated permutations of the switchboard controlling the lighting. His wife was a dancer and had studied with certain religious sects in Afghanistan and in this way had learned to develop amazing hypnotic powers of endurance.

Claudel had always advocated vertical scenery, on the grounds that when you read a book you held it vertically in front of you, not horizontally. Thus the aesthetics of the theatre of Hellerau exactly corresponded with his ideas. Later on I realized that in spite of the interest of such experiments, they led to a dryness and monotony of theatrical presentation which threw open the door to the most dubious form of expressionism. Some scenes in *L'Annonce* took place on two planes at once: the human and the divine. When Violaine broke off her engagement, she was playing on the upper plane, whereas her mother was seated down below in front of the fire, which was suggested by a reddish glow through a pile of blue cubes. When Violaine rose up to Heaven at the end of the play, her brilliantly lit silhouette stood out against a great shining cross behind the draperies representing the firmament. Light played a very important part at Hellerau and conferred a wonderful sense of mystery on the performances.

Claudel enjoyed considerable prestige in Germany. His works were displayed in the Hellerau bookshop, some of them translated into German. The King of Saxony attended the performance of his play, as well as many of the Czech friends whom he had made in Prague. After the play, we lingered for a long time in conversation under an arbour of flowers. The writer, Miloz Marten, the soul of the Czechoslovakia that was to be and who was killed in 1918 fighting for the freedom of his country, was there, together with Zdenka Braunerowa, Elémir Bourges's sister-in-law, who was also an ardent patriot. She was godmother to little Reine Claudel, who had been born in Prague. She used to draw and had done a lot of vignettes for the end-plates of Claudel's books.

First of all they had put me up in a *pension* for vegetarian girls which Claudel called 'the gazelles' enclosure', but my youthful appetite was too keen for me to be satisfied with a diet consisting of nuts and raw tomatoes washed down with tea, and I took a room in a baker's where the fare was more substantial. I divided my time between work and rehearsals. I had started to compose the *Agamemnon* music, and I worked at it lying in the fields. Claudel had clearly indicated where he wanted my music to intervene in the play. He had observed that in Aeschylus's style, especially in certain choruses or dialogues, there were sudden transitions to a lyrical utterance of such a pitch that it absolutely demanded the support of choir and orchestra. He would not have any music until Clytemnestra came out of the palace with her blood-stained axe in her hand and encountered the chorus of old men. It was from their violent altercation that the music sprang. I tried to avoid the usual type of incidental music, which is a form of expression I detested at that time. There is nothing more false than the intrusion of a musical phrase while the actors go on speaking their lines without a pause, since melody and speech exist on absolutely incompatible planes. To bring out this excess of lyrical content, what is wanted is a transition from speech to song. In my score the strophes sung by Clytemnestra (dramatic soprano) alternated with the anti-strophes sung by the chorus of old men (male voice choir) against the background of a normal symphony orchestra. I wrote variations on a fixed theme, which recurred unchanged at the heart of each new strophe, in the same key as at the beginning, and as a fanfare for the entry of Aegystheus after he has been proclaimed king. When he imposed silence on the crowd, the music came to an end, and the actors spoke their lines to the end of the play.

Aeschylus wrote a satirical drama of which only the title has been preserved; Claudel had brooded over the two syllables of this title, and so had come to write *Protée*, a work in which the most truculent fooling is mingled with the most exquisite poetry. He gave it to me to read before I left Hellerau, and I was able to tell him that, although he thought I was too 'serious-minded', this mixture of buffoonery and real emotion raised problems that I found enthrallingly interesting.

Chapter Nine

The 1913–1914 Season

I started to write the *Protée* music in a delightful country house owned by the Xavier Léons in Seine-et-Marne; it had formerly belonged to Madame Sans-Gêne. I had a very pleasant room and I loved to contemplate the landscape spread out before my eyes: lawns and woodlands, and the green flowers of two enormous American tulip-trees.

Claudel always worked amid a positive whirl of plans, most of which either came to nothing or turned out quite differently from what had been intended; this was the reason why I came to compose three different versions of the *Protée*. The first called for very little music: a little *a cappella* chorus to suggest the different levels of sound produced by the bleating of a flock of sheep; a fanfare for unaccompanied brass to illustrate the feeding of the seals; a *pianissimo* nocturne to be played during the nocturnal bacchanalia (for the latter I used a piece I had written for piano and violin: *Le Printemps*, which I now scored for string quartet and oboe); and a finale *A la Gloire du vin de Bourgogne* for male voice choir and full orchestra.

In 1916 Gémier planned to give some performances of *Protée* in a circus, and asked me to prepare a version for an orchestra of about fifteen, which would play above the theatre like a circus band. Gémier was obliged to abandon his project. Then in 1919 Gheusi tried to put on a very luxurious production of *Protée* at the Théâtre du Vaudeville, with scenery by José Maria Sert. He asked me to expand my music, and score it for full orchestra. Under these new circumstances, I composed overtures to each act, a prelude and fugue to precede the meal of the seals, and a finale for Act I, designed to accompany a film depicting the successive metamorphoses of Proteus. I re-scored the parts already written. Gheusi's theatrical ventures were short-lived, however, and came to an end just when rehearsals were due to begin.

Wearied by all these changes, I made another Symphonic Suite out of my *Protée* music. It is in this form that the work is now given in concerts and has been recorded.

In the absence of professional performances, '*Protée*' was staged by students on various occasions. It was played in Dutch at an important ceremony at the University of Groningen. Claudel and I were invited to attend, but he was at his post in Washington, and I suggested that his son Pierre should accompany me in his place. We were received at the station of Groningen by student representatives clad in their traditional university gowns. They escorted our four-horse carriage to the theatre. The perform-ance was a light-hearted and impromptu affair. In Geneva, as the students only had a limited number of instrumentalists at their disposal, I asked Jean Binet, an excellent musician from the French-speaking part of Swit-zerland, to adapt my music to their requirements. Finally, in Paris, the play was presented by the students of the Sorbonne with scenery by Jean Effel and — a piano. . . .

The Society of *La Libre Esthétique*, whose president was Octave Maus, organized many outstanding artistic events in Brussels. It was responsible for the first exhibition of Impressionistic painting in Belgium; Gide lectured there on *Criticism*, and on *Literary Influences*; Vincent d'Indy, Chausson and Magnard conducted concerts there. In 1914, for the first time, *La Libre Esthétique* engaged a musician belonging to my generation. They asked me to play my First Sonata with Georgette Guller. I was immediately struck with the hospitality of the Belgians, and with their respect for music. I stayed with a painter, Anna Bock. It was at this time that I completed my Sonata for piano and two violins, my first chamber music work that I did not later repudiate. Other older compositions, such as my first string quartet or my piano suite, although published, no longer satisfy me, and I do not like them to be played.

Jeanne Herscher was a great friend of the composer Charles Koechlin. I often met him at her house. I loved his music, his harmonic experiments, and the marvellous range of his mind. On his way to the Var he stopped for a few days at Aix. He was travelling with some hives of bees which he intended for his estate and had registered them with the luggage, which terrified the porters, especially when he had to change trains. He arrived at L'Enclos swathed in a great shepherd's cloak, with half a water-melon under his arm. We talked together about music, discussing the *Sacre du printemps* which we had hailed with such enthusiasm at its first perform-ance a year before. We not only admired its violent rhythms, its harmonic discords and polytonality, all of which had been foreshadowed in *Petrushka*, but, on quite a different plane, the novelty of the work. In it ballet was getting away from picturesque externals towards a dramatic and barbaric goal. Many musicians were quite unable to accept this rift with the past. Despite his admiration for Stravinsky, Debussy was anxious about the lines along which he was developing. Schmitt declared that 'all that was left to him was to tear up his music'. (What a pity he did not do so!) The younger generation, on the contrary, felt encouraged by this work, in spite of its profoundly Russian character, which kept it alien to our own aspirations. . . .

Georgette Guller followed Koechlin at L'Enclos; every day we went for long walks together. We would often be joined by Léo, who spent most of his evenings at L'Enclos. He would read his poems, while Georgette would play Chopin, whom she interpreted marvellously; I would sing the settings I had just made of Léo's latest poems, *La Tourterelle, Ma douleur et sa compagne*; then we would go and sit by the pool, with its myriad reflections of stars on nights when there was no moon, and listen in silence to the frantic warbling of the nightingales.

In July Léo asked me to go with him to see Jammes. A day or two later I left him at Orthez so that he and Jammes might attend the Eucharistic Congress at Lourdes, where the Papal Legate was to say the Pontifical Mass, and I went back to Aix to complete the second Act of *La Brebis egarée*, and write the third. I felt somehow that I ought to hurry. I wrote the last scene at one sitting, and finished it on the 28th July. Unfortunately, my presentiment had been only too justified: on 2nd August 1914, a gendarme came to stick the white mobilization poster on the walls of L'Enclos. War was declared! Caught in the Landes, where he had gone with Jammes and his wife, Léo hurriedly returned, travelling by military trains. He lost his luggage on the way, containing the latest volume of his Diary; he and Jammes made vain efforts to recover it. . . .

This was the first omen of grief to come, as was the sound of the tocsin at the Mairie, incessantly hammering out the announcement of war: I shall never forget its hurried tolling mingling with the shrill notes of the cicalas. . . .

Chapter Ten

The War

When the German thrust towards Paris had reached its farthest point, just before the battle of the Marne, many of my friends and relatives came and took refuge in Aix. Among them were my Aunt Lily and her two children, Etienne and Madeleine. Two of their neighbours in the country, Jeanne Thomassin and her mother, had come to join them. Jeanne was a former actress who had played with great success in the early plays of Tristan Bernard, and had made several tours in Russia where she had distinguished herself. This gay, amusing, affected, emphatic woman, who was never seen without her mother or her dog, a horrible little pug, improvised a theatrical atmosphere around her whetever she went. She was an excellent teacher, and had taken an interest in my cousin Madeleine, who had been studying with her to be an actress ever since the age of six. Madeleine was also very gifted musically, and we played together all the music that came to hand, from Beethoven to the *Sacre du printemps*. Although she was only twelve, Madeleine maintained a prodigious activity: she did all the housework for her mother, including the cooking if the need arose; she used to bring me delicious caramels cooked over a candle-flame; the remainder of her time was spent on her bicycle in the company of her brother, who worshipped her. These two children had such a profound understanding of one another that I always felt they were leagued together against the whole of the rest of the family. Whenever I used to go and see them at Vaucresson before the War, their whispers and conspiratorial airs only ceased when the whole family set out for the inevitable ritual walk to 'see the view' from the Bois de Villepreux, where they went to admire the sunset — *en famille* and in silence.

While I waited to receive my calling-up papers, I remained in Aix and resumed work. I orchestrated *La Brebis egarée* and started on my second string quartet. Léo had been posted to Briançon with the Chasseurs Alpins. He looked upon the war as a mission, a solution to his personal problems and got himself posted to the front as soon as he could. Gradually the first bad news filtered through to us: Albéric Magnard shot by the Germans and his house burnt down; my cousin Daniel Palm killed before Lunéville — his parents were notified the very day their youngest daughter Suzanne was repatriated from Germany, where she had been spending her holidays to perfect her German. When Etienne was called up with the 1915 class, Madeleine and I went with him in the tram as far as Pont de l'Arc, the first stop after Aix. We came back on foot along the little river, dark with shadows and lined with richly-hued trees. It was the first autumn I had spent in Aix since 1908.

I was rejected for military service on medical grounds, and went back to Paris in December. Apart from Henri Cliquet, who was in the auxiliary services acting as gardener at the Hospital of Versailles, and Honegger, who had only been mobilized for a few weeks in Switzerland, all my friends from the Conservatoire were at the front. Every year the Conservatoire awarded the Lepaulle Prize for composition. I won it with my Sonata for two violins and piano: that is the only time in my life I have ever won an award. . . . On my way to the Conservatoire I would stop every day at the window of my cousin Madeleine's room to chat with her for a moment — she and her mother were temporarily lodged in a ground-floor apartment almost opposite my place. I would also go across to keep her company during air raids by Zeppelins.

As I wanted to engage in some form of war work, I joined the Foyer Franco-Belge. This organization, whose headquarters were at the Galerie Druet in the Rue Royale, was partly supported by funds collected in America by Mrs Edith Wharton. Its aims were to assist refugees by giving them money and work. Gide played an active part in it and put me in the section run by Charles Du Bos. 'Charlie' was so overworked that he rarely left his office before midnight; he conducted every investigation like a psychological inquiry, hoping in this way to ensure the fairest possible distribution of the funds. Some of the poor refugees had difficulty in adjusting themselves to the idea of their misfortune: 'Ah, monsieur,' one of them said to Gide, 'we were so proud at Waterloo!' I often went home on foot with Charlie, and we engaged in endless conversations. He asked me to organize a series of concerts to raise funds for the good work. I leapt at the opportunity. Jeanne Herscher lent us her music-room and with the assistance of many artists, I gave a number of 'Foyer Franco-Belge' concerts. Gide called at my house several times, and I persuaded him to read me his notes on Chopin, which were still unpublished at that time. I was highly impressed by them; few men have felt so clearly as he that Chopin was first and foremost a tender and sensitive musician, and not the forlorn and morbid Romantic he was so often made out to be. Gide discerned the authentic purity and nobility of Chopin's music, and realized that the unfortunate reputation of 'morbidezza' under which he laboured was only due to performers who took liberties with tempi and rubatos, thus absurdly exaggerating the musical expression instead of strictly observing the time indicated. I told Gide of my intention to write a cantata on *Le Retour de l'enfant prodigue*, using only the passages of dialogue, and he gave me his permission to do so.

Cipa Godebski, the brother of Misia Edwards, who worked at the Foyer, invited me to go and see him. He and his wife Ida were at home regularly on Sunday evenings. Ravel often went there. Viñes used to play Spanish music and works by Debussy. You might also meet there Satie, whose music was still somewhat unfamiliar to me, Gallimard, closely attended by some of his contributors to the *Nouvelle Revue Française*, and Fargue, who would turn up just when everyone else was going. The Engel Bathoris also entertained a few friends on Sundays for musical evenings and I deserted the Godebskis to join them. What unforgettable times we spent together! Old Engel sang *L'Horizon chimérique*, we read through Ravel's choral music, and all the latest published music. In this way I came to play Debussy's Sonata for viola, flute and harp, with Manouvrier and Jeanne Dalliez. When Durand heard about this, he asked us to give the first performance at his house during one of the rehearsals, and sent me to Debussy's house to ask for advice on one or two points. This was the first and only opportunity I ever had of meeting the master. With what emotion I entered the room where the musician who held such sway in my heart, used to work. . . . He was already afflicted by the disease which was to carry him off, his face was deathly pale and his hands affected by a slight tremor. He sat down at the piano and played me his sonata twice. Through excessive modesty and discretion, although I had already written *Les Choëphores*, I made no mention of my own compositions.

During the summer of 1915, I took a short leave to go and see my parents. On the way back, I broke the journey to call on Claudel's father-in-law, the architect of the church of Fourvière at Lyons, Monsieur de Sainte-Marie-Perrin, with whom Claudel was staying for a few days before going back to his post of commercial attaché to the Embassy in Rome. All Madame Claudel's numerous family loved to congregate in that great château at Hostel en Valromay in the Ain. There were lots of children; in the evenings their cries gave way to the low-pitched murmur of the parents' conversation which came to me along the terrace like a muted echo of the noises of the afternoon. Before going back to Paris, I called on Jeanne Herscher, who owned an old priory near Vézelay. There I found Madame Claudel's brother and his wife, the daughter of René Bazin. Madame de Sainte-Marie-Perrin was a poetess and a writer who had written a very remarkable study of Claudel in which she showed proof of a profound understanding of his work. She translated some of Tagore's poems for me to put them to music. Delightful as it would have been to linger there in the vicinity of Givry with its lovely dark streams and pink Burgundian roads,

Darius Milhaud composing his opera *La Brebis égarée* in 1910

Milhaud at the piano, rue Gaillard, 1920

Milhaud with Francis Poulenc in 1921

3ᵉᵐᵉ CONCERT JEAN WIÉNER

LUNDI 16 JANVIER 1922, à 9 heures, à la SALLE GAVEAU, 45, Rue La Boëtie

PIERROT LUNAIRE

d'ARNOLD SCHÖNBERG

MÉLODRAME EN 21 PARTIES POUR VOIX ET PETIT ORCHESTRE

1ʳᵉ Partie : ι. Ivresse de lune - ιι. Colombine - ιιι. Pierrot dandy - ιν. Lune au lavoir - ν. Valse de Chopin - νι. Évocation - νιι. Lune malade
2ᵐᵉ Partie : νιιι. Nuit - ιχ. Prière à Pierrot - χ. Vol - χι. Messe rouge - χιι. Chant du pendu - χιιι. Décapitation - χιν. Les croix
3ᵐᵉ Partie : χν. Nostalgie - χνι. Insolence - χνιι. Parodie - χνιιι. Tache de lune - χιχ. Sérénade - χχ. Le retour - χχι. Le vieux parfum.

PAR

MARYA FREUND
JEAN WIÉNER
MM. FLEURY, DELACROIX, ROËLENS et FEUILLARD

SOUS LA DIRECTION DE

DARIUS MILHAUD

PIANO GAVEAU

AUCUN BILLET DE FAVEUR NE SERA DONNÉ

PLACES à 3, 4, 6, 10, 12, 15, 20 et 25 francs, à la SALLE GAVEAU, 45, Rue La Boëtie, chez DURAND, 4, Place de la Madeleine, au BUREAU MUSICAL,
20, Rue Trouchet et à l'Administration de Concerts A. DANDELOT, 83 Rue d'Amsterdam, Téléph. Gut. 13-29.

Poster announcing the first performance of *Pierrot Lunaire*
to be conducted by Milhaud

Darius Milhaud and Arnold Schoenberg in Vienna in 1922

With Jean Cocteau in London in 1921

Milhaud and Hindemith in Paris in 192

During the rehearsals for La création du monde in 1923: Blaise
Cendrars, Rolf de Maré, Milhaud, Fernand Léger and Jean Börlin

Milhaud in Baden-Baden with Burckhardt
and Béla Bartok in 1928

Darius Milhaud with Henri Sauguet in 1928

Darius Milhaud and Paul Claudel at l'Enclos, Aix-en-Provence, in 1930

The thirty years which separate these two photographs taken of the Group of Six (on the Eiffel Tower in 1921 and at home with Darius Milhaud in 1950) did nothing to change the friendship which bound together Francis Poulenc, Germaine Tailleferre, Georges Auric, Louis Durey, Arthur Honneger, Darius Milhaud . . . and Jean Cocteau

Milhaud in California in 1950

Darius and Madeleine Milhaud at Mills College in 1946

Darius and Madeleine Milhaud in 1948, in the Hans Richter film
Dreams That Money Can Buy

Darius Milhaud, together with Madeleine and their son Daniel, prepares
to return to France in 1947. Note the number of scores Milhaud
produced during his stay at Mills College

Milhaud with his son Daniel during rehearsals for *Bolivar* at the Paris Opera in 1950

Darius Milhaud and Armand Lunel arriving in Israel in 1952
for the first discussions on their opera *David*

Students at Mills College, along with Dave Brubeck and Leland Smith,
help celebrate Milhaud's sixtieth birthday

At home with Darius Milhaud at Mills College in 1958:
Françoise Arnoul, Micheline Presle, Gérard Philipe, Jean Marais
and Jean Renoir. Josepha Heifetz is at the piano

Darius Milhaud and Olivier Messiaen at Aspen in 1962

Milhaud and Jean-Luis Barrault during rehearsals for *Judith* in 1961

At the first ecumenical concert, given for Pope Paul VI at the Vatican, in 1965

Milhaud with Shostakovich and Jean Wiéner in 1960

Overleaf: Darius Milhaud with his grandchildren, Solange and David, in 1966

and the fascinating evenings when poetry was followed by music, I had to get back to Paris and work.

I had undertaken a thoroughgoing study of the problem of polytonality. I had noted — and interpreted as a sign for myself — that a little duet by Bach written in canon at the fifth really gave one the impression of two separate keys succeeding one another, and then becoming superimposed and contrasted, although of course the harmonic texture remained tonal. Contemporary composers like Stravinsky or Koechlin, made use of chords containing several tonalities, often handled contrapuntally or used as pedal. I set to work to examine every possible combination of two keys superimposed and to study the chords thus produced. I also studied the effect of inverting them. I tried every imaginable permutation by varying the mode of the tonalities making up these chords. Then I did the same thing for three keys. What I could not understand was why, although the harmony books dealt with chords and their inversions, and the laws governing their sequences, the same thing could not be done for polytonality. I grew familiar with some of these chords. They satisfied my ear more than the normal ones, for a polytonal chord is more subtly sweet and more violently potent. I built up the music for *Les Choëphores* on the basis of my research, and added to my manuscript the sub-title: 'Harmonic Variations'. For each strophe and antistrophe, indeed, I established in most cases a definite line of harmonic research, applying to sequences of chords the technique used for variations. The essential part of the music, however, remained the general melodic line. Even when I studied chords containing twelve notes, I only used them to sustain a diatonic melody, remembering Gédalge's advice: 'Just write eight bars that can be sung without accompaniment.'

The score of *Les Choëphores* was constructed in the following way: a Funereal Vociferation for choir and orchestra to accompany the entry of the Choephori bearing libations to Agamemnon's tomb; a chorus *a cappella* entitled 'Libation' which was my first attempt to write a chorus in two simultaneous keys, with the lines of chords in the male voices set over against the women's voices and both forming a background for a soprano solo; an 'Incantation' sung by Electra (soprano), Orestes (baritone) and chorus before Agamemnon's tomb; and then 'Presages' and 'Exhortations', two scenes so violent in character that they created a problem which I solved by having the words spoken in time with the music by one woman narrator, while the choruses uttered words or disjointed phrases, the rhythm of which was indicated, but not the pitch. To support all these various speech elements I used percussion instruments having no definite pitch — quite ordinary instruments listed in all the treatises on orchestration; finally, I ended with a 'Hymn to Justice' for choir and orchestra, and a spoken 'Conclusion' for voices and percussion.

On September 27th, 1915, as I was going across the Place de Villiers, I felt an exceedingly acute physical pang, which lasted several seconds. I immediately thought of Léo and feared that some disaster had befallen him. Later I was to learn that I had felt this pain at the very moment of his death. It was at the height of an offensive in Champagne; he had been wounded but, although no longer able to handle a rifle, refused to be evacuated so that he might take part in the attack with his comrades. He was mown down by the German machine guns at the head of his company while encouraging his men. His family sent me a copy of his will; he had left me his Diary. He had deposited it, together with my letters, in an old wooden chest, an eighteenth-century sailor's trunk; I added the letters I had received from him. Subsequently, Dr Latil had a selection of his letters and extracts from his diary published by Plon. This supreme testimony of his pure Christian faith and spirit of self-sacrifice was singled out for mention by Barrès on account of the distinction of its thought. While I was in Brazil I had a hundred copies of Léo's poems privately printed. A few months after his death, I wrote my third string quartet, dedicated to his memory. This consists of two very slow movements, in the second of which I introduced a soprano voice singing a page from Léo's diary ending: 'What is this longing for death, and which death does it mean?' This sentence had haunted my imagination ever since I had read it. I have refused to publish this quartet so long as I am alive, but the firm of Durand is under contract to publish it within six months of my death.*

I left the Foyer Franco-Belge to work at the Maison de la Presse, grouped with the propaganda services directed by Philippe Berthelot, and therefore came under the Ministry of Foreign Affairs. I was sworn into the Army, and attached to the Army photographic service. I made friends with a number of young diplomatists. We used to meet occasionally at a restaurant in the Place Gaillon. We had delightful meals, enlivened by the spicy anecdotes of Paul Morand and René Chalupt, the musician-poet, and by Saint-Léger Léger's tales of the West Indies, to all of which Henri Hoppenot and I listened in silence. I had just finished my *Poèmes juifs*, settings for some anonymous poems I had come across in a revue, and I was seriously thinking of composing music for the *Eumenides* in Claudel's translation. I mentioned it to him one day when I met him at the Maison de la Presse. He complained of having too much to do at Rome; he needed a secretary, and proposed that I should get Berthelot to send me there on detachment. Before this scheme could materialize, however, he was appointed Minister to Brazil. He renewed his request, and the idea of going with him so far away, and the great longing for solitude I had felt since Léo's death, made me decide to accept.

At the end of December, my parents and my friend Yvonne Giraud accompanied the great man and his 'secretary' to the Gare d'Orsay.

* In fact Durand published the quartet in 1956 (Translators' note).

Chapter Eleven

Brazil

I shall never forget the effect which the sight of neutral Spain produced in me. What a startling contrast with France, where in the streets you now only met aged civilians and old horses rejected for military service, spavined old hacks formerly used for farmwork. No sooner had you crossed the frontier at Irun than you saw crowds of young men and mettlesome horses, and apart from the customs officers and gendarmes, not a single uniform. Portugal on the other hand had begun to feel the effects of war, and the convoy escorting our English steamer the *Amazon* out of territorial waters was conveying to France the first Portuguese military contingents.

The crossing took eighteen days. At night, on the completely blacked-out upper deck, I felt caught mid-way between the starry firmament and the sea. From that vantage-point, I witnessed the transition from northern to southern skies at the equator: the Great Bear still glittered on the horizon as the Southern Cross, closely attended by the twinkling glow of the two stars in the constellation of the Centaur, rose to meet it.

We reached Rio on February 1st, 1917, on a blazing hot day like midsummer. Claudel found quarters for me with him at the French Legation; magnificently situated in the Rua Paysandu, a street bordered with royal palms from the isle of Réunion sometimes more than two hundred feet in height and crowned with swaying fronds over twenty feet long. Throughout these two years, Claudel's activity was a constant source of wonder to me: he would get up at six in the morning and go to mass, then he would work until ten a.m. After that he devoted his time entirely to his diplomatic duties until five p.m. when he would go off on his own for a walk. I would sometimes see him striding along the sea-front, nervously rubbing his hands together and so absorbed in his thoughts that he failed to see me. I would never accost him. Sometimes he took me with him for his walk along the foreshore, but it was usually on Sundays that we went out together. As soon as dinner was over, he would retire to his own room and go to bed early. His thoughts were always centred on the Bible. Every day he would write commentaries on verses from both Testaments. He let me read some of them, impressively lofty in their inspiration. At that time he was much preoccupied with the topic of water, which looms so large in mystical thought, and he would choose verses from Genesis naming water in all its manifold forms: sea, lake, cloud, rain, spring, river, wetness, dew, mist, well — and write commentaries on them. Claudel the Minister was no less amazing than Claudel the writer: he had a very catholic conception of his diplomatic function, and took a passionate interest in all economic and financial problems, for which he invariably found some ingenious solution. He only entrusted copying work or enciphering and deciphering to his secretaries, and personally drafted all telegrams and dispatches.

Rio had a potent charm. It is difficult to describe that lovely bay, ringed with fantastically shaped mountains covered with a light shading of forest or crowned with solitary red-brown pinnacles of rock, sometimes topped with lines of palm-trees that stood out like ostrich feathers in the murky light of the tropics against a sky shrouded in pearly grey cloud. I would often stroll in the centre of the city where — a refreshing contrast with the broad Avenida Rio Branco — the cool, shady streets were too narrow for wheeled traffic. In the most colourful of them all, the Rua Ouvidor, antique shops crowded with furniture from the Imperial period stood next to displays of luscious fruit where I tasted delicious *refrescos* of mango or coconut. Not far away, on the hill, the little Gloria church, eighteenth-century baroque in style, like most of the ecclesiastical architecture in Brazil, displayed its colours of pink, blue and tender green, and its *azulejos* among which were to be seen magnificent examples of wood carving. I would also sometimes go to Copocabana beach, facing the Atlantic. Along it stood a few houses, including one delightfully amusing one by the architect Virzi. In the evenings I often walked around the Tijuca. I loved to see the panorama of Rio gradually spread out before me, with the bay clearly outlined in glittering lights; or else I would take a boat to the other side of the bay, near Nichteroy, and lie on the lonely beach for a whole part of the night with the moonlight so bright that I could read easily.

The Botanical Gardens of Rio are most impressive: on either side of a long central path lined with gigantic royal palms, various kinds of exotic trees — mangoes, giant bamboos, bread-trees, cocoa trees, different types of coffee plants, sugar-cane and tea — grew in rich profusion. This array of foods and beverages stood next to lyre-shaped latanias known as the Traveller's-tree, because the stalks secrete a refreshing liquid. In a pond fringed with trees no less picturesque, water-lilies floated on their enormous leaves, and towering above all else, rose extraordinary banyan trees with roots springing half way up their trunk, as if they were carrying them on their shoulders. What hours I spent in this garden of wonders! But the lure of the forest was greater yet. It began even inside the city, for so luxuriant was the vegetation that it invaded the least patch of unoccupied land. Any site that was not built over immediately fell victim to an invading horde of plants, and the roads on the outskirts of Rio passed through enchanted forests. Claudel and I often took the Corcovado funicular as far as Paineras. From there we followed a little track along a rivulet from whose banks we looked down on the mountainside drowned in a torrent of dense vegetation in which glittered the shiny, silvery leaves of the bilo-bilo. No sooner had the sun set than, as if operated by an invisible switch, all kinds of crickets, cooper-toads which imitate the sound of a hammer banging on a plank of wood, birds with dull, sharp or staccato cries, peopled the forest night with their different noises that sometimes rose swiftly to a pitch of paroxysm.

In order to recruit our strength after the dank heat of Rio, we would sometimes go and spend the week-end in the mountains at Therezina. The inn there was run by a Frenchman called Norbert. We could do some riding there, but what we liked best was to go on foot into the heart of the forest, accompanied by two negroes who hacked a way for us through the tangle of trees, giant ferns and intertwining lianas. They would also keep up a great fire for us all through the night. We slept under a vault of foliage from which occasional long trailing clusters of orchids hung down amid the lianas. The contrast was equally striking between the inhabitants of the city and of the forest; for in Rio, on the very fringe of the forest, lived descendants of the Nordic races who had gradually reverted to savagery and now inhabited miserable huts, surrounded by hordes of half-naked children and having a wretched field of maize or one or two banana trees for sole possessions.

A month or two after our arrival in Rio, Henri Hoppenot was appointed secretary to the Legation. Overjoyed, I went to the boat to meet him and his wife Hélène. Already I felt how much their presence was going to mean to me. Henri Hoppenot was a young writer and a great admirer of Claudel. What a curious Legation that was, with two writers and a musician. . . . During our long walks together, we got to know one another better and our friendship deepened. We would carry our friends off for the week-end to Therezina or Petropolis; the latter was the summer residence for diplomats, members of the Government or wealthy *cariocas* — inhabitants of Rio — and was too artificial for our liking, but we were drawn thither by Audrey Parr, a delightful friend of dazzling beauty and irrepressible high spirits. She was the wife of the Secretary to the British Legation and had got to know Claudel in Rome. As she could draw, he used to get her to do sketches for all the illustrations that thronged his ever fertile imagination.

My first contact with Brazilian folklore was very sudden. I arrived in Rio right in the middle of the Carnaval, and immediately sensed the mood of crazy gaiety that possessed the whole town. The Carnaval in Rio is an important event whose coming is most laboriously prepared in advance. Several months beforehand the newspapers carry announcements of the formation of 'Carnaval clubs', together with the name of their president, secretary and members. These little groups meet daily in preparation for the festivities, and often spend large sums, occasionally all their savings, on fancy dress adorned with elaborate decorations of ostrich feathers. Six weeks before the Carnaval is due to begin, groups of *cordoes* perambulate the streets on Saturdays and Sunday evenings, select a little square and dance to the music of *violao* (a kind of guitar) and a few percussion instruments like the *choucalha* (a kind of round copper container filled with iron filings and terminating in a rod to which a rotatory motion is given, thus producing a continuous rhythmical sound). One of the dancers' favourite amusements is to improvise words to a tune which is repeated over and over again. The singer has to keep on finding new words, and as soon as his imagination begins to flag, someone else takes his place. The monotony of this never-ending chorus and its insistent rhythm end by producing a sort of hypnosis to which the dancers fall victim. I remember seeing a negro completely carried away by the music, dancing frenziedly all on his own, holding in his hand a huge ice-cream which he would lick with his pink tongue in time with the music. . . .

The crowds in the ballrooms were much more elegant. The Carnaval organizers decree one single shade for the ladies' dresses; they must wear a different one every night. They go to the ball in all their finery, leaning on their husbands' arms. As most of the negro dancers are servants, they borrow their masters' clothes and even sometimes their names and titles. One evening I heard 'The President of the Senate' and 'The British Ambassador' announced, and saw two negro couples, dressed up to the nines, proudly come forward. For six weeks, the whole populace is passionately given over to dancing and singing; there is always one song which wins more favour than the others, and thereby becomes the 'Carnaval song'. Thus 'Pelo Telefono', the Carnaval song for 1917, was to be heard wherever one went, ground out by little orchestras in front of the cinemas in the Avendia, played by military bands and municipal orchestras, churned out by pianolas and gramophones, whistled and sung after a fashion in every house — and it haunted us all the winter.

I was intrigued and fascinated by the rhythms of this popular music. There was an imperceptible pause in the syncopation, a careless catch in the breath, a slight hiatus which I found very difficult to grasp. So I bought a lot of maxixes and tangoes and tried to play them with their syncopated rhythms that run from one hand to the other. At last my efforts were rewarded and I could both play and analyze this typically Brazilian subtlety. One of the best composers of this kind of music, Nazareth, used to play the piano at the door of a cinema in the Avenida Rio Branco. His elusive, mournful, liquid way of playing also gave me deeper insight into the Brazilian soul.

Before I left Paris, I had met André Messager, back from Brazil, who had recommended me to get to know the music of Glauco Velasquez. When I had done so, I was struck by its resemblance, both structurally and in inspiration, with that of Guillaume Lekeu. An uncanny likeness, since both composers died at the age of twenty-six! One Sunday, a young pianist named Luciano Gallet took me to see an aged relative of Velasquez who lived on the enchanting Isle of Paqueta. Her delightful, rather tumbledown, old house, surrounded with overgrown gardens, dated from the colonial period. I was shown the rough draft of a Trio by Velasquez, which I found to be complete. I edited it, and had it played at one of my lectures at the Lycée Français. The Director of the Conservatoire, Henrique Oswald, often invited me to dine with him on a Sunday. He was married to a vivacious and witty Florentine lady who, with her children, kept up a constant flow of high spirits all the evening. At their house I met the conductor of the Symphony Orchestra of Rio, Francesco Braga, who had been taught by Massenet in Paris, as well as a young newly-wedded couple of musicians, the Oswald Guerras. Oswald composed music steeped in the French tradition, while his wife Nininha, who also composed, was above all an excellent pianist. Her father Leao Velloso was a piano teacher, and had encouraged her to play a great deal of contemporary music. He instilled a taste for it in all those around him, his daughter, his pupils, and even his dog, who answered to the name of 'Satie'. I became friendly with the Vellosos, and often went to see them. They introduced me to the music of Satie, which was imperfectly known to me at that time, and I ran over it with Nininha, who was extremely good at reading any contemporary music.

Every mail brought me piles of letters from my mother and my faithful friends. Bathori would keep me up to date with musical life in Paris. As soon as I received a copy of *En blanc et noir*, which had just been published by Durand, Leao Velloso and his daughter played it. I had organized concerts in aid of our war charities, and the Vellosos' unwearying devotion enabled me to give several recitals of chamber music in which I included the sonatas of Magnard and Debussy, and my Second Sonata for piano and violin which I had just completed.

In the course of a lecture tour which I undertook on behalf of the Red Cross and Prisoners of War Comforts Fund, I visited the state of Minas Geraes, which is rich in gold and diamond mines. Our train was boarded at Bello Horizonte by a very strange individual wearing a great cloak and a pistol belt, and with a wide-brimmed hat pulled down over his eyes. In the luggage van he registered 40 kilograms of rough diamonds. The goldmine of San Juan del Rey, considered at that time the deepest mine in the world, was run by Englishmen. It was situated near the pleasant little town of Ouro Preto, and when you saw the latter spread out over several hill-tops and crowned with a picturesque church, it was difficult to imagine the infernal underground workings so near at hand. . . . I visited the mine, going down 5,000 feet in the cage and another 6,000 feet in a kind of basket. Down below, there was an old mule that had not seen the light of day for many years, tirelessly hauling trucks piled high with broken stone, which half-naked negroes streaming with sweat hacked from the living rock. The whole scene had the grandiose beauty of an ancient bas-relief.

As soon as I arrived in Rio, I started work on *Les Euménides*. In *Les Choëphores* I had used chords superimposed in masses; the nature of the musical thought in *Les Euménides* led me to adopt the same device. When I wrote the *Récit de la Pythie* for narrator and a few percussion instruments, I mentioned it to Ansermet, who at the time was conducting the rehearsals of the Ballets Russes, and he suggested he should get together the players required for this scene and have them play my music at the end of a rehearsal, in order to give me an opportunity of hearing what it sounded like. I gladly accepted. I have seldom been surprised by the sound of my orchestrations, but this time the performance surpassed my fondest hopes; it expressed for me an authentic intensity of dramatic feeling such as I had imagined.

I also composed and completed *L'Enfant prodigue*. I chose an orchestra of twenty-one players to accompany the voices of the singers (piccolo, flute, oboe, cor anglais, clarinet, bass clarinet, bassoon, horn, trumpet, trombone, timpani, harp and percussion, and two quartets of strings placed one on either side of the conductor). What I wanted was to eliminate all non-essential links, and to provide each instrument with an independent melodic line or tonality. In this case, polytonality is no longer a matter of chords, but of the encounter of lines. Owing to the intricate mingling of the instrumental parts, I could only make an arrangement for two pianos, which I hastened to play with Nininha. In composing this music, I had recaptured the sounds I had dreamed of as a child when I closed my eyes for sleep and seemed to hear music I thought I should never be able to express. I was attracted by the unusual quality of small groups of instruments, and embarked on a series of *Petites Symphonies* for seven or eight different instruments. I was most anxious to hear the effect of these experiments in tonal independence: Braga played the *Première Symphonie* at one of his concerts. The audience did not seem to object to the sound of my music, but ignorant or forgetful of the fact that in the days of Monteverdi the word 'symphony' was sometimes used to denote a single page of instrumental music, it expected to hear a huge work played by a huge orchestra and was shocked by the brevity of my piece.

Various troupes succeeded one another in Rio that winter: Régina Badet and André Brûlé came, and Caruso sang at the Opera. There were also several concerts. Arthur Rubinstein's recitals were a veritable triumph. At one of them, just when Arthur was about to play the first bars of one of his pieces, an enthusiastic negro rose to his feet in the upper gallery and made a seemingly interminable speech, at the conclusion of which he threw the pianist, who was amused and remained motionless, an enormous bouquet which missed its target and fell in the orchestra pit. Rubinstein often visited the Legation. What grand times we had! Hardly had he finished telling, or rather miming, one of his stories than he sat down at the piano and played us all his repertoire, as well as transcriptions of orchestral works. He played in the most masterly fashion the subtlest of scores such as *L'Après-Midi d'un faune* or *Le Sacre du printemps*, the soul of which he managed to convey. Rubinstein was one of the first to make known in Europe and the United States the music of Villa Lobos, the composer who is now so famous, but in those days was compelled to play the cello in a cinema, to keep body and soul together.

Diaghilev's Ballets Russes also gave a series of performances in Rio that winter. The troupe came to spend the evening at the Legatin. We were eager to hear the details of Cocteau's ballet *Parade*, for which Satie had written the music and which had just been given its first performance in Paris. Ansermet described the scenery and costumes by Picasso; and the accessories with which Satie had augmented the orchestra, such as a typewriter, a roulette wheel and a siren. Dressed in their working clothes, the dancers Chabelska, Idzikowski and Woydzikowski now reproduced Massine's choreography in the tropics, and although it had scandalized the Parisian public, it delighted the Minister for France and his friends, perched on piles of woollens in the Grand Ballroom of the Legation which had been transformed since the War into a sewing-room for war charities.

Nijinsky and his wife also came to see us. How handsome he looked, glancing up over his shoulder to talk to someone standing behind his chair! His head turned, but the head only, and with such a swift and precise movement that it was as if not a single muscle had moved. Claudel was so impressed by his dancing that he immediately conceived the subject of a ballet for him. In order to explain it to him more clearly, he took him off into the forest. Nijinsky liked the idea, but his health prevented him from carrying it out. We did not know then how ill he really was, so hagridden with anxiety that he had surrounded himself with detectives. Shortly after our meeting, his reason gave way altogether. Nevertheless Claudel and I continued work on our projected ballet. This is the subject of *L'Homme et son désir* as described by Claudel in the programme note he wrote for its performance:

This little plastic drama was born of the Brazilian forest, in which we lived submerged, as it were, and which has almost the uniform consistency of one of the elements. How unearthly the moment when the night begins to be peopled with movements, strange cries and furtive glimmers of light! It is precisely one such night that our Poem is intended to portray. We have not attempted to reproduce with photographic exactitude the impenetrable tangle of the *floresta*. We have simply draped it like a carpet of blue, purple and green around a central pattern of sable, over the four tiers of our stage. The latter is conceived vertically, held perpendicularly to the beholder's eye like a picture, or book. If you like, it also resembles a page of music, on which every action is noted on its own particular stave. Along the topmost crest move the Hours, all in black with golden head-dresses. Below them the Moon, escorted across the sky by a cloud, just like a great lady preceded by her servant. Underneath, in the waters of the vast primeval swamp, the reflected images of the Moon and her servant follow the regular progress of the heavenly pair. The action proper takes place on the intermediary platform between the sky and the waters below. And the principal character is Man, over whom the primitive forces have resumed their sway, and who has been robbed by Night and Sleep of Name and Countenance. He enters, led by two identical veiled shapes, who spin him around like a child that is caught in the game of hide-and-seek, and make him lose his way. One is Image and the other Desire, one Memory and the other Illusion. Both sport with him for a moment, and then vanish.

He remains standing, with arms outstretched; he sleeps in the blaze of the tropical moon like a drowned man in the depths of the waters. And all the beasts, all the sounds of the everlasting forest come to gaze at him, and fill his ears with their music: the Bells and the Pan-pipes, the Strings and the Cymbals.

Man begins to stir in his dreaming. Now he begins to move and to dance. And his dance is the eternal dance of Desire, Longing and Exile, the dance of captives and abandoned lovers, the same that sets those who are tortured by insomnia fever-ishly pacing their verandah all night long, or makes animals in captivity hurl themselves again and again aginst the unyielding bars. Now it is a hand from behind him that pulls him back, now a perfume that saps all his strength away. Then the theme of his obsession becomes ever more frantic and violent, and one of the women returns and revolves around him as if fascinated.

Is it a living woman, or a dead one? The sleeper snatches the corner of her veil as she turns and spins around him, unwinding herself until he himself is wrapped up like a chrysalis and she is almost naked. . . . Then, joined to him still by one last strip of cloth, tenuous as the fabric of our dreaming, the woman covers his face with her hand and both move off towards the side of the stage. Of the Moon and her Follower only one last faint reflection below remains.

The Dark Hours have now passed by, and the first Daylight Hours begin to appear.

During the weekends at Petropolis, Audrey Parr and 'Cacique' — the nickname she gave to Claudel — prepared the sketches of the scenery. He would suggest all the colours of the vast carpet which was to cover the four tiers and link them together by draping their walls; the appearance of the characters, which Audrey would cut out in cardboard and paint straight away; and the dimensions of the steps on which the musicians were to stand. I was enchanted by this last notion. Already I could visualize several independent groups: on the tier, to one side a vocal quartet, and on the other an oboe, trumpet, harp and double-bass. On the second tier, on either side, the percussion. On one side of the first tier, the piccolo, the flute, the clarinet, and the bass clarinet; on the other a string quartet. I wanted to preserve absolute independence, melodic, tonal, and rhythmic, for each of these groups. I realized my desire, and in order to facilitate the execution of my score, written for some instruments in common time, for others in triple time, and for others in six-eight, etc., I inserted an arbitrary bar-line every four beats, adding accents to preserve the authentic rhythm. The percussion faithfully evoked for me the nocturnal sounds of the forest; I used it unaccompanied, though very discreetly and never for more than thirty bars at a stretch, in the scene in which the elements tempt Man as he sleeps. The complexity of the score made a piano arrangement practically impossible, but Nininha did not despair, and finally managed to produce a version for piano duet; the individual notes were blurred, but it was possible to follow the thread of the music. She also made the piano duet arrangement of my fourth string quartet, composed in Brazil, and my fifth, composed later in Paris.

On the invasion of Belgium on 2nd August 1914, Brazil was the only neutral to protest to Germany. Thereafter, Senator Ruy Barbosa pleaded the cause of the Allies. He used to win the attention of crowds by his very lengthy speeches pronounced in a scarcely audible voice. After a number of diplomatic incidents, Brazil declared war on Germany.

Claudel undertook two journeys to study the various enterprises in which French interests were involved, and I went with him. We went to Santos on a French warship the *Marseillaise*, which was then on an official visit to Rio. We went on to Sao Paulo, the kingdom of coffee, via the new highway whose bends and twists revealed landscapes of grandiose and impressive beauty. We passed through the States of Parana and Santa Catharina whose inhabitants are mostly Germans and have retained the customs and schools of their land of origin. At that time, both were in a state of ferment because of the contested ownership of a coniferous forest, which was in any case quite abandoned. The dispute had become so envenomed that it had become necessary for Federal troops to intervene. This was the reason why we saw soldiers even in settlements lost in the depth of the forests, sometimes seated in front of their tents, playing the guitar with a parrot perched on their shoulders.

We were travelling by special train. The commander of the *Marseillaise* and two hundred of his men had joined us on their way to Rio Grande do Sul to take over tugs chartered by the French Government. One night there was an incident worthy of the Théâtre du Châtelet: a band of outlaws with drawn revolvers boarded the train and immobilized it by keeping the driver covered, while their confederates prevented the station telegraphist from notifying the police. Claudel was called. Escorted by Commandant de Closmadeuc impeccably dressed and wearing tails, Claudel in pyjamas calmly called for an explanation of the situation. All that the bandits asked him to do was to set down one of their number at the following station. In order to avoid provoking an incident, Claudel agreed to do so, and the train crew, still at the point of the pistol, drove the train on. The remainder of the night passed quietly. Next morning when we arrived at a little town, the representative of the military authorities, Colonel Virgilien de la Porcioncule offered Claudel his Government's apologies and discreetly refrained from telling him that he had enabled a rebel leader, who was being actively pursued by the Federal troops, to make good his escape. With no ill feeling, he invited us to a *vin d'honneur* at the station buffet, where there were assembled delegations of Syrians and Poles who wished to demonstrate their loyalty to the representative of France. The military band struck up with the Brazilian National Anthem, that of the State of Rio Grande, and finally the Marseillaise. The thunderous strains were suddenly interrupted by a fearful crash: the unaccustomed weight of the spectators had caused the floor to give way beneath us, while the tables, flung in every direction, hurled their piled-up crockery to the ground. After this day was over, our journey continued with no further tragi-comic incident. At Porto Alegro, the last town we passed through, the shops belonging to Germans had been looted on the declaration of war. As we entered the plain, we could see as far as the eye could reach gauchos galloping after their cattle, deserts strewn with the bones of oxen and horses, and little ostriches, like gigantic hens, their plumage ruffled by their frantic running. What an amazing contrast with the pines of Santa Catharina!

After a few weeks in Rio, Claudel was obliged to set out on a study trip towards the Bolivian frontier. Once more I accompanied him. The train only left Sao Paulo three times a week, and steamed through the forest for five consecutive days. We installed ourselves on a little seat in front of the locomotive, which was an ideal position during the heat of the day. Hordes of monkeys fled before our approach, as well as hundreds of parrots and clouds of innumerable Morpho butterflies fluttering so slowly that we could see the velvety black undersides of their enamel blue wings. Throughout this region only the dozen yards or so required for the railway line bore any trace of human labour. We crossed the great River Tieté, so famed for its prodigiously extensive low falls, and the River Paraná, two kilometres wide and bordered by trackless forest wastes. Claudel and I felt as if nothing in this country had been changed since the first chapter of Genesis. The Indians lived in the woods, and rarely ventured out, except at the halts when one or two were occasionally to be seen wearing canvas trousers and shirts just like Portuguese peasants, though like their ancestors they still used their feet to fire the arrows from their bows. When we reached our destination, we were invited to visit a model farm on the plain, which could only be reached on horse-back. This lovely ride was only disturbed by herds of wild oxen or *caracus* (a kind of buffalo whose horns are used to make delightful walking sticks) that galloped across the vista towards the unknown.

In August 1918, at the end of the southern winter, the Spanish 'flu made its appearance in Brazil, and rapidly reached epidemic proportions; 4,000 deaths were recorded daily. The authorities were overwhelmed. In the hospitals the dead were removed from the beds before they were cold, in order to make way for the dying. The supply of coffins gave out, and you constantly saw cartloads of corpses which were thrown into common graves in the cemeteries. Nininha lost her mother, and she herself was dangerously ill. I did not see her again until the day I left. She was still in bed, pale and emaciated. I realized she had had a narrow escape from death.

After November 11th gloom was succeeded by gaiety. The crowds poured into the streets to celebrate the return of peace at last. Claudel was sent to Washington to represent France on an inter-allied economic mission and took me with him. Afterwards we would go on to France. I was very happy at the thought of going back to Paris, and of seeing my parents and friends again, but my joy was tinged with a certain nostalgic regret: I had fallen deeply in love with Brazil.

Chapter Twelve

A Difficult Voyage

It was not easy to find a boat going to New York. All the regular services were English and had been suspended for the repatriation of troops. Claudel decided to take one of the German ships seized by the Brazilians and chartered to the French Government. They offered him the *Leopoldina*, of the Hamburg America Line, which, like most of the German vessels, had been sabotaged by her crew during internment and had had to undergo serious repairs.

There were not many passengers on board: a few Government officials rejoining their posts, and six sailors going home to France. Our accommodation was therefore very comfortable. The officers and crew were all Brazilians.

The engines did not seem to be running very well, and we put into Bahia for a brief halt in order to have them overhauled. There are three hundred and sixty-five churches in this town, and one of them, situated on a hill a little way outside the town, is a famous resort of pilgrims, who throng the roads leading to it every Sunday. All along the way you see beggars, blind men and paralytics, exhibiting their crippled limbs, their stumps and their sores, with mumbled prayers or loud cries to attract attention, pity and alms. The church is very rapidly filled, and the congregation gathers outside the porch. All the negresses in Bahia wear charms attached to the belt of their coloured crinoline-like dresses. These charms are nearly always held together by a clasp in the shape of a hand, a piece of wood mounted in metal, a guava or a bunch of grapes. Although they are Christians, most of the negroes practice voodoo rites. Since these are forbidden, the ceremonies are held at night in the country. The Secretary of the Consulate took me there one night. The worshippers sit on the ground, around the leader or sorcerer, who selects an individual and puts him into a trance. When the subject falls, screaming and foaming at the mouth, the sorcerer dabbles his fingers in the saliva and touches the lips of all the adepts, who immediately become possessed and also fall into a trance. At this point the ceremony reaches its climax, and we deemed it prudent to jump on our horses and ride back to the 'city of three hundred and sixty-five churches'.

Another breakdown of the engines enabled us to go ashore in Pernambuco. The sea was as translucent as an emerald. *Jamgadas*, or little fishing craft, consisting merely of rafts on which the negroes fix a chair, criss-crossed it in all directions. As we left, we were accompanied for a long way out to sea by the faint chimes, muffled by distance and the dense heat, of the bells of the city's innumerable convents and churches.

About two hundred miles out of Pernambuco, the engines failed completely. The sabotage must have been more thorough and more complicated than had been thought, for even the wireless was not working. What was to be done? The weather was magnificent and the sea perfectly calm. All we had to do was to wait patiently in the midst of the sea. The vessel was transformed into a luxury hotel. Claudel translated the Psalms (I wrote musical settings for some of them a few weeks later in New York). I was composing *Les Euménides*. The officers remained on deck all day long, and the men fished. One day, contrary to all expectations, the ship began to move slightly. Miracle of miracles! We were in the Gulf Stream! An attempt was made to get the engines going again, but they only went for a few moments. The current pulled us along at two knots, and a day or two later, Barbados hove into sight. We wanted to get to the French West Indies, where the Messageries Maritimes had fairly large ship-repairing yards, so we only stayed a few hours in Bridgetown; just time enough to visit the market where the negresses gabble English, go for a stroll in the countryside among the sugar-mills, and taste some pretty little fruit that caused such indigestion that we hastened back on board. At every step in Barbados, English influence is apparent in the cottages and grass lawn tennis courts, but at Fort-de-France we found ourselves back in the atmosphere of a typical French *sous-préfecture*; on the Grand'Place a statue of the Empress Joséphine stood amid innumerable palm-trees and the inevitable green park seats. On closer examination we found that the engines stood in need of lengthy and extensive repairs. Having received orders from Paris, Claudel decided we would take the *Pérou* which was leaving for Saint-Nazaire and would call at Porto Rico, where we could easily get a boat for New York. Until our departure, the Governor took us all over the island in his little Ford. We were struck by the silence of the West Indian forests, less luxuriant than their Brazilian counterparts; not a single bird seemed astir in them. We were told that the reptiles destroyed them and that a few years before an attempt had been made to remedy this situation by importing a whole ship-load of mongooses, which are enemies of snakes and eat their eggs — but apparently a truce was gradually established between the two inveterate foes, for the forests had fallen silent again, and teemed with snakes. We had to give up an excursion to Mont-Pelé owing to bad weather. We spent the night at Saint-Pierre where the incessant sound of the rain was only interrupted by the furtive and continual rattle of a tropical insect called the 'Kid of the Woods'. Next morning we were again confined to our quarters in the hotel by a downpour so violent that it noisily tore away the topmost fronds of the palms. In the West Indies the manifestations of Nature, including catastrophes, reach gigantic proportions, and as you travel around you are constantly coming across traces of them: 'Here', they will tell you, 'is where the church steeple was destroyed by a typhoon', or else, 'This is where a village was submerged by a tidal wave'. Not to mention Saint-Pierre itself, twice destroyed by a volcanic eruption. . . .

No sooner had the *Pérou* come alongside than we went on board. It was Christmas, our first since the Armistice. In order to celebrate the victory, the officers organized a ball, and invited all the society of Fort-de-France. The Martiniquais came in force: Government officials, Creole families, wealthy negro planters wearing long frock coats and accompanied by their daughters, lightly made-up and clad in brightly coloured evening gowns. As they danced, they all mingled together and joyfully rediscovered the habits of peace-time, the climate of happiness. In the Bal Doudou, to which a young officer took me a few days later, the atmosphere was the same: the typical *bal musette* orchestra, the Guests' dance, quadrilles, beguines, the women in their printed cotton dresses, gold necklaces, and all the grace and charm of a solemn occasion.

The *Pérou* was taking a contingent of young soldiers from Guadeloupe home to be demobbed. Lying on the decks in the ship's stern, they sang all night long enchantingly lovely melodies (some of these I later used in the vocal quartet *Le Brick*, based on a poem by René Chalupt). Our stay in Porto Rico interested me because of the continual contrast between United States influence and the traces of Spanish colonization: (the modern port has shower baths for the stevedores, while the old town is surrounded by Spanish turrets and ancient ramparts). In the club opposite the hotel, strictly reserved for Spaniards, I could see from my room dark-skinned, bright-eyed women wearing shawls and mantillas, dancing the tango with slim young men with side-whiskers, while on the main square the American military band played marches by Sousa and fox-trots. While I was there I heard dances by Cuban composer Romeo, in which he seemed to be juggling with Bach-like allegro themes and the sharp syncopated rhythms of popular music, all underpinned by the emphatic grinding rhythm of the *guitcharo*. I bought one of these in the market, and introduced it later on into one or two of my orchestrations; it is a percussion instrument made of a long gourd on which a series of very close grooves have been traced. To play it these grooves are violently rubbed with a piece of iron mounted on a handle.

Two days after leaving Porto Rico and its dank heat, we ran into our first snowstorm at sea. We arrived in New York with its forest of skyscrapers at the beginning of January. The voyage had lasted fifty-nine days. . . .

Like all other cities after the war, New York was in the throes of a housing shortage. Claudel was provided with a divan in one of the drawing-rooms of the Hotel Lafayette, while I slept on a plank laid across a bath. It was the last few days before the introduction of Prohibition and the town was in a ferment. On all sides you could hear speeches in favour of Prohibition. Even music hall audiences were asked to write their opinion on slips of paper and drop them in urns at the exits. It was a genuine national issue.

This was the first winter for me since 1916. . . . Thanks to my mother's far-sightedness in sending me my fur-coat and warm underclothes, I was able to face the cold and have a good look round New York. I went about on the upper deck of the buses, especially 'down town'.

During a soirée given by Monsieur de Coppet, I met once more the Flonzaley Quartet with whom I had become acquainted in Switzerland through Céline Lagouarde. They told me they had played my quartet several times during their tours. I believe they were the first to perform my works in the United States. They played a quartet by an aged American composer of German origin born in Alsace, Charles Martin Loeffler and later they introduced me to him. A few days after I went to see Marion Bauer, the composer and musicographer. She introduced me to a charming young man called Charles Tomlinson Griffes who composed sensitive works, slightly tinged with the influence of Debussy and Ravel. I met him again several times and showed him my music. He thought that the publishing firm of Schirmers might be interested in *Love Poems* by Tagore which I had set to music both in the English words and in the French translation by Elisabeth Sainte-Marie-Perrin. He put me in touch with the head of the firm, who agreed to publish them.

Claudel was delighted to see Copeau again in New York, where he had set up his theatre during the war. In the meantime Jane Bathori directed the Vieux-Colombier. She had put on several musical shows; the latest of which, Paul Méral's *Dit des jeux du monde* had scandalized the public by the novelty of its presentation. It was not at all surprising that they should be shocked by the masks made by Guy Pierre Fauconnet to confer upon the characters a new kind of unity and grandeur, or by Honegger's score, but I could not understand the fatuousness of audiences who were so sure of never being in the wrong that they always mistook youthful daring for wanton extravagance.

I little thought that soon I too, and for a long time, was going to experience, the ill will of the public.

Chapter Thirteen

Paris

I returned to a Paris jubilant with the Victory celebrations. But it was as a stranger that I took possession of my old flat again, for my eyes still retained too much of the murky light reflected from Brazilian skies, my ears were still too full of the sumptuous sounds of the forest night and the subtle rhythms of the tango. I took out of my trunk all sorts of knick-knacks that I had bought in South America: nutshells engraved and painted by the Indians, clay whistles in the shape of birds, Morpho butterflies, heavily ornamented toothpick-holders, and specimens of Portuguese colonial silverware. I placed all these silent witnesses to the lovely voyage I had made on the mantelpiece of my room.

Fortunately I was soon caught up in the artistic movement that developed around me and tore me away from these memories. The nightmare of the war as it faded had given birth to a new era. Everything was changing, both in literature, with Apollinaire, Cendrars, Cocteau and Max Jacob, and in painting; exhibitions followed close on one another, the Cubists were beginning to make names for themselves, and pictures by Marcel Duchamp, Braque and Léger were hung beside those of Derain and Matisse. In music, activity was no less intense. Reacting against the impressionism of the post-Debussy composers, what musicians asked for now was a clearer, sturdier, more precise type of art which should yet not have lost its qualities of human sympathy and sensitivity. Durey and Poulenc had come to swell the numbers of the musicians I had known before the war. I met Poulenc at René Chalupt's while he was still in the army. He played us his *Mouvements perpétuels* and sang the *Bestiaire*, which he had just completed. I thought that day of a saying by d'Indy concerning the development of music: 'French music will become what the next musician of genius wants it to be.'

After all the vapours of impressionism, would not this simple, clear art renewing the tradition of Mozart and Scarlatti, represent the next phase in the development of our music? At all events, I remember feeling that day that Poulenc would achieve greatness and would attain a place in music's history. He reminded me that he had met me one day in the country at the house of some mutual friends, in 1915, when he was fifteen, and that we had played tennis together. I was still at the Conservatoire at the time. Shortly after this, young Francis had written to me for an autograph or to ask me about some musical question, I do not remember which, and I had answered with the affectionate solicitude of an elderly man addressing a young musician. We often had a good laugh at this first contact of ours! The fresh charm of Poulenc's music was the most endearing feature of that period. Having been mobilized with the 1919 class, however, he had not had the opportunity to practise his technique adequately. Wisely, he was not content with his immediate successes, and placed himself in the hands of Charles Koechlin in order to learn his trade. That admirable teacher, whose treatises on harmony and counterpoint are monuments of learning and pedagogical method, was the only way to carry on the tradition of Gédalge. I have always felt that it was a deplorable injustice that he should not have been appointed to the Conservatoire after the latter's death.

There were many concerts that winter. A young conductor, Vladimir Golschmann, presented a series of new works at the Salle des Agriculteurs. Delgrange abandoned the cello to devote himself wholly to the cause of the new, art; he organized concerts in a little hall in Montparnasse, the Salle Huyghens; the backless benches were uncomfortable, and the air unbreathable because of the fumes of the stove, but all that was elegant in Parisian society, as well as the artists and devotees of the new music, rubbed shoulders there. Jane Bathori and Ricardo Viñes, the faithful pioneers, and the (female) Capelle Quartet, the pianists Juliette Meerovitch and Marcelle Meyer, and the actor Pierre Bertin who also sang, lent us their devoted help and disinterested services. There was also a very important centre of intellectual activity, placed under the aegis of Shakespeare and of contemporary literature, in the two neighbouring bookshops of Adrienne Monnier and Sylvia Beach in the Rue de l'Odéon. There you might often meet Joyce and other authors and poets, both French and foreign. Valéry and Fargue used to read their verse there, Ballguerie gave the first performance of *Socrate* with Satie playing the piano, and Bathori sang my *Alissa* for the first time.

I had met Satie again at a reception given by the Comte de Beaumont in honour of the Queen of Rumania, at which he had been accompanying a few of his songs. At once he told me he had often heard me practising during the summer of 1916; whenever he went to call on some friends of his who lived opposite to me, he had heard me through my open windows, tirelessly repeating over and over again the same phrases on the piano. He had been greatly intrigued by this, for he did not know at the time who the tenant of the flat, from which these little fragments of music proceded, was. In the course of the winter, Cocteau published a book which created a great stir: *Le Coq et l'Arlequin*. In this little treatise on aesthetics, he attacked the so-called serious music — the kind one listens to with one's head in one's hands — and the 'Russian pedal', that is the influence of Mussorgsky and Rimsky-Korsakoff, and impressionism in the manner of Debussy. He exalted the barbarian feeling of Stravinsky's *Sacre du printemps*, the purity of *Socrate*, and the astringent art of Auric; he called for a decisively French type of music. Always prone to generalize, the critics lost no time in hailing Cocteau as the prophèt, theoretician and animator of post-war music.

After a concert at the Salle Huyghens, at which Bertin sang Louis Durey's *Images à Crusoë* to words by Saint-Léger Léger and the Capelle Quartet played my Fourth Quartet, the critic Henri Collet published in *Comoedia* a chronicle entitled 'Five Russians and Six Frenchmen'. Quite arbitrarily he had chosen six names: Auric, Durey, Honegger, Poulenc, Tailleferre and my own, merely because we knew one another, were good friends, and had appeared on the same programmes; quite irrespective of our different temperaments and wholly dissimilar characters. Auric and Poulenc were partisans of Cocteau's ideas, Honegger derived from the German Romantics, and I from Mediterranean lyricism. I fundamentally disapproved of joint declarations of aesthetic doctrines, and felt them to be an unreasonable limitation on the artist's imagination, who must for each new work find different, often contradictory means of expression. But it was useless to protest. Collet's article excited such worldwide interest that the 'Group of Six' was launched, and willy nilly I formed part of it.

This being so, we decided to give some 'Concerts des Six'. The first was devoted to our works; the second to foreign music. The latter programme consisted of works by Lord Berners, Casella, Lourié who was then People's Commissar for the Fine Arts in Soviet Russia, and Schoenberg and Bartók, whose latest works we had been unable to hear owing to the War. Satie was our mascot. He was very popular among us. He was so fond of young people that he said to me one day: 'I wish I knew what sort of music will be written by the children who are four-year-olds now.' This purity of his art, his horror of all concessions, his contempt for money and his ruthless attitude to the critics, were a marvellous example to us all.

The formation of the Group of Six helped to draw the bonds of friendship closer between us. For two years we met regularly at my place every Saturday evening. Paul Morand would make the cocktails, and then we would go to a little restaurant at the top of the Rue Blanche. The dining-room of the *Petit Bessonneau* was so diminutive that the Saturday customers filled it completely. They gave free rein to their high spirits. We were not all composers, for our numbers also included performers: Marcelle Meyer, Juliette Meerovitch, Andrée Vaurabourg, the Russian singer Koubitzky; and painters: Marie Laurencin, Irène Lagut, Valentine Gross, Jean Hugo's fiancée, Guy Pierre Fauconnet; and writers: Lucien Daudet, Raymond Radiguet, a young poet who was brought to us by Cocteau. After dinner, lured by the steam-driven roundabouts, the mysterious booths, the 'Daughter of Mars', the shooting galleries, the games of chance, the menageries, the din of the mechanical organs with their perforated rolls seeming to grind out simultaneously and implacably all the blaring tunes from the music halls and revues, we would visit the Fair of Montmartre, or occasionally the Cirque Médrano, to see the Fratellinis in their sketches, so steeped in poetry and imagination that they were worthy of the Commedia dell'Arte. We finished up the evening at my house. The poets would read their poems, and we would play our latest compositions. Some of them, such as Auric's *Adieu New York*, Poulenc's *Cocardes* and my *Boeuf sur le toit* were continually being played. We even used to insist on Poulenc's playing *Cocardes* every Saturday evening: he did so most readily. Out of these meetings, over which a spirit of carefree gaiety reigned, many a fruitful collaboration was to be born; they also determined the character of several works strongly marked by the influence of the Music Hall.

Belgium was the first foreign country to devote a concert to our works. This was done under the auspices of Madame Vandervelde, the wife of the Minister of Fine Arts. Satie, who had just withdrawn from the Socialist party to join the Communists, asked me to inform her that 'Erik Satie, of the Soviet of Arcueil, kissed her feet.' Our programme began with an Introduction by Cocteau, then Auric and I played *Parade* as a pianoforte duet, as well as my Second Sonata for violin and piano (for at that time I still played the violin), Germaine Tailleferre her *Jeux de plein air* for two pianos. During the concert I noticed a young man following from the score all the music we played. He introduced himself; he played the piano and knew all about our movement. His name was Paul Collaer.

Delgrange decided to extend the range of his activities to include conducting concerts of contemporary music. He performed *Petrushka, Parade*, and my music for *Les Choëphores*. Owing to the small funds at his disposal, he found some difficulty in staging my work. The devoted Bathori came to the rescue by recruiting and rehearsing singers. She took the main singing role (Soprano solo) and that of Narrator. The *Exhortation* scene for spoken chorus and percussion called for seventeen additional instrumentalists, which was far more than the resources of Delgrange's budget could stand. He therefore engaged professionals at union rates only for the drums, and asked Cocteau, Auric, Lucien Daudet, Poulenc and Honegger to play the others. The concert was given on June 19th, 1919. The *Exhortation* scene was tremendously effective and was encored.

I postponed my departure for Aix in order to see the Victory march-past. On the night preceding July 14th, the scene in the streets was unforgettable. There was dancing at every street corner to the strains of little bal musette orchestras. On the 14th at dawn, Honegger, Vaurabourg, Durey, Fauconnet and I made our way towards the Etoile. We managed to clamber up on a seat from which we had a view over the heads of the crowd. There were people everywhere; every tree, every roof, every balcony had its cluster of human faces, and from all sides the crowds continued to arrive in an uninterrupted stream. . . . The march-past began at eight o'clock. Now at last the Victory that had been paid for so dearly was felt to be something tangible, visible, making our hearts swell with boundless hope. All the great Allied leaders, whom we only knew by their photographs or the newsreels in the cinemas, were now before us in the flesh: Marshal Foch, Marshal Joffre, Field Marshal Lord Haig and General Pershing preceded the French regiments each with the flag they had covered in glory, the English who had grouped their flags like a sea of banners, the Americans marching to the rhythm of their march, 'Over there', the Belgians, the Serbians. . . . Everything at that time seemed to us to be big with promise for the new era of peace.

During the holidays, my friends the Hoppenots came to spend a few days at L'Enclos; to our great joy they were always in the habit of dropping in on us, on their way from one distant outpost to another. At the same time, Cocteau and Louis Durey were making a short stay at the Hôtel Sextius in Aix. Jean kept us in fits of laughter with his descriptions of the peculiarities of that delightful hotel. The manager was also an antique dealer and accumulated most of his acquisitions in his clients' rooms, but whenever he found a buyer for them, he would take them away without notice, and if some Louis XV chest-of-drawers had been sold, the unfortunate hotel guests were apt to find all their things scattered on the floor in the middle of the room. The hotel organized operatic performances in the grounds, which created a fearful din: to the infernal caterwauling of the undermanned orchestra, supported by a piano, would be added towards midnight the sound of Werther's pistol-shot. . . . I toyed with a musical setting for one of Jean's poems: *L'Hymne au soleil*. (It proved a failure, and I destroyed it.) We all wanted to hear it but it was no easy matter to recruit musicians in Aix. I appealed to the town band for the brass and hired a big drum and several other percussion instruments. We all sat on the terrace. Jean read his poem; a few of our friends, Hélène Hoppenot and Louis Durey provided the percussion, and the Marquise de Grimaldi-Régusse who unexpectedly turned up was roped in to play the triangle. The result was a frightful cacophony, and the experiment did nothing to improve my reputation among those amateurs of music accustomed to hearing marches by Ganne and fantasias on airs from operettas played by the town band.

Still haunted by my memories of Brazil, I assembled a few popular melodies, tangoes, maxixes, sambas and even a Portuguese fado, and transcribed them with a rondo-like theme recurring between each successive pair. I called this fantasia *Le Boeuf sur le toit*, which was the title of a Brazilian popular song. I thought that the character of this music might make it suitable for an accompaniment to one of Charlie Chaplin's films. At that time, the silent films were accompanied by fragments of classical music, rendered by large or small orchestras, or even a single piano, according to the financial means available. Cocteau disapproved of my idea, and proposed that he should use it for a show, which he would undertake to put on. Cocteau had a genius for improvisation! Hardly had he conceived the idea of a project than he immediately carried it out. To begin with, we needed some form of financial backing. Jean took the seating plan of the Comédie des Champs-Elysées to the Comte de Beaumont, who undertook to book in advance, at a high price, the boxes and the first rows of the stalls. A few days later, as if at the wave of a magic wand, the whole theatre was booked up, and the Shah of Persia even paid ten thousand francs for a front seat from which he could not see a thing, but was himself in full view of everyone. The expenses of the show being covered, all that remained to be done was to set to work.

Cocteau produced a pantomime scenario which could be adapted to my music. He imagined a scene in a bar in America during Prohibition. The various characters were highly typical: a Boxer, a Negro Dwarf, a Lady of Fashion, a Red-headed Woman dressed as a man, a Bookmaker, a Gentleman in evening clothes. The Barman, with a face like that of Antinous, offers everyone cocktails. After a few incidents and various dances, a Policeman enters, whereupon the scene is immediately transformed into a milk-bar. The clients play a rustic scene and dance a pastorale as they sip glasses of milk. The Barman switches on a big fan which decapitates the Policeman. The Red-headed Woman executes a dance with the Policeman's head, ending up standing on her hands like the Salome in Rouen Cathedral. One by one the customers drift away, and the Barman presents an enormous bill to the resuscitated Policeman.

Jean had engaged the clowns from the Cirque Médrano and the Fratellini to play the various parts. They followed implicitly all the extremely precise orders he gave them as producer. Albert Fratellini, being an acrobat, could even dance on his hands around the Policeman's head. In contrast with the lively tempo of the music, Jean made all the movements slow, as in a slow-motion film. This conferred an unreal, almost dream-like atmosphere on the show. The huge masks lent peculiar distinction to all the gestures, and made the movement of hands and feet pass unperceived. Guy Pierre Fauconnet designed them, as well as the costumes. We got together one Sunday at my place to arrange the entrances and dances in accordance with my score, as well as for Fauconnet to draw the characters as Jean described them to him.

We worked so late that I offered to put Fauconnet up for the night, but he refused and preferred to go home to Montparnasse, after arranging another rendezvous with us. He did not turn up. Anxiously, Jean rushed to his house and learnt that the poor fellow had died trying to light a fire. He was, unknown to us, extremely ill, apparently having an enlarged heart. In him we lost a very dear friend. This was the first loss our little group was to sustain. Later we were to lose Meerovitch, Radiguet, Emmanuel Fay, Nininha Guerra. . . .

Raoul Dufy agreed to take over the work on the scenery for *Le Boeuf*, keeping our friend's masks and designs for the costumes. During rehearsals, Lucien Daudet was devotedly helpful. His mother, Madame Alphonse Daudet, kept up with all the latest literary and artistic movements and received us most kindly. One evening she even prepared a most delicate surprise for her guests: she engaged two Hawaiian musicians for Prince Firouze, who was the Persian Minister for Foreign Affairs at the time and was so crazy about Hawaiian music that he always took some with him when he went to a restaurant, while for Jean and me she had served for dessert a little house of caramel surmounted by an ox, the whole garnished with vanilla ice-cream.

We announced three performances of *Le Boeuf*. Cocteau was so nervous that he was afraid no one would come after the first, which was not open to the public. He persuaded Lucien Daudet to send three hundred *pneumatiques* (express letters) each entitling the bearer to 'a little box'. There was an indescribable crush at the doors which only the skilful handling and diplomacy of Lucien Daudet, who consented to take charge of the situation, managed to keep in hand.

The programme included *Trois Petites Pièces Montées*, especially written by Erik Satie for our show, Auric's *Fox-Trot* and Poulenc's *Cocardes* sung by Koubitzky, accompanied by violin, trumpet, clarinet, trombone and big drum. Golschmann conducted our orchestra of twenty-five instruments. This isolated demonstration was taken by both critics and public as a declaration of aesthetic faith. The light-hearted show presented under the aegis of Erik Satie and treated by the newspapers as a 'leg-pull', was regarded by the public as symbolizing a Music Hall Circus system of aesthetics, and for the critics it represented the so-called post-war music. . . . Forgetting that I had written *Les Choëphores*, both public and critics agreed that I was a figure of fun and a showground musician . . . I, who hated anything comic and, in composing *Le Boeuf sur le toit* had only aspired to create a merry, unpretentious *divertissement* in memory of the Brazilian rhythms which had captured my imagination but had certainly never made me laugh. . . .!

Chapter Fourteen

Scandals

I showed Gabriel Pierné the Symphonic Suite I had written, based on the incidental music for *Protée*, and at the same time Honegger brought him an *Interlude* he had composed for a play by Max Jacob called *La Mort de Sainte Alméenne*. Pierné decided to perform both our works at the Concerts Colonne on 24th October 1920. They were grouped together in a programme under the heading of 'Polytonality': in my opinion, this was a mistake, for the development of music should take the form of a natural growth and not follow the imposition of a system. The audience is always in a sceptical frame of mind at the first performance of a new work, and this description with its air of saying, 'You will see what you will see,' did nothing to improve matters. In fact it was I who was to see. . . . Pierné rehearsed our works so carefully that, in order to have more time for them, he included only pieces from the repertoire in the programme of the concert that preceded ours.

My parents came to Paris for the occasion and we shared a corner box. I had never for one moment dreamt that my music could possibly be provacative, yet the audience was already restive before the end of the overture, expressing its feelings by cries of, 'Take it away!' and animal noises, whereupon counter-demonstrations of bravos and clapping broke out, all of which did nothing to help win a hearing for the music. I began to have my fears for the fugue, in which the insistent use of the brass might cause some bewilderment. It was written for three trumpets and three trombones, and was accompanied by an *ostinato* for double-basses and four bassoons. I was not mistaken; with the fugue an indescribable tumult broke out, a real battle in the course of which Monsieur Franck, the organist from the Temple de la Victoire, had his face slapped by Durey. The sound of the orchestra was swamped; the din grew worse; the police intervened. The balconies were cleared by the *Gardes municipaux*. I had the satisfaction of seeing Monsieur Brancour, the critic of *Le Ménestrel*, thrown out by two policemen. Before starting the third piece, Pierné made a speech, in which he said: 'If I include a work in the programme for the Concerts Colonne, it means I think it is worthy to figure there. It is your right not to approve of it and to express your opinion accordingly, but only *after* it has been played, not before.' This speech was succeeded by a brief respite, and a start was made on the *Pastorale*. The audience was too excited, however, to calm down completely. After a short while the uproar broke out again, and the noise covered the sound of the orchestra right to the end of the piece. From the box next to mine, I caught a reassuring glance from Madeleine; she left her place to come and sit beside me till the demonstration was over. My parents were horrified; not that they had the slightest doubt concerning the value of my work, but because of their fears for my future. As for me, I was extremely proud: this genuine, spontaneous, violent reaction filled me with boundless confidence. It is the indifference of the public which is depressing; enthusiasm, or vehement protests, are a proof that your work is *alive*.

The history of music is littered with the débris of such scandals: Wagner had to exercise extraordinary cunning to get the Ninth Symphony accepted in Leipzig; Berlioz had all the difficulty in the world in persuading the orchestra of the Conservatoire to play Beethoven's Third Symphony, and his own music was never appreciated during his own lifetime. Not to speak of *Carmen*, or *Pelléas*. . . . Is not the *Sacre*, which had been given such a stormy reception not so long ago, now listened to in a religious silence? All this reassured me, but I wondered anxiously what Pierné thought. He set my fears at rest immediately. 'If that is the way it is, I'll play your work again in my next programme,' said he and was as good as his word. There was another uproar, but it was less spontaneous this time. I had gone up into the galleries with Claudel, Audrey Parr, Madeleine and a few friends, in order to study people's reactions. The newspapers had made such a splash about the 'Scandal at the Concerts Colonne' that large numbers of people had only come out of curiosity, and to demonstrate. Much later, I learnt that Pierné's courageous attitude had earned him the unanimous disapproval of the musicians at the Institute and delayed his own election to that august body. The *Ménestrel* reproduced a letter written to Pierné by Saint-Saëns from Algiers. From it I took the following extract which I had framed and hung on the wall of my studio in Aix: 'I am grieved to see that you are opening the doors to all sorts of Colney Hatch aberrations and trying to force them down the public's throat when it protests. Several instruments playing in different keys have never produced music, only a filthy row!'

Next year Golschmann conducted my *Cinq Etudes* for Piano and Orchestra, with Marcelle Meyer as soloist. In this work I had employed a musical language based on a long tradition; each study dealt with a different problem of harmony and construction. (In the *Art of the Fugue* and the *Musical Offering*, Bach used much more complicated combinations.) I adopted the language of polytonality and in this way obtained a more subtle sweetness and a greater intensity of violence. The third *Etude*, 'Fugues', consists of four simultaneous fugues, one for the wind instruments in A, one for the brass in D Flat, one for the strings in F, while the one for the piano is in two parts based on the notes common to all three keys and states the theme and answer of the fugue while the orchestral fugues provide the *divertimenti*, and *vice versa*. The Fourth *Etude*, both violent and dramatic in its content, is constructed crab-wise, i.e., the piece is divided into two, the second being an exact replica of the first, but reversed. From the mid-point, it runs backwards to the beginning. The audience was bewildered by this device and lost no time in showing it: the hall became rowdy. Marcelle Meyer took no notice, but went on playing, wringing out the violent harmonies with all the force of her finely tempered technique. My old friend Engel walked out of the Salle Gaveau in disgust. The attendant, a half-breed who had known me for years, was worried about my physical safety and went to fetch a policeman to sit beside me. I was not disturbed by this new outburst, for I was determined to go ahead with my research whatever the public might think of me.

Diaghilev's *Ballets Russes* had opened the season triumphantly with *Le Sacre du printemps*. The critics who had at first had considerable difficulty in getting accustomed to this work now listened to it with fervent enthusiasm and praised its composer, though they hoped he would not change his manner again. Diaghilev, who was strongly influenced by the theories advanced by Cocteau in *Le Coq et l'Arlequin*, was distinctly attracted by the amusingly direct art personified by Poulenc and Auric; on the other hand, he was not very fond of my music. Nevertheless, to please José-Maria Sert, who was a great admirer of Claudel's, he asked me to play *L'Homme et son désir*. The audition took place in Misia Edwards's drawing-room. (She was to marry Sert a few weeks later.) She was a great friend of Diaghilev, and lent him devoted assistance in putting on his shows. He placed great confidence in her judgement, which was trenchant. Like Diaghilev himself, she was always on the alert for the novelty of the day, or rather the latest minute, and if she liked a work, she would take it up, otherwise. . . . Satie used to say, 'If you keep a magnificent pedigree cat, you should hide little birds from it!' and, acting on this principle, he kept the music for *Parade* (which he had nevertheless dedicated to her) a secret from her until the day of its first performance. It was therefore amid an atmosphere heavy with scepticism and unspoken reserves that I played my score. The icy silence which followed it was broken by a conversation in Russian between

Diaghilev and Massine. I soon realized that my symbolic and dramatic ballet no longer corresponded with the needs of the day.

That winter another troupe of dancers, the Ballets Suédois, gave a series of performances at the Théâtre des Champs-Elysées. A Swedish Maecenas named Rolf de Maré devoted all his leisure to it and provided its financial backing. These dancers had not the virtuosity of the Russians, but their sincerity and love of the art were very captivating. At first their repertoire consisted of Swedish works and folk-dances, but on the advice of their conductor Inghelbrecht they extended it to include Albéniz's *Iberia*, Ravel's *Tombeau de Couperin* and Inghelbrecht's *El Greco*. The choreography was by Jean Borlin.

Honegger had composed a very fine ballet called *Horace Victorieux*, and Fauconnet had prepared designs for the scenery, costumes and masks. To honour the memory of his dead friend, the composer submitted this work to de Maré, but the latter preferred to commission a new ballet from him to be called *Skating Rink*, with scenery by Fernand Léger. Yet when I submitted to him my *L'Homme et son désir*, he agreed to put it on in spite of the singers, the orchestra of soloists and the large number of percussion instruments required. Through his generosity, the fruit of our Brazilian collaboration came to see the light of day. Audrey Parr designed the costumes on the basis of suggestions by Claudel. The latter had just been appointed Ambassador to Japan, and as the Heir to the Imperial Throne, Prince Hirohito was passing through Paris at the time, he often had to escort him. He would suddenly appear on the stage of the Théâtre des Champs-Elysées wearing a morning coat and top hat and interrupt the rehearsal at the most unexpected moments to suggest some new steps to Borlin.

Apart from Honegger's music, Inghelbrecht had no great love for the works of Les Six. My relations with him were far from cordial; indeed, once when I asked him in the nicest possible way to alter a nuance slightly, he retorted very gruffly: 'You have no business here!' In spite of this incident, however, I had no fear, for I knew of his artistic integrity and was sure he would conduct my music flawlessly. I was right, too. There was a young flautist in the orchestra called Roger Désormière, who struck up for me unceasingly. He lived opposite me and often came to take me out with his motorcycle and sidecar, visiting the country round about Paris, which he knew intimately.

The first performance of *L'Homme et son désir* took place on June 26th, 1921. I was anxious about the passages for unaccompanied percussion, but they did not provoke any hostile demonstration, for they were only short, and the music that followed immediately soothed the audience's irritation, and the vocal quartet acted as a sedative. . . . On each occasion, the reaction of the public was different, ranging from restlessness to solemn attention.

De Maré paid no heed to these fluctuating responses and kept my ballet in the repertoire.

Auric had been asked to write a score on a subject proposed by Cocteau, but was unable to carry this out for lack of time. So Cocteau decided to put on a show by Les Six. We all agreed to take part, except Durey. The décors for *Les Mariés de la Tour Eiffel* were by Irène Lagut, and the costumes were the first revelation of the talent of Jean Hugo, who advanced from strength to strength thereafter. The dancers wore masks and painted costumes; they had a sort of *trompe-l'oeil* effect which was really very charming. Cocteau and Pierre Bertin read the running commentary which accompanied the ballet between the various pieces of music through cardboard loudspeakers placed on either side of the stage. The plot was very simple: a newly-married couple, accompanied by their relatives and an old friend, a General, have come to have their wedding banquet on the first-floor terrace of the Eiffel Tower. During the banquet, the General mimes a speech. A wedding group photograph is taken, but every time the fateful words, 'Watch the birdy!' are uttered, some unexpected apparition interrupts the proceedings. First of all it is the 'Bathing Beauty from Trouville', then 'Telegrams' — for the Eiffel Tower has been the handmaiden of the Post Office ever since its aerial was erected — and finally a lion that devours the General. This is only the beginning of the misfortunes that befall this unlucky wedding party, for it ends by being 'massacred', as in a coconut shy at the Fair, by the 'Child of the Future'. We were all interested and amused at taking part in such an extraordinary mixture of different ingredients the fanciful nature of which would not have been disowned by the Dadaist movement that was then at its height. Auric composed a brilliant *Overture* and a series of enchanting ritornelles; Poulenc *La Danse de la baigneuse de Trouville* and *Le Discours du Général*; Tailleferre *La Valse des dépèches*; Honegger *La Marche funèbre du général*, and I *La Marche nuptiale* and *La Fugue de massacre de la noce*. Apart from Poulenc's polka, whose deliberate drollery was a great success and the pieces by Auric, the whole work was rather feeble. Only Honegger's contribution was taken seriously, and when they began to play it, a well-known critic exclaimed, 'Ah! Some real music at last!' without recognizing the Waltz from *Faust* which Arthur had used in the bass in order to give his composition the required authentic touch of satire.

The Opéra-Comique decided to put on *La Brebis egarée* in November 1923. I have often been reproached for authorizing performances of this youthful work, but I do not disown it and will never be against its being played. In spite of the prosody, which derives undoubtedly from that of *Pelléas*, and the themes representing the varius aspects of the work which enabled me to use the so-called 'cyclic' method of treatment, as well as the excessive use of chords of the ninth and the doubling of instruments in the orchestra, I think my score reflects a certain lyrical spirit which is highly personal to me and which found expression in this work to a much greater extent than in any other of my youthful compositions. The revivials of *La Brebis* in Germany for the 150th Anniversary of the Berlin Opera, and on the Paris and Belgian radio on the occasion of Francis Jammes's death did nothing to make me revise my opinion.

The production of *La Brebis* at the Opéra-Comique was most elaborately planned. I had asked Jammes's old friend Lacoste to collaborate, and he produced carefully painted little *trompe l'oeil* tableaux, in which the accessories were reduced to a minimum, in order to facilitate changes of scenery — this was essential, for there were twenty different scenes. The play was very cleverly staged by Albert Carré, who introduced a second curtain, smaller than the main one, and operated by three narrators who sang the description of the various changes of scene. The narrators played the part of a Greek chorus, although more descriptive than dramatic. They were dressed in the fashions of 1910 with garlands of flowers like those you see on the picture postcards of the period. This was the first occasion on which an opera had been performed using 1912 costume, but I had insisted that it should owe its character to the period when it was written, even if that period was one of excruciatingly bad taste. . . .

Although the opera was flawlessly produced, it roused violent demonstrations of feeling, for which I believe that the familiar language of the text was more responsible than the music. For instance, when Pierre, who is about to abduct Françoise, nervously consults a railway timetable, his understandable agitation raised a laugh. Yet it was little touches like that which created the characteristic atmosphere of the play and, better than lyrical outbursts, expressed the ideas of love, moral indigence, repentance and forgiveness. . . . The incidents followed the familiar pattern of whistles and catcalls succeeded by untimely applause. The outcry led to counter-demonstrations in my favour and gradually degenerated into complete disorder with everyone shouting violent insults at one another. Albert Wolff continued to conduct the orchestra with fervour, unperturbed. During the third performance he scathingly addressed the audience as follows: 'If you don't like this, come back tomorrow night, we're playing *Mignon*!' That evening, I was sitting in the gallery — I like to mingle with the people in the cheaper seats during performances of my works — and the students were all for me, calling the jeerers in the boxes and orchestral stalls 'dirty bourgeois'. Next to me, a young man wearing an enormous *lavallière* kept vigorously applauding. Unable to stand any longer my impassive attitude, he turned to me and said: 'Why don't you clap, shout, cheer? You ought to come back every time they play this opera! I'm always here to defend it!' During the interval, I introduced myself to my youthful admirer, and thereafter never omitted to invite him to my first nights. Shocked by the attitude of the public, Albert Carré went so far as to place on every seat a copy of the sarcastic reviews which had greeted the first performance of *Pelléas*, together with the one phrase: 'Be careful!' I was deeply touched by this gesture, but it only irritated the audience, and my work was withdrawn after the fourth performance.

In 1920–21, I undertook to write some articles of musical criticism in the *Courrier musical*. It was a pleasant task to assume the defence of contemporary music, which was being assailed from all sides, and freely express my own opinions. I also felt it was an opportunity to explain one or two points of view and dissipate certain misunderstandings. In this connexion I was given a demonstration of the perfidious nature of some of my colleagues. Emile Vuillermoz, who pontificated in *L'Excelsior*, never let an opportunity pass of attacking my supposed anti-Debussy views. I requested a meeting with him in order to disabuse him. I have never attached any importance to criticisms of my own work, but this concerned my attitude to a musician whom I held in veneration being called in question, and I brought along all my articles to prove he was labouring under a mistaken impression. I even took the trouble of underlining in blue all the references to Debussy. Vuillermoz pretended to be delighted, but went on to deplore my attitude towards Ravel and Florent Schmitt, whereupon I explained to him my reasons. He thanked me for having enlightened him on all these points. A few days later he did not fail to treat me once more as a thankless 'anti-debussyite' . . . which led me to suspect that the politics of music held many a mysterious secret.

The Sunday concerts were a sort of musical 'Salon Carré', an exhibition of the masters of past centuries. I loved classical music, but protested in my articles against the excessive number of Beethoven-Wagner and Wagner-Beethoven programmes. It was very tiresome. Every Sunday, the Fifth, the Third, the Leonora Overture. And Wagner every Sunday. . . . Apart from one or two of his overtures, his works should never be performed in the concert-hall. When the Concerts Pasdeloup announced yet another Wagner Festival, I headed my article simply, 'Down with Wagner!' which provoked a veritable scandal. I received protesting letters, insults, and even anonymous letters. Wagner was worshipped like the Golden Calf. And I hated his music more with every day that passed, for it represented a type of art that I detested; yet I could never have guessed that it would one day become the standard-bearer of Nazi philosophy until the day when its high-priests would be swallowed up in a new Götterdämmerung.

Since that time I have often attended admirable performances of Wagner's works in Germany, but have been unable to revise my opinion. My Latin mind refuses to swallow this music that Debussy used to call 'tetralogical tin plate'; since, however, our criticisms are wasted, and we shall always have to put up with festivals of this kind, I may say I am prepared to shout, 'Long live Beethoven!' even after the hundred thousandth performance of the Fifth, but — oh, yes! certainly — always ready to cry, 'Down with Wagner!'

Chapter Fifteen

My First Encounter with Jazz

In June 1920 Claudel, who was then Minister to Denmark and High Commissioner for the Schleswig-Holstein Plebiscite, came to Paris for a few days and invited me to motor back with him to Copenhagen. I gladly accepted. We waited just long enough for me to obtain all the necessary papers and then set out. We had with us Copeau's daughter, little Marie-Hélène, who was going to spend her holidays with her grandmother in Denmark. We were favoured by the weather and had a very pleasant journey despite the fact that it was rather hurried because Claudel had to attend an official dinner on the occasion of the plebiscite which had just been held. So we sped across Belgium and Holland and through the empty harbours of a Germany in the deadly grip of inflation, across the Great Belt and the Little Belt, and over the plains of Denmark. One hour after our arrival at the Legation, Claudel, hatless and wearing the Grand Cordon of the Order of Danbrog, chewing leaves, which he idly plucked from the bushes as we went by, set out on foot for the Royal Palace.

I loved Copenhagen, with its old sixteenth-century quays, its beautifully laid out ancient palaces rubbing shoulders with huge colourful modern buildings of brick reddened by the sun. The Museum amazed me by the size of its collection of sculptures by Carpeaux of the famous personalities of the Second Empire. Claudel took me to Elsinore. As we gazed at the portrait of the Royal Family, whose members had wedded so many sovereigns, Claudel confided in me that he would like to see a performance of *Hamlet* in a décor like that in the picture, with its padded furniture and satin cushions. As we went back to Copenhagen, the car seemed to be floating through a sea of cyclists lured out into the countryside by the long bright evenings. I took advantage of my free time to make a start on my first two *Etudes* for piano and orchestra and a dance suite for the piano, inspired by South American rhythms and not based on folk music, entitled *Saudades do Brasil*. Each piece bore the name of a district of Rio.

I was to join Cocteau in London for some perfornaces of *Le Boeuf sur le toit*. I went via Esbjerg. We soon realized that the charming young man who acted as our manager had only the vaguest ideas of how our show should be organized; instead of acrobatic dancers he had engaged some weird-looking youths who looked as if they had come straight out of Whitechapel. . . . The rehearsals were held at the Baroness d'Erlanger's house, Lord Byron's former town-house in Piccadilly. Our dubious-looking actors came every day to study their dance movements among the priceless furniture of a richly appointed drawing-room. The bar was represented by a splendid Coromandel screen laid across two chairs. *Le Boeuf* was to play for two weeks at the Coliseum, London's biggest music hall. This seemed rather risky to us, but its audiences were apparently used to the most heterogeneous programmes; the Ballets Russes had played there with great success. The rehearsals were difficult, with musicians unaccustomed to playing music like mine, and I often had to berate the lady horn-players. To mollify me, they would show me photos of their babies during the intervals. I conducted the first performance, and all went well. *Le Boeuf* was sandwiched in between a number by Japanese acrobats and Ruth Draper's highly original sketches. In any case, this was not the last time *Le Boeuf* was given in a music hall. Madame Rasimi, the manager of the *Ba-ta-clan*, put it in one of her revues, famous for their displays of nudity and its comedians' broad humour. One night, Cocteau heard one of the audience — a workman wearing a cloth cap — say to his wife: 'It ain't that it makes you laugh; but it's different, see, so it makes you laugh!'

It was during this visit to London that I first began to take an interest in jazz. Billy Arnold and his band, straight from New York, were playing at the Hammersmith Palais de Danse, where the system of taxi-girls and taxi-boys had been introduced. A dozen or so young men in evening dress and girls in blue dresses with lace collars sat around in a box, and for a charge of sixpence any timid young man or neurotic old maid could have one of them to dance with. For the same fee they could have another dance with the same, or any other, partner.

In his *Coq et l'Arlequin* Cocteau had described the jazz accompaniment to the number by Gaby Deslys at the Casino de Paris in 1918 as a 'cataclysm in sound'. In the course of frequent visits to Hammersmith, where I sat close to the musicians, I tried to analyze and assimilate what I heard. What a long way we had travelled from the gypsies who before the war used to pour their insipid, treacly strains intimately into one's ears, or the singers whose glides, in the most dubious taste, were borne up by the wobbling notes of the cimbalom, or the crudity of our bals musette with the unsubtle forthright-ness of cornet, accordeon and clarinet! The new music was extremely subtle in its use of timbre: the saxophone breaking in, squeezing out the juice of dreams, or the trumpet, dramatic or languorous by turns, the clarinet, frequently played in its upper register, the lyrical use of the trombone, glancing with its slide over quarter-tones in crescendos of volume and pitch, thus intensifying the feeling; and the whole, so various yet not disparate, held together by the piano and subtly punctuated by the complex rhythms of the percussion, a kind of inner beat, the vital pulse of the rhythmic life of the music. The constant use of syncopation in the melody was of such contrapuntal freedom that it gave the impression of unregulated improvisa-tion, whereas in actual fact it was elaborately rehearsed daily, down to the last detail. I had the idea of using these timbres and rhythms in a work of chamber-music, but at first I had to penetrate more deeply into the arcana of this new musical form, whose technique still baffled me. The musicians who had already made use of jazz had confined themselves to what were more or less interpretations of dance music. Satie in the *Rag-Time du paquebot* from *Parade* and Auric in the fox-trot *Adieu New York* had made use of an ordinary symphony orchestra, and Stravinsky had written his *Rag-Time* for seven solo instruments, including a cimbalom.

I had lost sight of Jean Wiéner since the war. Life had not been easy for him, and he was married and had a little daughter. Putting a bold face on things, he now earned his living by playing the piano in a night club. He came to me and suggested that we should transfer our Saturday evening meetings to the place where he worked. I was attracted by this idea and hurried off to see Cocteau whom I greeted with the words: 'I have got a bar for you!' The very next Saturday, my apartment was abandoned in favour of the Bar Gaya in the Rue Duphot. We were given a warm welcome from the owner, Moyses, who had even adorned the walls with little many-coloured posters, each bearing one of our names. As the bar's customers invariably arrived later than we did, and left before us, there was always one part of the evening when we were all alone and free to make music to our hearts' content. Jean Wiéner played syncopated music with aerial grace and sensitivity, with an especially light rhythm. We loved to listen to his playing, and to that of his partner, the negro Vance, who was an admirable saxophonist and banjo-player. Without any transition, these two would pass from fashionable rag-time and fox-trots to the most celebrated works of Bach. Besides, syncopated music calls for a rhythm as inexorably regular as that of Bach himself, which indeed is firmly established on the same basis.

In May 1921, Pierre Bertin put on an *avant-garde* show. The programme included a play by Max Jacob, imbued with the spirit of chivalry, and Radiguet's charming one act play *Le Pélican*, with music by Auric. I remember one very amusing scene in which Monsieur Pélican points out to his son that he ought to think of taking a nom-de-plume if he wanted to be a poet, to which the young man retorts: 'Pelican is no sillier than Corneille (crow) or Racine (root). . . .' Together with these plays, a play by Cocteau called *Le Gendarme incompris* was given which rather audaciously introduced a whole passage from Mallarmé. This is so apt in the new context that, pronounced with the traditional comic accent of the stage policeman, no one ever suspected its origin. Poulenc had composed music which was so witty and pungent that I have always felt sorry he would not allow it to be played again. The negro Graton danced a 'shimmy' composed by me and entitled *Caramel mou*. (Cocteau had written some words for it; it was scored for clarinet, saxophone, trumpet, trombone and percussion.) But the *pièce de résistance* was undoubtedly Satie's extraordinary play *Le Piège de Méduse*, whose dialogue was full of his own inimitable wit. The unbridled fantasy of this play bordered on the absurd. In the role of Baron Méduse, Bertin wore make-up that made him look like Satie himself; it was as if he had assumed the latter's actual bodily presence. The action was interrupted from time to time by a stuffed monkey, which came down from its pedestal to execute a little dance. Satie had written quite short dance tunes scored for a small group of instruments that was to be conducted by Golschmann, who, however, withdrew at the last minute as the result of a tiff.

Shows of this kind, so variegated in character, were excellent training for us, enabling us to experiment in all sorts of technqiues and to strive constantly after new forms of expression.

Chapter Sixteen

'Furniture Music' and Catalogue Music

Just as one's field of vision embraces objects and forms, such as the pattern
on the wallpaper, the cornice of the ceiling, or the frame of the looking-
glass, which the eye sees but to which it pays no attention, although they are
undoubtedly there, Satie thought it would be amusing to have music that
would not be listened to; 'furniture music', or background music that would
vary like the furniture of the rooms in which it was played. Auric and
Poulenc disapproved of this suggestion, but it tickled my fancy so much that
I experimented with it, in collaboration with Satie, at a concert given in the
Galerie Barbazange. During the programme, Marcelle Meyer played music
by Les Six, and Bertin presented a play by Max Jacob, called *Un figurant
au théâtre de Nantes*, which required the services of a trombone. He also
sang Stravinsky's *Berceuses du Chat* to the accompaniment of three
clarinets, so Satie and I scored our music for the instruments used in the
course of these various items on the programme. In order that the music
might seem to come from all sides at once, we posted the clarinets in three
different corners of the theatre, the pianist in the fourth, and the trombone
in a first-floor box. A programme note warned the audience that it was not
to pay any more attention to the ritornelles that would be played during the
intervals than to the candelabra, the seats, or the balcony. Contrary to our
expectations however, as soon as the music started up, the audience began
to stream back to their seats. It was no use for Satie to shout: 'Go on talking!
Walk about! Don't listen!' They listened without speaking. The whole
effect was spoilt. . . . Satie had not bargained on the charm of his own
music. This was our one and only public experiment with this sort of music.
Nevertheless Satie wrote another 'ritournelle d'ameublement' for Mrs
Eugene Meyer of Washington when she asked him, through me, to give her

an original manuscript. But for this *Musique pour un cabinet préfectoral* to have its full meaning, she should have had it recorded and played over and over again, thus forming part of the furniture of her beautiful library in Crescent Place, adorning it for the ear in the same way as the still-life by Manet adorned it for the eye. In any case, the future was to prove that Satie was right: nowadays, children and housewives fill their homes with un-heeded music, reading and working to the sound of the wireless. And in all public places, large stores and restaurants, the customers are drenched in an unending flood of music. In America, every cafeteria is equipped with a sufficient number of machines for each client to be able, for the modest sum of five cents, to furnish his own solitude with music or supply a background for his conversation with his guest. Is this not 'furniture music'; heard, but not listened to?

We frequently gave concerts in picture galleries. At Poiret's Auric and I gave the first performance of Debussy's *Epigrammes antiques* for piano duet. At the Galerie la Boétie, Honegger played violin sonatas with Vaurabourg, and the pianist André Salomon pieces by his friend Satie. Delgrange conducted my *Machines agricoles.*

I had written musical settings for descriptions of machinery taken from a catalogue I had brought back from an exhibition of agricultural machinery which I had visited in the company of Madame de B. and Mademoiselle de S. who wanted to choose a reaper for their estate in the Bordeaux area. I had been so impressed by the beauty of these great multicoloured metal insects, magnificent modern brothers to the plough and scythe, that I thought of celebrating them in music. I had put away in a drawer a number of catalogues which I came across in 1919. I then composed a little suite for singer and seven solo instruments in the style of my little symphonies: the titles were *La Faucheuse* (reaper), *La Lieuse* (binder), *La Déchaumeuse-Semeuse-Enfouisseuse* (harrow-plough, seeder, stubble-burier), *La Moissonneuse Espigadora* (harvester), *La Fouilleuse-Draineuse* (subsoil plough and draining plough), *La Faneuse* (tedder). A few months later, I used the same group of instruments for settings to some delightful poems by Lucien Daudet inspired by a florist's catalogue: *Catalogue de fleurs.*

Not one single critic understood what had impelled me to compose these works, nor that they had been written in the same spirit as had in the past led composers to sing the praises of harvest-time, the grape harvest, or the 'happy ploughman', or Honegger to glorify a locomotive and Fernand Léger to exalt machinery. Every time people wanted to prove my predilection for leg-pulling and eccentricity they quoted the *Machines agricoles.* I have never been able to fathom why sensible beings should imagine that any artist would spend his time working, with all the agonizing passion that goes into the process of creation, with the sole purpose of making fools of a few of them. . . .

Chapter Seventeen

Paul Collaer and Jean Wiéner

Paul Collaer, the young man we had met at the concert we gave in Brussels, assumed the direction of all the *avant-garde* musical functions in Belgium. About the same period, four young men, Alphonse Onnou, Laurent Halleux, Germain Prévost and Quinet, formed the Pro Arte Quartet. By dint of talent and artistic intergrity, they quickly rose to the top of their profession. Their exceptionally wide repertoire was most carefully rehearsed, and they brought to a modern quartet, which they would only have an opportunity of performing once in public, the same earnest application they gave to one of the classics. In order to earn their living, they played in the orchestra at La Monnaie, or in those dismal ensembles whose function it was to besprinkle film shows liberally with music. These four lent Collaer their enthusiastic and devoted support, and it was largely thanks to them that he was able to carry his enterprise through. He was also assisted by a charming singer, Evelyne Brelia, who interpreted our songs with superlative intelligence. She had married the cellist Quinet, whose place was taken by Maas when the former left the quartet to become Director of the Conservatoire in Charleroi. A few months later he underwent a cruel ordeal, for his wife was murdered, no doubt by a lunatic, for no trace of her assassin was ever found. Collaer's concerts were re-christened Les Concerts Pro Arte. They listed chamber-music recitals among their aims, as well as works for small ensembles. Arthur Prévost, the viola-player's brother, undertook to conduct the orchestra. He was the bandmaster of the excellent regimental band of the *Guides*, from which he was able to recruit the woodwind and the brass for the orchestra. Moreover, Collaer was not obliged to pay them, which was a considerable relief for him in view of the slender financial resources at his disposal.

Paul Collaer carried on a bewildering range of multifarious activities: he was an excellent pianist, admirable at sight-reading, and rehearsed all his soloists personally. He advised them and, if necessary, won them over to his own way of seeing. He also looked after the administrative side: hire of the hall, printing the programmes and tickets, getting new subscribers. In the evenings, when a concert was over, he loved to refresh his spirit in the company of his fellow-musicians at the café, but would rise hurriedly to his feet towards midnight in order to catch the train to Malines where he lived. Next morning, in accordance with a long-established family tradition — all the members of his family were either teachers or headmasters of lycées – – he would quietly walk, pipe in mouth, to the Athenaeum where he taught physics and chemistry. Thus Collaer divided his time between music and science, and in summer, in his wife's native Switzerland, he would go off into the mountains to pursue his investigations into 'the influence of light on chlorophyll'. As soon as he got home from school, and while his wife prepared one of her succulent repasts, he would rush to the piano and enthusiastically play over scores both classical and modern. He was also an ardent gardener, and would get up in the middle of the night to keep an eye on the temperature of the greenhouse in which he grew rare orchids. From his house on the banks of the canal on the outskirts of the town, you could just hear the peals of the carillon in the Cathedral, and the bay-window of his drawing-room looked out on the heavy barges constantly going to and from Holland. I frequently stayed with him. I have heard my chamber music works played in the Concerts Pro Arte so often that I hardly think there is one that Collaer did not have performed. I took advantage of the concerts to go and spend a few days in Malines and work in that incomparably calm and friendly atmosphere.

A few years later, Collaer tried to extend the range of his activities. There was in Brussels an organization giving symphony concerts known as Les Concerts Populaires, whose finances were guaranteed by Monsieur Henri Leboeuf, to whom Brussels also owes the Hall of the Palais des Beaux Arts. Like most associations of its kind, it was not much inclined to welcome contemporary works, although the Belgian public, less sceptical than the French, always listens respectfully before passing judgement. Collaer was a great fighter, and set out to modernize their programmes, sometimes successfully. Through him, I was engaged in 1924 to conduct my *Deuxième Suite symphonique*. He also persuaded Louis de Vocht to produce my *Choëphores* in Antwerp. Whenever the Director of the La Monnaie orchestra summoned me to play one of my works, Collaer always took time off to come with me to help me perform my music. He became enamoured of ancient instruments and bought several of them. He trained a quartet of recorders; he produced Purcell's *Faery Queen*, Monteverdi's *Orfeo* and *La Rappresentazione di anima e di corpo*. He wrote a very good book on

Stravinsky and one on myself, containing very shrewd analyses of my work. But so many diverse activities ended in overtaxing his strength, and when he was offered the post of Artistic Director in the Flemish Broadcasting system, he gave up teaching in order to devote himself wholly to music.

When the Bar Gaya was transferred to new premises, its owner Moyses asked Cocteau and myself to allow him to use the name *Le Boeuf sur le toit*. The idea tickled our fancy, and we agreed. We had no inkling that this would cause so much confusion: from then on, it was supposed that we were the owners of this bar, an error which was all the more deeply rooted because we went there so often, and it was stated in programme notes for concerts that I had called my ballet after a night-club. . . . Jean Wiéner played there regularly, together with Clément Doucet, an excellent pianist. To a remarkable extent they were complementary to one another; they performed all syncopated music with rare distinction. Their records are a valuable addition to the history of jazz during this epoch; they were the first to give concerts of this type of music in Europe and went on many tours. Yet all this activity was not enough for Wiéner, who decided to organize a series of concerts at his own expense. He became our 'Artist-Maecenas'.

For the first concert he engaged the Billy Arnold orchestra, which had gone from strength to strength since I had heard them in London. The public, accustomed to concerts of so-called 'serious' music, was indignant at first that anyone should dare to play dance music or restaurant music in a hall which had been graced by the presence of so many distinguished virtuosos; but gradually it yielded to the lure, that is, the languorous charm of the 'blues' and the exciting clamour of rag time, and the intoxicating freedom of the melodic lines. When the concert was over, the audience in the Salle des Agriculteurs seemed to have been overcome by vertigo: they had encountered an unknown force. Although the quality of the music was often questionable, at least it was firmly rooted in the soil from which folk-music sprang. Through it, the voice of America made itself heard, fresh, vital, compelling, as well as husky or melancholy; and sometimes peaceful, slightly sentimental, or imbued with a kind of desperate poetry.

Jean Wiéner decided to give a first performance of Schoenberg's *Pierrot Lunaire*, and asked me to conduct it. The work consists of twenty-one pieces based on poems by the Belgian poet A. Giraud, written in a decadent style and rather dubious taste. In it, Schoenberg uses a kind of recitative halfway between speech and song, but on very precisely indicated notes. After continuous practice, our admirable Marya Freund succeeded in 'speaking' the words without singing them, and 'singing' them without falling over into speech. As we felt that it would be essential for the words of such a musical innovation to be clearly understood, she agreed to translate, or rather adapt them. The simplest thing would obviously have been to substitute the original words for the German text, but this was out of the question because Schoenberg's prosody was based on a translation into German. Marya therefore made a translation of this translation. In spite of its ultra-expressionistic character bordering on morbidity, this wholly atonal music composed in 1913 was tremendously evocative. We had twenty-five rehearsals. The orchestra consisted of four players, one of whom played the violin or viola according to requirements, another the flute or piccolo, the third the clarinet or bass clarinet, and finally Jean Wiéner at the piano. *Pierrot Lunaire* was such a success that we repeated it twice in Paris, and Collaer engaged us for Brussels. After conducting this work so many times, all my nerves were on edge. I was exasperated by the recitative running over the whole range of the vocal register with the most unexpected leaps and intervals. After conducting it in London, therefore, I decided that this would be the last time. Yet the other day I listened with genuine pleasure to the recording made by Schoenberg himself and I find that, in spite of the years that have come between, this music has kept an authentic freshness.

Other works by Schoenberg were presented by the Concerts Wiéner, among them *Herzgewächse* on a poem by Maeterlinck. This was sung by Mathilde Veillé-Lavallée who had a very shrill voice, while Poulenc played the celesta, Wiéner the Harmonium, and I conducted the weird ensemble. In his love for contemporary music Wiéner bore all the material responsibility for these concerts, and was so modest that he seldom appeared himself as a soloist. He engaged the Pro Arte Quartet to play the Czech composer Alois Hába's quarter-tone quartet. I had then, and still have now, no prejudice against this kind of experiment, provided the works concerned are powerful, sincere and moving, but this was not the case in this instance: we found it both boring and weak. Wiéner had several of my works performed. He had singers who had been rehearsed by Collaer in preparation for a concert in Brussels a few weeks later come from there to play my *Cantate du retour de l'enfant prodigue*. He organized several Stravinsky Festivals, too. He presented the *Symphonies pour instruments à vent* and *Mavra*. This *opéra-bouffe* which was first performed by the Ballets Russes at the Opéra in 1922, represented an important stage in Stravinsky's development. It marked the break with the period leading up to *Le Sacre* and *Les Noces* and with the period which was really a prolongation of the other, including works such as *Renard* or even *L'Histoire du soldat*. The atmosphere of France, in which Stravinsky had been living for so many years, as well as his admiration for Tchaikovsky, had perhaps induced him to substitute for his vividly coloured, oriental, Russian art, which was almost Asiatic in feeling with its complicated harmonies and barbaric rhythms that had the violence of a hurricane, a type of music that was spare, stripped of inessentials, economical in the means it employed and imbued with a sense of proportion that by no means excluded grace or grandeur but conveyed a feeling that was pure, quintessential, devoid of artifice. *Mavra* was the first step along this path, from which Stravinsky never strayed again; from then on, his works, while retaining a precisely defined style, adequate to their subject, and full of an individual flavour and richness, all took on a more austere character. Later, in his marvellous *Apollon Musagète, Perséphone, Symphonie des Psaumes* and even *Ode* for orchestra and the pellucid Sonata for two pianos, a serene tenderness, of a quality previously unknown in his work, was to make itself felt.

The public that had taken ten years to swallow *Le Sacre* was scandalized by the simplicity of *Mavra*. It could not bear the idea that Stravinsky should change his manner just when they had him neatly labelled as the composer of *Le Sacre*. The Press showed a pitiful lack of comprehension; it screamed that Stravinsky no longer wrote like Stravinsky, that he was no longer capable of expressing himself, that his music was dull and insipid, that his melodies were 'old-fashioned'. . . . Vuillermoz's article was so full of incomprehension that Stravinsky could not resist pasting it on the first page of his manuscript. A small number of musicians, Auric, Poulenc, Roland-Manuel, Rieti, Sauguet and myself, were so deeply moved by this work that Jean Wiéner gave us another opportunity of hearing it. Courageous defenders such as he and Paul Collaer reward the efforts of composers, who so often have to contend with incomprehension and scepticism.

Chapter Eighteen

United States 1922

Robert Schmitz and his wife had been living in New York since 1918; they worked hard to spread the knowledge and appreciation of contemporary music, more especially of French music. They were good enough to put me in touch with their manager, Miss Bogue, a white-haired spinster lady who booked for me a sufficient number of engagements to justify a trip to the United States. Some of these involved difficulties. I had been invited by certain conductors to appear as a pianist and, as I was no virtuoso, I had to compose *for myself* an easy work which would give the audience the impression that it was difficult. This was how I came to write the *Ballade* for piano and orchestra. In 1927, and again in 1940, a similar set of circumstances led me to compose *Le Carnaval d'Aix* and my Second Piano Concerto, some of the passages in which were beyond me. A few weeks before leaving France, I received a telegram from my manager telling me that I was to conduct a concert in Philadelphia. It stipulated that the programme should be half modern and half classical. This was a new complication. I had no experience as a conductor beyond conducting my own works. . . .

On arrival in Philadelphia, I learnt that Stokowsky had appointed Enesco, Casella and myself to take his place during his absence in Europe. Naturally, neither he nor my manager Miss Bogue nor Mr Judson, the manager of the orchestra, had ever imagined that I should have the audacity to make my début as a conductor with his orchestra. . . . I was not too nervous, however; since I had to begin some time, it was all to the good that it should be with the finest symphony orchestra in the world. I think it was the prospect of this that turned my head and prevented me from realizing what an adventure I was rushing into. I chose a relatively easy programme: a concerto by Carl Philipp Emanuel Bach, the Italian Symphony, the second suite of *L'Arlésienne, Parade,* Auric's *Nocturne des Fâcheux,* Honegger's *Pastorale d'été,* an overture by Poulenc based on the finale of the Sonata for two pianos which I had orchestrated, my *Sérénade* and one or two *Saudades.* The contemporary works bothered me less than the others. I studied the scores very thoroughly, and the rehearsals did not go too badly. The orchestra must have found me very awkward, but they were very kind. My friends the Schmitzes came over from New York, terribly anxious. It was a dreadful shock for them to find me, half an hour before my concert was due to begin, calmly seated at table eating my dessert. I endeavoured to conduct with simplicity and precision, and this was my salvation. I even had the satisfaction of reading in one newspaper that I was a good conductor, but a rotten composer. But I still tremble when I think of my audacity, or rather my innocence at that time. Ignorance is bliss. . . .

I made my debut as a pianist under Dirk Foch, a Dutchman who conducted the New York City Symphony Orchestra. I played my *Ballade* and conducted my *Sérénade* in the same programme. Miss Bogue had booked other engagements for me, of the most varied character. I gave a little talk on Satie and the music of Les Six from the pulpit of the Church of St Joan of Arc, in the middle of the service, while Robert Schmitz illustrated my talk with extracts on the piano. The congregation was eager for instruction, and the day before, in similar circumstances, had heard a lecture on grapefruit-growing. I also went to Princeton University and Vassar College. At the latter, the audience, wholly composed of young ladies, intimidated me; I certainly had no idea that I should spend several years of my life teaching musical composition in a similar college. The wife of the editor of the *Washington Post,* Mrs Eugene Meyer, a great friend of Bibi Picabia and Germaine Survage, asked me to play some contemporary music at her home. She owned some very lovely modern paintings, as well as sculptures by Brancusi whom she had induced to come to the United States for an exhibition of his works, and the two had remained on excellent terms. A year or two later, I met her again in Paris at a dinner in Brancusi's house, to which Satie had also been invited. We ate a delicious dinner cooked in the sculptor's great furnace.

In Boston I took part in a concert of my works given by a group of players from the Boston Symphony Orchestra and conducted by the flautist Laurent. I gave a lecture at Harvard, and the members of the Harvard Glee Club prepared a surprise for me by singing the *Psalm* I had composed for them at the request of their Director, Dr Davidson, whom I had met in Paris on the occasion of a lunch given in his honour and in honour of the members of the musical delegation from Harvard University, by Marshal Foch. The lunch took place at the Cercle Interallié, and the Marshal had invited musicians of all generations, from members of the Institut to the so-called rebels. When the dessert was served, the young Americans had greeted the Marshal with some of their sporting yells and Indian war-cries. . . . In Boston, Dr Davidson introduced me to some of his friends, who at once decided to offer me a party. This was right in the middle of Prohibition, and the tiniest authentic drink cost a small fortune. Whisky was served in tea-cups, which were filled underneath the table. . . . Dr Davidson had chosen the Hotel Brunswick for the party, because it had an excellent jazz orchestra and he knew I should like to hear it. When I arrived in New York, I had told the newspapermen interviewing me that European music was considerably influenced by American music. 'But whose music?' they asked me, 'Macdowell's or Carpenter's?' 'Neither the one nor the other,' I answered, 'I mean jazz.' They were filled with consternation, for at that time most American musicians had not realized the importance of jazz as an art-form, and relegated it to the dance-hall. The headlines given to my interviews prove the astonishment caused by my statements: 'Milhaud admires Jazz', or 'Jazz dictates the future of European music'. Of course, my opinions won me the sympathy of Negro music-lovers, who flocked to my concerts. The Chairman of the Negro Musicians Union even wrote me a touching letter of thanks. Little suspecting what complications this would cause, I immediately invited him to lunch: no restaurant would serve us, but at last Germaine Schmitz solved this delicate problem by asking the manager of the Hotel Lafayette to receive us. I was also called upon by Burleigh, the famous arranger of Negro Spirituals, who played me Negro folk-tunes and hymns which interested me keenly, for I wished to take advantage of my stay to find out all I could about negro music. The jazz orchestra of the Hotel Brunswick was conducted by a young violinist called Reissmann, who got from his instrumentalists an extreme refinement of pianissimo tones, murmured notes and glancing chords, whisperings from the muted brass and barely formulated moans from the saxophone, which had a highly individual flavour. The regular rhythm was conveyed by the muffled beat of the percussion, and above it he spun the frail filigree of sound from the other instruments, to which the high notes of the violin lent an added poignancy. It made a great contrast to Paul Whiteman's lively orchestra which I had heard a few days before in New York and which had the precision of an elegant, well-oiled machine, a sort of Rolls Royce of dance music, but whose atmosphere remained entirely of this world and without inspiration

I owe to Yvonne George my introduction to the pure tradition of New Orleans jazz. In the course of a little reception which followed a lecture I gave at the Alliance Française, she came up to me and said: 'You look bored, come and have dinner with me, and afterwards I'll take you to Harlem when I've done my number!' She lived in the Hotel Lafayette. In the next room to hers, Isadora Duncan and her Russian poet Essenin used to quarrel and chase one another right out on to the fire escape. . . . Yvonne introduced me to Marcel Duchamp, an old friend of Satie and Picabia, whose paintings were closely associated with the beginnings of cubism and had played a dominant part in its development. After dinner I heard Yvonne George give her number. She was on Broadway, singing French songs of an intensely realistic character in a style that was both plain and charged with desperate feeling.

Harlem had not yet been discovered by the snobs and aesthetes: we were the only white folk there. The music I heard was absolutely different from anything I had ever heard before, and was a revelation to me. Against the beat of the drums, the melodic lines criss-crossed in a breathless pattern of broken and twisted rhythms. A Negress whose grating voice seemed to come from the depths of the centuries, sang in front of the various tables. With despairing pathos and dramatic feeling, she sang over and over again, to the point of exhaustion, the same refrain to which the constantly changing melodic pattern of the orchestra wove a kaleidoscopic background. This authentic music had its roots in the darkest corners of the Negro soul, the vestigial traces of Africa no doubt. Its effect on me was so overwhelming that I could not tear myself away. From then on, I frequented other Negro theatres and dance-halls. In some of their shows, the singers were accompanied by a flute, a clarinet, two trumpets, a trombone, a complicated percussion section played by one man, a piano and a string quintet. I was living in the French House of Columbia University, enjoying the charming hospitality of Mademoiselle Blanche Prenez; the Schmitzes were my close neighbours. As I never missed the slightest opportunity of visiting Harlem, I persuaded my friends to accompany me, as well as Casella and Mengelberg who were in New York at the time.

When I went back to France, I never wearied of playing over and over, on a little portable gramophone shaped like a camera, 'Black Swan' records I had purchased in a little shop in Harlem. More than ever I was resolved to use jazz for a chamber-music work.

Chapter Nineteen

Austria — Poland — Holland — Italy

As Francis Poulenc and I were anxious to renew our contacts with the Austrian musicians from whom we had been separated by the War, we went on a journey to Central Europe. Marya Freund went with us. Vienna had suffered a terrible food-shortage from which it was only just recovering and was still a prey to inflation and poverty; yet its artistic life continued. At the Redoutensaal, an enchanting little rococo theatre, we saw a performance of the *Marriage of Figaro* and at the Opera Strauss's *Ariadne auf Naxos*. The libretto by Hofmannsthal, Strauss's collaborator-in-chief, was of the greatest interest. He had contrived a double plot, most skilfully worked out, of the adventures of Ariadne and of scenes from Italian comedy. We met Hofmannsthal at the house of Frau Mahler, the widow of the composer, who entertained the intellectual and artistic élite of Vienna. This lady, whose beauty was only equalled by her kindness, wanted us to meet all her friends: Alban Berg, for whom we had the greatest admiration; Anton Webern with some of whose grippingly interesting quartets the Pro Arte Quartet had regaled us a few weeks previously; Egon Wellesz, a very erudite composer and a specialist in Byzantine music who showed us real friendship when, a week or two later, Poulenc fell seriously ill and had to be operated on for an abscess in the throat. I shall never forget how Wellesz brought him a pot of jam, which at that time represented a real sacrifice for a Viennese, especially if he had children.

Erika Wagner, who sang Schoenberg's works in Germany, happened to be in Vienna at the same time as ourselves, and Frau Mahler thought it might be a good idea to organize a double performance of *Pierrot Lunaire* in the German and French versions. Schoenberg agreed, and we used the same instrumentalists, including the pianist, Steuermann, an ardent devotee of Schoenberg's work. It was a most exciting experience; Schoenberg's conducting brought out the dramatic qualities of his work, making it harsher, wilder, more intense; my reading on the other hand, emphasized the music's sensuous qualities, all the sweetness, subtlety and translucency of it. Erika Wagner spoke the German words in a strident tone, with less respect for the notes as written than Marya Freund, who if anything erred on the side of observing them too closely. I realized on that occasion that the problem of recitative was properly insoluble.

After the performance of *Pierrot Lunaire*, in such widely varying interpretations, Schoenberg and I discussed our respective points of view, so different yet each equally justified. He invited us to call on him at Mödling, in the neighbourhood of Vienna. We spent a wonderful afternoon together. At his request, I played my Second *Suite*. Francis played his *Promenades* for the piano, which he had just completed. Schoenberg talked to us at length of his works, especially of the operas *Glückliche Hand* and *Erwartung*, whose scores I had just bought. He gave me a copy of his *Five Orchestral Pieces*, the score he had himself used for conducting the first performance, with all his pencilled annotations. A princely gift! Then he took us into his dining-room to have tea. The room was decorated with haunting pictures painted by himself, and all representing parts of faces in which only the eyes were visible.

Marya Freund, who was Polish, had organized concerts for us in Warsaw and her native town of Kalish. There too we found traces of the war's ravages: poverty, cold and famine. . . . Our hosts, Marya's relatives, spent a fortune on keeping us warm. As all the pipes had burst because of the cold, we gave our recitals by candle-light, huddled in our overcoats.

In September 1922, I was invited, together with Roussel and Ravel, to attend the Festival of French Music organized at the Concertgebouw by Mengelberg. This was the first occasion on which a work of mine had been included in a programme given under official auspices. Apart from my *Suite symphonique*, Ravel's *La Valse*, Roussel's *Pour une fête de printemps*, Fauré's *Requiem* and Debussy's *Fantaisie* were played. Ravel enjoyed considerable prestige abroad, but I had a greater admiration for Roussel, whose development and unremitting research had led him to a complete mastery of his art, while he never lost the freshness of his imagination.

During my stay in Amsterdam, I often went out with Bob de Roos, a young composer whose acquaintance I had made in Paris when he called on me to show me his music, in which I immediately detected sterling qualities. Whenever Dutch reporters plied me with the inevitable question: 'What do you think of Dutch music?', I used to answer, imitating in this Satie who never let an opportunity pass of praising the young: 'I won't talk to you about musicians who are already well-known, but of Bob de Roos, in whom I have the greatest hopes!' When the questioners expressed their astonishment at this unknown name, I would add: 'He is only fourteen, but remember his name!' When, ten years later, his two Symphonies were played, as well as his Studies for piano and orchestra and his music for *Ajax* which classed him among the best Dutch composers, I wonder whether any one of these reporters thought of my prediction. I stayed with the Curator of the Rijks Museum, Mr Van Notten, who took me to see Van Gogh's sister, a very old lady inhabiting a modest little flat and so conventional that she did not have a single canvas by her brother on her walls. She only possessed a few of them, and they were relegated to the attic. I strolled a lot around the silent streets of Amsterdam, austerely bordered by ancient houses and interrupted by sluggish canals that hardly seemed to move at all. What a contrast with the modern districts where the white and airy buildings were triumphant examples of all that was best in modern architecture! It was a pleasure for me to go back to Amsterdam a year or two later when Mengelberg engaged me to play my *Ballade* and Monteux to perform my *Carnaval d'Aix*. It was also in Amsterdam that I heard Hindemith give the first performance of the Concerto for viola that I had written for him.

Poulenc and I had such good memories of our previous trip together that we were on the look-out for an opportunity to undertake another. The idea of going to Italy was attractive, but we needed a pretext. Casella tried to get us an engagement with the Santa Cecilia, the oldest chamber music society in Rome, but the reputation enjoyed by the 'Groupe des Six' was not calculated to appeal to the Society's reactionary audiences. We therefore contented ourselves with a private concert in the house of Count Lovatelli as a justification for our journey.

In the course of my travels, I have often visited towns as a tourist does, hurrying from museum to church and from church to museum, without wasting a single moment. In Rome, however, I had such a sense of being at home that my only ambition was to bask in the sunshine on the steps of the Piazza di Spagna, nibbling shiny black olives sprinkled with chopped garlic. But after a few days spent in idling, my cousins, Marcelle and Renée Milhaud, who were staying with one of their aunts, persuaded us for our own delectation to explore the city in earnest. We went everywhere: Tivoli, Frascati, the Villa d'Este — the latter conjuring up for us the conversations between Lamartine and Madame de Girardin accompanied by the murmur of those same cascades that Liszt, too, glorified in song. . . . We often ate in little *trattorie* outside which, in market-days, innumerable painted carts with the hood folded back would call a halt, to enable the driver to rest before going on to Rome to unload his cargo of wine.

Claude Delvincourt, who held the Prix de Rome at that time, invited us to meet some of his colleagues. The immediate surroundings of the Villa Medici have an unutterable charm; you go in through a little square adorned with a broad-based fountain splashing into a pool. It is an ideal haven for the artists who, for three long years, are freed from material cares to work, meditate at leisure and exchange ideas with their gifted colleagues. Just as my voyage to Brazil had given me that change of scene that is desirable for any young man or woman beginning to take stock of his or her own abilities, the Villa Medici serves to develop the imagination of these young artists, while at the same time giving them the opportunity of seeing new faces and a new country.

In Naples, a disagreeable surprise awaited us at our hotel: there would be no room available for two whole days. Rather than sleep in the open, we decided to take a boat and sail to Palermo. We arrived in Sicily early in the morning in dazzling sunlight, and endeavoured to cram as many things into our visit as we could: the lovely old palaces, the cathedral of Monreale on the outskirts of the town, and even the catacombs of the Carmelite Convent, in which the skeletons of prelates and bishops stand ceremoniously clad in their most sumptuous robes. This macabre sight is more Spanish than Sicilian in taste.

Once back in Naples, we went for long walks around the harbour area, in the working-class quarters where the steep, narrow streets are festooned with lines of many-coloured washing stretched from window to window like gaudy rainbows. One night we hired a strange sort of vehicle driven by what appeared to be half a driver — he had only one eye, one leg and one arm — who leapt up to his seat on the box and took us to see all the puppet theatres in the Neapolitan suburbs. Everywhere we went, we saw the same scenes of medieval battle enacted before a noisy, exuberant audience that greeted every line with a roar and consisted solely of men and little boys, mostly wearing caps and no waistcoats, often no jackets either, and revelling in their untidiness. (In Naples, working-class women never go to the theatre. A year or two later, when I happened to be in Liége, I went to the Petit Théâtre des Marionnettes in the Rue de la Roture. This was the pompous way in which a little bistro in one of the most populous quarters of the city described itself. There you could drink 'Gueuse' beer, foamy and bitter, in a little back-room like a fairground booth, with narrow backless benches set too close together, on which were huddled a mass of noisy ragged urchins, poverty-stricken old women, and a few idle drinkers. Twice a week for years, these spectators had crowded to see the same spectacle showing the adventures of Sir Corydon at the Court of Charlemagne. . . . There were interminable battles between the infidels and the glorious warriors of the Emperor, conversations and conspiracies between officers, the arrival of a princess who recited long poems in Walloon dialect that excited wild enthusiasm. During the battle scenes, the action was accompanied by a single drum, supported by the regular percussion supplied by the sound made by the legs of the puppets as they fought. What interested me most about these helmeted heroes in medieval armour, or these princesses in hennins and dresses adorned with gold and brocade, was that the puppets and their actions were the same as those I had seen in the little theatre in Naples, the home of Pulcinella. . . . Out of this primitive form of art had sprung the prettiest theatre that could possibly be imagined, that of I Piccoli in Rome: an ideal theatre in which every effect is obtained by means of machinery so complicated that the puppets are capable of miming an actor's every gesture and of dancing a ballet in perfect time and with absolutely accurate steps. The puppets represent all kinds of things, animals or fairy chariots. All that seems unreal and impossible in an ordinary theatre becomes easy and possible in this little theatre, where the most extravagant fantasy has been let loose. The repertoire of I Piccoli is amazingly extensive. Its director Podrecca puts on ballets and classical operas, or sketches by Casella and other modern composers in decors by contemporary painters.

Before leaving Naples, we visited the museum, which contains some magnificent bronzes from Herculaneum and a 'secret' collection of a rather special character, to which women are not admitted, and the Aquarium where there are wonderful kinds of tiny fish, some as bright as golden nails, others elegantly adorned with wavy crinkled gills like the lace collars worn by seventeenth-century noblemen. We spent an unforgettable day at Pompeii, where one can still see traces of nearly all the everyday customs of that community so suddenly engulfed by death.

There is a local superstition to the effect that those who throw a coin into the Fountain of Trevi in Rome come back to Rome again. Like most tourists, I had of course performed the traditional rite, with a smile on my lips, but hope in my heart. Was it to those two or three sous that I owed the fact that I was engaged in 1924 to play my *Ballade* at the Symphony Concert at the Augusteo? Casella and Malipiero warned me straight away that the Roman public was not enamoured of contemporary music, to which it always gave a stormy reception. The rehearsals went off very well, cordially even. The same was not true of the concert itself. At the very first bars, the audience started to shout. They stopped while I was playing but shortly afterwards the tumult broke out again and lasted to the end of the piece. I bowed coldly and walked slowly off into the wings, where I found Molinari who had fled so rapidly before the last note had properly died away, that to me he had looked as if he were swimming out through the violins. Some of my friends in the Ambassador's box, and my host Jacques Truelle, were already convinced there was going to be an anti-French demonstration. I was able to set their minds at rest in this respect and to assure them that the audience at the Augusteo was just as hostile to the works of contemporary Italian composers.

Vittorio Rieti invited me to his house to meet Labroca and Massarani. They played me some of their music; a little *a cappella* chorus by Rieti called *Barabau* which I found so pleasing that I carried away with me a copy which I showed to Diaghilev on my return, when he asked me what I had heard in Rome. He immediately commissioned a ballet from Rieti, to be based on this little choral work of the folk-music type, steeped in malicious jollity. The ballet, for which Utrillo painted the scenery and Balanchine did the choreography, was an enormous success. After that, Rieti fell into the habit of coming often to Paris for long stays, and took part in all our musical activities.

Although I did not bring back with me from these later travels any musical inspiration, they at least gave me the opportunity of forming bonds of friendship with Vittorio Rieti and the Managing Director of Universal-Edition in Vienna, Emil Hertzka, who was to be for me not only a devoted publisher but also a faithful friend.

Chapter Twenty

Ballets

As soon as I came back from the United States, I got into touch with Fernand Léger and Blaise Cendrars, with whom I was to work on a new ballet for de Maré. Cendrars chose for his subject the creation of the world, going for his inspiration to African folk-lore, in which he was particularly deeply versed, having just published a Negro anthology. On this occasion, I remained more closely in contact with my collaborators than for any other of my works. They were great frequenters of bals musette, and often took me with them, thus revealing to me a side of Parisian life with which I had not previously been familiar. Wearing cloth caps and with mackintoshes slung over our shoulders, we would set out from the little restaurant in the Rue de Belleville, famous for its tripe, where we had had dinner, and make our way to the Rue de Lappe. From every café came the strains of the accordeon, sometimes accompanied by the clarinet, the cornet, the trombone or the violin. Men wearing caps and soft coloured shirts with a bright-hued scarf wound round their throats danced with their pleasant-faced girls, so well trained that they would never consent to dance with anyone else. Their 'man' paid for the right to dance, handing the money to the lessee of the dance-hall who went about among the couples constantly repeating the words: '*Passons la monnaie!*' (Pay up please), dropping the coins into a broad pouch she wore slung round her shoulder. Sometimes the cries of customers calling for a drink — a *fraisette* or a *rince-cocon* — drowned the sound of the music. Here the scene was always gay and animated. On the Boulevard Barbès or the Place des Alpes the atmosphere was quite different. Behind the Bastille, the Auvergnats of Paris danced the Bourrée to the sound of the hurdy-gurdy, while in the Rue Blomet the West Indians, with their women-folk wearing printed cotton headdresses, met to dance the beguine, whose irregular rhythm conjured up the palm-trees and savannahs of their islands. During our explorations, Léger, Cendrars and I were working out the details of our ballet. Léger wanted to adapt primitive Negro art and paint the drop-curtain and the scenery with African divinities expressive of power and darkness. He was never satisfied that his sketches were terrifying enough. He showed me one for the curtain, black on a dark brown background, that he had rejected on the grounds that it was too bright and 'pretty-pretty'. He would like to have used skins representing flowers, trees and animals of all kinds, which would have been filled with gas and allowed to fly up into the air at the moment of creation like so many balloons. This plan could not be adopted because it would have required a complicated apparatus for inflating them in each corner of the stage, and the sound of the gas would have drowned the music. He had to content himself with drawing his inspiration from the animal costumes worn by African dancers during their religious rites. At last in *La Création du monde*, I had the opportunity I had been waiting for to use those elements of jazz to which I had devoted so much study. I adopted the same orchestra as used in Harlem, seventeen solo instruments, and I made wholesale use of the jazz style to convey a purely classical feeling.

I wrote *La Création* in the new flat I had just taken at No 10 Boulevard de Clichy. Paul Morand had changed houses at the same time as myself, and as his flat was very tiny, and we had so many friends in common, he proposed that we should combine forces and celebrate our house-warming at my place. I piled up my furniture in every corner, and still the congestion was terrible. Our friends thronged the staircase outside and even invaded the café of 'La Chope Pigalle' on the ground floor. Through the open windows came the blaring of the *Limonaires*, shots from the shooting-galleries and the growls of wild beasts from the menageries, for the Fête de Montmartre had been in full swing since the beginning of June. We had arranged a surprise for our guests. Morand would have liked to have brought a lion, but as the lion-tamer had told us that it would refuse to come down the stairs again, we had to content ourselves with a Bird Theatre. What a charming show it was! Tame canaries and sparrows perched on their master's fingers and shoulders and head, or flew round the room performing a thousand different tricks. Then they enacted a little sketch. One canary shot another bird with a tiny cannon, and its victim lay still on the ground. They laid him on a little hearse which was drawn by two birds around the table, and to conclude the performance a canary-magician revived him by stroking him with his wing, whereupon he flew off as fast as he could go.

A little while after this party, I went to stay with my parents at Aix, to enjoy a week or two of solitude and work in the peace of L'Enclos. Désormière and Paul Collaer and his wife were to join me there in order that we might all go on to Sardinia together. I was intrigued by this country which the travel bureau never mentioned and none of my friends had ever visited. Paul Collaer, that admirable organizer, had prepared our expedition a long time in advance, and he had contacted the Italian Touring Club for information on all the peculiarities of Sardinia. He had prepared an interesting itinerary based on market-days and popular feast-days and attached especial importance to the Feast of Fonni, which was among the most famous.

We took advantage of a short halt in Genoa to visit the Campo Santo, which startled us by the pompous 'ninety-ish' style of its funerary monuments adorned with statues of the deceased, wearing frock-coats or dresses in the fashion of 1900. We saw the living replicas of these when we attended that evening a ridiculous performance of *Aïda* in which there was such a straining after effect that the dramatic feeling was swamped by a flood of sham lyricism. We embarked at Civita Vecchia where Stendhal had once been French Consul.

Sardinia is so well protected by its insularity that it has remained unspoilt, authentic, wild. If it had not been for the War, few of its inhabitants would ever have seen the continent. In one little village the children ran after us shouting: 'Cinesi! Cinesi!' (Chinamen!) for we were the first foreigners they had ever seen. Our only luggage consisted of the haversacks we carried on our backs, and this enabled us to travel by horseback as well as by bus. On market-days the latter did not serve the most outlying villages. We also took the local trains, crammed with peasants. It was not unusual to find them lying in the corridors, helpless with malaria, which was endemic on the east coast.

The villagers wore extremely picturesque costumes, with short skirts, resembling those worn by the Montenegrins, over their bare legs, waistcoats of tanned skins lined with lambswool and adorned with brilliant designs and a kind of bonnet of black wool shaped like a stocking on their heads. The younger men wore dark-coloured European-type suits. On Sundays they met to dance local dances to the strains of the accordeon and the *sampogna*, a kind of rustic oboe. The custom of serenading is still very popular in Sardinia, and it was not uncommon to hear in the early part of the night a song that was repeated over and over again to the accompaniment of the guitar. The music would never come to an end unless the 'fair one' or the friend to whom it was addressed did not appear at the balcony and distribute thanks and little gifts to the musicians. I noted down several of these melodies, of Spanish or Saracen origin, little thinking that I should have the opportunity to use them soon.

It was a very attractive country. We visited a great number of villages perched on the heights and looking down over vast landscapes, often intersected by the prehistoric structures known as *nouragues*. In the little towns, architectural details, balconies and window gratings of forged iron, bore witness to the period of Spanish domination of the island. We stopped for a few days at Cagliari, the capital, and the well-stocked shops were a pleasant change after the harsh austerity of the villages. In the museum there is an antique collection of old Sardinian bronzes, most of which go back to the mists of antiquity, and twelfth-century fabrics with complicated friezes representing stylized birds and geometical designs. . . . We took the train to go to the Feast of Fonni and at every little station we would get out of the train to stretch our legs. Once we picked some of the fruit of the prickly pear, and as we did not know how to skin it, our fingers were full of little prickles which were very difficult to extract. We were so enchanted by the prospect of seeing the Feast of Fonni that we were full of high spirits; this intrigued our fellow-travellers, who asked us where we were going. 'Andiamo per la Festa di Fonni!' we said, and as they did not seem to understand this, we explained in our halting Italian what the purpose of our journey was. Immediately our peasants shook their heads and informed us that the Feast of Fonni, of which we had read a glowing description in our up-to-date guide-books, had long since ceased to exist. The beauty of the surrounding landscape made up for our disappointment, and we went for some wonderful rides on horseback around Gennargentu, the highest mountain in Sardinia.

We had to think of getting back to our respective countries and jobs, however, and so we re-embarked at Porto Torres. A policeman asked us suspiciously what the significance of the colour of our shirts might be, and what party Déso[1] and I belonged to. The poor Fascist would no doubt have been incapable of understanding that we had bought the shirts in the market of Aix because we liked their blue colour and thought they were practical.

The Collaers had never been to Rome before. We tried to show them as much as we could in twenty-four hours, and then we parted. Before coming back to Paris, Déso and I spent a day or two in Florence which, in spite of the lovely country round about and the splendour of its buildings, seemed to me to be more of a museum than a town, and when we had thoroughly explored it I was not sorry to leave.

A few weeks afterwards, the Ballets Suédois gave the first performance of *La Création du monde*. Léger's contribution helped to make it an unforgettable spectacle. The critics decreed that my music was frivolous and more suitable for a restaurant or a dance-hall than for the concert-hall. Ten years later the self-same critics were discussing the philosophy of jazz and learnedly demonstrating that *La Création* was the best of my works.

De Maré was to undertake a tour of the United States, and wanted to put on an authentic American work, but did not know whom to approach. He

[1] This was the nickname we had given to Désormière.

was afraid of coming across some composer struggling along in the wake of Debussy, or someone composing music *à la* Brahms or *à la* Reyer. I had met Cole Porter several times at the house of the Princesse de Polignac. This elegant young American, who always wore a white carnation in the buttonhole of his faultless evening-dress, sang in a low, husky voice songs having just the qualities that de Maré was looking for: I introduced them to one another. De Maré immediately asked him to treat a subject admirably suitable for his music: the arrival of a young Swede in New York. As Cole Porter had never had any experience of orchestration, Charles Koechlin undertook to orchestrate his score, which was redolent of the pure spirit of Manhattan, with wistful blues alternating with throbbing rag-time rhythms. This odd partnership between the technician of counterpoint and fugue and the brilliant future 'King of Broadway' was an outstanding success. Fernand Léger asked an American artist, Gerald Murphy, to paint the scenery, and the skyscrapers of Times Square were seen to rise on the stage of the Théâtre des Champs-Elysées.

Despite all the praiseworthy efforts by the Ballets Suédois, and all the esteem in which they were held, the Ballets Russes achieved a greater technical perfection. On the instigation of Stravinsky, their indefatigable promoter, Diaghilev even attempted a very interesting experiment. Together they picked out one or two of the little comic operas that were no longer played, and Diaghilev decided to produce them. As, however, most of the arias were linked together by passages of spoken dialogue, he decided to follow the precedent set by Berlioz in providing musical settings for the recitatives in *Der Freischütz* and by Guiraud, who did the same thing for *Carmen*, and asked Satie, Auric and Poulenc to compose some music for the spoken passages in three of Gounod's little operas: *Le Médecin malgré lui*, *La Colombe* and *L'Education manquée*, but had not yet chosen a composer for the recitatives. Satie, who had had many arguments with Diaghilev about me, took the opportunity of mentioning my name. He pointed out that bearing the stamp of Chabrier's style, my music would be less likely to incur his displeasure, and during the summer I received the following letter from Satie:

Saturday, 21st July, 1923.

My very dear friend,

I have been requested by Diaghilev to ask you to do him a favour: to complete *L'Education Manquée* for him. I told our dear Director that you were the *only possible* one able to complete the work as it ought to be done, thanks to your so noble inspiration and your unerring craftsmanship.

I pulled his leg a little about his ostracism of you, and he seems to be better disposed towards you now.

What do you say?

Loyally, I cannot advise you. I must tell you that one thousand francs is the price mentioned, and that the work is only short, but . . . *most important*, and *deserves*

to be followed by some form of *compensation*. Yes.
Judge for yourself.
P.S. Poulenc has already done wonders for *La Colombe*. So I understand. Lucky
fellow!

In view of the aversion that I felt Diaghilev entertained for me, I hesitated
to accept this work, which would certainly be very amusing, but less
interesting than an original composition, and no doubt leading nowhere.
Satie, who was devoted to me, did not lose hope of winning me over to his
point of view and wrote me again:

Sunday, 28th July 1923.

My very dear friend,
Diaghilev is not here. I have just written to him and told him to write to you
himself.
Your letter gave me very great pleasure. You are absolutely right. Once you get
into the company, they will adore you, and Diaghilev will see for himself what a
magnificent artist you are. I have told you already: he is coming round to better
feelings towards you. Our friend Stravinsky was working him up a bit against you,
if I may say so.
Let's forget the past — and even the future too!
I am working on the *Docteur qui s'imagine l'être*, I'm not getting on at all.

Sunday, 19th August 1923.

I am working like a mad man . . . Yes . . . It's a jolly joke (for me) . . . I am
churning out 'Gounod' like a house on fire. It's all very Reber-ish (and *all tripe* if
I may say so . . . Yes).

Saturday, 25th September 1923.

Dear Friend,
Come back soon and let us have a talk together. . . . I am overjoyed to think that
(at last) Diaghilev has written to you. It's a victory over X (I'd like to know who
X is. Yes.)
I am working like a worker at work (a rare phenomenon). I have just finished Act
II of *Le Médecin malgré lui*. Someone (?) told Jean I was going to let it drop.
Hm. . . . Could that 'someone' have been — our friend Auric?

In the end, my friend Satie's persistence wore down my resistance. I
accepted the work and found it engrossing. *L'Education manquée* is written
for three singers; but as there are only arias for the baritone and the tenor, we
wanted to give the soprano one. Madame Bretton-Chabrier and the publishing firm of Enoch gave me access to Chabrier's unpublished manuscripts,
among which I discovered an enchanting melody which I could use without
change. René Chalupt wrote words that fitted in with the dramatic situation,
and the gap was filled. For the connecting passages between the scenes, I
endeavoured to stick close to Chabrier's style in order to ensure continuity
in the musical development and in the orchestration. I believe I was
moderately successful in this aim, for during rehearsals I heard Diaghilev

asking in an undertone: 'And what about this? Is this Chabrier?' He could not tell the true from the false.

The hereditary Princess of Monaco had given her patronage to the troupe of the Ballets Russes, which thus had the further advantage of working at Monte Carlo, free from material cares. Diaghilev therefore always went there to prepare his plans for the new season. The operettas were given such a cool reception at the Casino de Monte Carlo that he abandoned the idea of presenting them in Paris, with the exception of *L'Education manquée* (décors and costumes by Juan Gris). As nearly always happens, the public proved to be lacking in imagination and spurned the unexpected. It felt itself cheated, and clamoured: 'Bring on the ballets' so noisily that *L'Education* had to be withdrawn from the programme.

The Paris season of 1924 was a particularly brilliant one from the choreographic point of view, with Diaghilev's troupe vying with Massine's. The latter had left the Ballets Russes in order to strike out on his own, and like the noble patrons of the Renaissance, the Comte de Beaumont gave him the means of producing, with his own troupe of dancers, the works he had commissioned. I agreed to accept a libretto by Albert Flament on an old subject from the Commedia dell'Arte entitled *Insalata*, a mixture of Punchinello farces and love intrigues thwarted by jealous guardians; in short, a very highly complicated imbroglio bedevilled by a series of disguises and mystifications. I took as my inspiration some ancient Italian music that Massine showed me and used a few of the serenade themes I had brought back from Sardinia. I kept the same title, *Salade*, and wrote a ballet with singing.

The first rehearsals were held in the lovely drawing-rooms of the Comte de Beaumont at what was formerly the eighteenth-century Spanish Embassy, and later at the Théâtre de la Cigale. A series of literary evenigs, dance recitals and musical concerts were announced to take place under the auspices of the Soirées de Paris. These included a dadaist play by Tristan Tzara called *Mouchoir de nuages* and a very abridged adaptation of *Romeo and Juliet* by Cocteau, whose startlingly original production, in conjunction with the scenery by Jean Victor Hugo, marked an important date in theatrical history. Roger Désormière, a young conductor full of talent and extremely accomplished, who directed all of the musical side of the Soirées de Paris, had composed a score reminiscent of the bagpipes of the Elizabethan period. It was a very successful combination. Massine produced my ballet with décors painted by Braque, and Satie's *Mercure* with décors by Picasso.

In the meantime, Diaghilev's season promised to be exceptionally brilliant. The rivalry between the two troupes gave rise to quite a number of incidents and dramas, particularly as Massine had carried off with him several of the dancers of the Ballets Russes. However tempted he might have been to do so, Diaghilev could not prevent artists like Braque and Picasso from collaborating on these two ballets, but he warned Auric and Poulenc that he would ignore the success achieved at Monte Carlo by their ballets *Les Biches* and *Les Fâcheux* and would not produce them in Paris if they agreed to co-operate with the Comte de Beaumont. My two friends had to give way to his demands. To lend these young men's works more prestige and ensure their success, Diaghilev engaged André Messager to conduct them, thinking that the presence of the man who had conducted the first performance of *Pelléas* would create a favourable impression on both critics and public.

I was working on *Salade* one day when I received an unexpected visit from Diaghilev. He had come to task me whether I would write a ballet for his next season. While holding out the lure of the immense advantages that would accrue for me from such a collaboration, he advised me to break off my relations with the Comte de Beaumont on the grounds that there was no future in the Soirées de Paris. I pointed out that I was under contract and intended to honour my commitments, but that, in the absence of any clause forbidding me to undertake any other form of work, I was at his disposal. Diaghilev had no real choice in the matter; he needed a new work in a hurry for the debut of the young English dancer Anton Dolin and he knew that I worked quickly. Before finally agreeing, I consulted the Comte de Beaumont, who was most understanding. So I wrote *Salade* between February 5th and 20th, and *Le Train bleu* between February 15th and March 5th. I call these works my twins.

Le Train bleu was an operetta without words. By asking me to treat this subject of Cocteau's, gay, frivolous and frothy in the manner of Offenbach, Diaghilev was perfectly aware that I should not be able to go in for my usual kind of music, which he did not like. The action takes place in a fashionable resort where the elegant train known as *Le Train bleu* daily discharges new crowds of visitors who wander about the stage indulging in their favourite sports: tennis, golf, etc. . . . Dolin had every opportunity to perform his acrobatic feats and show his skill with the 'light fantastic toe'. Throughout the rehearsals, Messager was fatherly, charming and solicitous. The décors were by Laurens, and the costumes by Chanel. There were no incidents during rehearsals.

On the other hand, the performance of *Mercure* at the Soirées de Paris was disturbed by a band of surrealists who organized a demonstration, whose motives escaped us. They kept shouting: 'Up with Picasso! . . . Down with Satie! . . .' This left Satie quite unmoved; indifferent to what these incidents might lead to, he left the box where we were all together, in order to catch the last train for Arcueil. 'On my way out,' he wrote next day, 'I passed through a group of "pseudo-Dadaists", but they never said a word to me.' With the exception of a strike by the musicians ten minutes before the curtain was due to go up, the performances of *Salade* went off quite normally. On the night of the strike, I had to play my own score at the piano, by candle-light. My singers, the faithful Bathori among them, stood around me. Massine's choreography was very vivid, bringing out some of the dramatic aspects of the subject, whereas Lifar's production at the Opéra ten years later (with highly Mediterranean décors by Derain) was designed more exclusively to express the light-hearted, frolicsome side of Italian comedy.

Only a few days separated the production of my two ballets. Later on, I had the opportunity of conducting *Le Train bleu* at Monte Carlo and London. A year or two later, both works were given in the same programme at the Berlin Opera, and *Salade*, which was produced at the Opera in Budapest in 1938, was put on again immediately after the liberation.

Chapter Twenty-One

Cross-currents, from *Le Roi David* to *the School of Arcueil*

In the history of music, distinct and opposite tendencies have often confronted one another, and frequently led to open strife, either in the sphere of teaching methods (e.g. the Conservatoire and the Schola Cantorum), or between composers like Debussy and d'Indy or Roussel and Florent Schmitt, who were poles apart or again between musical societies such as the 'Nationale' and the 'S.M.I.', or the 'Sérénade' and the 'Triton' whose programmes were utterly different from one another. I myself came up against this state of affairs when musical writers, critics and a number of fanatical friends systematically opposed and compared Honegger's music and mine. Our friendship and mutual admiration were strong enough to take the strain of these violent attacks.

Honegger's career is a fine example of success rapidly reached in all fields. Whereas at every one of my new works the critics bared their teeth, they accepted his at first hearing; they treated me as a leg-puller and joker incapable of serious thought, but they regarded Arthur as both serious and profound. In addition, his pleasant manner and jovial character won him friends without difficulty, whereas I was sometimes violent, outspoken and, at one and the same time, both curt and bashful.

Nearly all Honegger's compositions won him immense success. When he was asked to write a work devoid of technical difficulties, to be sung by mountaineers at the theatre of Mézière in Switzerland, he composed *Le Roi David*, and its success was so great that it was not confined to Switzerland. Performances rapidly followed in Paris, in the course of which several sections of *Le Roi David* were regularly encored. The Parisian public which hitherto had persisted in its inability to understand modern music, now felt that it had grasped the secret of it. In his symphonic writings Arthur hit the bull's eye with the same unerring aim: he sang the praises of an American locomotive in a symphonic poem, and his *Pacific 231* soon went round the world. He only had to touch the operetta, seemingly so remote from the profound thinker idolized by so many writers on music, for it to be an immediate and overwhelming success: as witness *Le Roi Pausole* with its run of a thousand performances. When he turned to the cinema, as soon as the film producers had agreed to collaborate with a so-called 'symphonic' composer, Arthur was the only man capable of writing the scores for long films on great subjects. . . . He has such a sure sense of atmosphere, and is so skilful in putting himself at the level of the public by the extreme simplicity of his means, that soon he was unable to cope with the innumerable demands made upon him by the film industry. After *Le Roi David* it was *Judith*, also for Mézière, but a more personal and consequently less direct work than the previous one. *Pacific 231* was followed by *Rugby*, in which he celebrated sport and agility and freedom of movement. To me his masterpieces are *Horace Victorieux*, sombre and difficult, and not sufficiently direct in its appeal to be played very often, and the opera *Antigone*, a magnificent flowering of his personality, first produced in Essen, then at Brussels before the war, and in Paris during the occupation. Finally, there is *Jeanne d'Arc au Bûcher*, a huge fresco in which elements derived from films and film sound-tracks augment the orchestral and choral textures. The result realizes in masterly fashion Claudel's wonderful poetic drama of French purity and fire.

Despite the fact that Arthur's works were admired by the same musicians and critics who attacked mine, while my music was appreciated by a group of young musicians who were profoundly unjust in their attitude towards his, our affection remained unchanged. We were above these petty disturbances and were fond of giving concerts together. *Le Roi David* and *Les Choëphores* often figured on the same programme, each of us reaching his own public whose rival clans looked askance at one another with unconcealed animosity both during and after the concert. Trends opposed to Honegger had definitely set in with the works of Auric and Poulenc, but these only served to demonstrate the independence of Les Six, and the fact that they had no style in common. These trends became more marked in the work of younger musicians, especially those forming the School of Arcueil, who used them as aesthetic shock-tactics in a kind of election campaign.

In homage to Erik Satie, a number of young men had grouped themselves together to found *L'Ecole d'Arcueil*. The oldest of them was my old classmate at the Conservatoire, Henri Cliquet. (He had taken his mother's name to add to his own, and now called himself Cliquet-Pleyel.) Few of his works were ever performed, although he wrote a great deal. Roger Désormière, on the other hand, was not a prolific composer; he had not the time, devoting himself mostly to his conducting. As their emeritus leader, he became the promoter and defender of his comrades' music. Baron Jacques Benoist-Méchin was a strange fellow. Very much influenced by my music, he had undeniable lyrical gifts. Perhaps from megalomania, he chose to collaborate with only the very greatest — Shakespeare or Michelangelo. He was generous by nature and loved to act as a Maecenas. He bought manuscripts, and had an extensive collection of Claudel's first editions, a real 'Claudelium'. For a period of several months he acted as buyer for a wealthy American Press magnate, sending him antiques, ancient churches, cloisters, and even a Flemish carillon that played *Tosca* and could be operated by the collector from his bathroom . . . at least that is what Benoist-Méchin told us, though he was a great story-teller! He published an essay on *Music in the Work of Proust*. He spoke fluent English and German; he translated many works, and wrote one very remarkable text on the German Army. He was to become one of the Ministers at Vichy during the Occupation. His record as a collaborator made me feel no regret at having broken off, for personal reasons, my friendly relations with him in 1930. The artistic contribution that Maxime Jacob brought to the Group was one of aerial grace and freshness of vision. He would come and see me on his way home from the lycée, weighed down by the big dictionaries he carried under his arm. He would bring me some simple, sentimental, rather over-facile piece of music written in a style not far removed from that of the operetta. He was a Jew from Bayonne and remembering his origins he sometimes set to music fragments of the Psalms. A few years later, this fashionable young man who seemed to be wedded to worldly success and easy living, made the most edifying of conversions: he entered a Benedictine monastery. He did not give up music, however, but became the organist of his monastery. I met him again in Paris during his father's illness and again at L'Enclos during the War, when he came to spend his leave from the Army with me. Whether he was wearing his monastic robes, or a military uniform, I found him the same gifted, merry-hearted, lively man, but his eyes were deeper, purer, more luminous than before. He played a part in the Resistance, and I have a letter from him here: all the members of his family were murdered in a concentration camp. He is back in the monastery now, and still composing: for Dom Clément, music is the very breath of his soul, a gift of God.

Of all the members of the School of Arcueil, the most unquestionably gifted was Henri Sauguet. At the time of our Saturday meetings, Cocteau had brought us along one or two pianoforte pieces and a song, *Oceano Nox*, that Sauguet had sent him from Bordeaux. The talent revealed in them was still not very sure of itself, but had an authentic poetry of its own. I immediately began a correspondence with him, and invited him to come and stay with me for a few days. This brief visit enabled him to get to know us and attend a few concerts. We were all captivated by Sauguet's charm of manner, his subtle, refined intelligence, his profound culture and love of fun. A year later he definitely took up residence in Paris. To earn his living, he occupied successively the posts of salesman in the big store Paris-France, secretary to Monsieur Maître, a very learned Oriental scholar who, as a friend of Désormière, and finally took a job with an oil company. In the meantime, he continued his studies under Koechlin. Madame Beriza, who organized performances of modern operatic works, produced his *Plumet du Colonel*, an opéra-bouffe whose libretto he had also written himself. This was a charming work, consistently lively and poetic; shortly afterwards Diaghilev commissioned a ballet from him, *La Chatte*, which was so successful that it enjoyed a run of over 100 performances. . . . Sauguet's most important work is undoubtedly *La Chartreuse de Parme*, based on a libretto made by Lunel from Stendhal's novel of that name: the music is marvellous, often light-hearted, tender and broad in its treatment, but rising in the last act to genuine heights of emotion. I love it so much that when it was produced at the Opéra in Paris, I not only attended the last rehearsals, but also seven consecutive performances.

Office work had begun to lose its charm for Sauguet and, after the success of *La Chatte*, he was able to decide to give it up altogether and make a living by means of his literary gifts. He became a critic, one whose utterances were feared. His violent articles attacking Honegger and his followers' artistic tendencies penetrated Arthur's guard. On one occasion he even went to the length of hurling himself on Sauguet at the Théâtre des Champs-Elysées, snatching off his glasses — without these the poor fellow was absolutely helpless — and threatening to 'knock his face in' if he persisted in his attitude towards him. Sitting beside Sauguet, I felt caught between the devil and the deep blue sea. . . .

At a remove of several years, I can now see that, although opposition offers a stimulus to a young artist, and is even essential for his development, it is useless once works have won an established reputation; and it was with an equal emotion that I received Honegger's *Danse des Morts* and Sauguet's *La Voyante*, the first recordings from France to reach me after the Liberation.

Chapter Twenty-Two

Les Malheurs d'Orphée *and* Esther de Carpentras

The Princesse de Polignac, who was an excellent pianist and organist, had often given the first performance, in her own drawing-room, of works commissioned by herself: among these were Fauré's *Suite de Pelléas*, Ravel's *Pavane pour une infante défunte*, Manuel de Falla's *El Retablo de Maese Pedro*, Stravinsky's *Renard*, Satie's *Socrate*, Kurt Weill's Symphony, Poulenc's Concerto for two pianos and orchestra and his Concerto for organ, strings and timpani, and the *Pièces pour deux pianos* by Sauguet. In 1924 she asked me to write a work for her. I had for a long time been wanting to transpose an ancient myth to modern times. I was attracted by the legend of Orpheus, whom I imagined as a peasant of the Camargue, living on that wonderful plain where mirages hover above the blue horizons. I wanted Eurydice to have nothing in common with him, to be a stranger to his country and his settled ways. I pictured her as one of the gypsies who go on pilgrimage to Les Saintes-Maries-de-la-Mer and belong to a fiery, mysterious, passionate race.

Armand Lunel had now been a philosophy teacher in Monaco for several years and I had kept up my correspondence with him. Gallimard had published a number of books by him, which I admired enormously and in which I saw the fulfilment of the promise of his youth. It was with genuine pleasure that we met again at Aix each summer. I told him of my idea, and in the course of long conversations we worked out the details of a libretto which Lunel undertook to write for me. He fell in with my wishes admirably: *Orphée charmeur d'animaux* became *Orphée guérisseur des hommes et des bêtes*. The action is brief and dramatic. Orpheus lives in a little village of the Camargue, from which he absents himself from time to time to tend sick animals, even visiting their dens for the purpose; his villager friends, the Wheelwright, the Basket-maker and the Blacksmith are worried about him; Orpheus reassures them and tells them that he is going to settle down in the village for good because he is going to marry Eurydice, one of four gypsies who arrived in the village a few days before. Suddenly Eurydice comes in, tracked down by her nomadic relatives who are revolted at the idea of her proposed marriage and are determined to win her back, dead or alive. The villagers advise the young couple to flee. Act II takes place in the mountains where the lovers have sought refuge, but Eurydice has been smitten by a mysterious illness which Orpheus for all his skill is unable to relieve. She dies, after recommending her husband to the old Bear, the Boar, the lame old Fox and the Wolf 'that has lost the taste for blood'. The animals carry away her mortal remains, singing a funeral chorus. Act III discloses Orpheus once more back in his home, which is a cross between a chemist's shop and a natural history laboratory, adorned with ex-votos and crutches and plaster casts of limbs. Everybody believes him to have got over his grief, but he sings now of his despair that nothing can alleviate. Blinded by false appearances, the three sisters of Eurydice, like the Bacchantes who in the ancient myth tore Orpheus's body to pieces, now come to accuse him of their sister's death and pierce him with a pair of shears. As the unhappy man expires, yearning with all his soul and being towards his beloved, they realize their mistake.

In Lunel's hands, the libretto was beautifully balanced. He built it up in short scenes, with separate arias, duets and choruses. This made my task all the easier, and I composed *Les Malheurs* straight off, working all day long and then going out for a drive with Madeleine Milhaud, who was spending the summer with us at L'Enclos. There could be nothing more restful than to drive through the light of the setting sun, able, thanks to the motorcar, to explore roads that lay off the beaten track and discover yet another aspect of the wonderful scenery around Aix.

I invited Jean Victor Hugo, who was staying at the time with his grandmother, Madame Ménard-Dorian, to come and meet Armand Lunel. We wanted to talk to him about our plans for *Les Malheurs d'Orphée*, and for *Esther de Carpentras*, on which we intended to start soon. Our projects seemed to interest Jean, and he immediately did one or two sketches. He had an admirable grasp of what Lunel had imagined: the Camargue villagers, the gypsy women with their striped skirts and long shawls that made them look like 'black and gold bees', the animals swathed in bandages, worn out with weariness and old age. We had to wait till some years later to see these lovely sketches translated into reality in Madame Beriza's production of our work; for when the opera was played at the Théatre de la Monnaie in 1926, a Belgian painter was commissioned to do the scenery. The Honeggers came with us to Brussels to see the first performance. Vaurabourg, Madeleine and I squeezed into the little Renault under a pile of blankets and luggage, while Arthur, wrapped up in a great overcoat and wearing a sou'wester like those worn by fishermen on the Newfoundland banks, slept in the dickey, heedless of the rain. Elsa and Paul Collaer attended all rehearsals. When she heard *Die Entführung*, which was being produced at the same time as *Les Malheurs*, Elsa, who was more used to hearing contemporary music than Mozart's, was as startled as most people are on hearing a modern work for the first time. . . .

Les Malheurs d'Orphée is the first of a series of chamber operas that I wrote. The music is stripped to its bare essentials. Apart from Orpheus and Eurydice, the characters are grouped together, and while each preserves his or her own individuality and character, more often than not they sing together, thus forming a little choir. I scored it for only thirteen instruments. I knew that such an ensemble was as capable of filling a large hall as a drawing-room, but the Director of the Orchestre de la Monnaie, Monsieur Corneil de Thoran, who conducted the work, doubled the strings for fear that the solo instruments might prove inadequate. He soon realized that in doing so he was destroying the balance of my score, which was based on solo instruments only, so he suppressed the doubling.

Apart from the full-scale productions at Brussels and in Paris at the Théâtre Bériza, performances of *Les Malheurs* were given both in the concert-hall and on the radio. I conducted it myself at a Pro Musica concert given in New York, and at a concert at the Salle Pleyel devoted to works dedicated to the Princesse de Polignac. It was conducted at Königsberg by Scherchen, several recitals were given on the French wireless, and the University of Chicago included it in the same programme as my ballet, *The Bells*, produced in 1946.

Lunel had written a comedy inspired by old family stories and an eighteenth-century play written in the Jewish dialect of the county of Avignon: he called it *Esther de Carpentras*, and Gallimard had just published it. I found it the ideal subject for a comic opera. The scene is laid in Carpentras, before the Revolution. In the first act, three Israelites come to the Cardinal-Bishop to ask for permission to present the traditional play of Esther on the town square for the Feast of Purim. The young Bishop, newly arrived from Rome, allows himself to be influenced by his valet Vaucluse: he grants their request but plans to interrupt their performance in order to urge all Jews to renounce their faith. Act II takes place in front of the synagogue, where all the houses are bedecked with flags. There are two plots interwoven. In accordance with tradition, the actors are recruited from among the spectators. The play is given on a little wooden stage, and all the roles except that of Esther are taken by amateurs. At first everything goes off as usual. Then, just when the famous scene of Esther is due to begin, the

Bishop and Vaucluse turn up and read an edict threatening the Jews with death or exile if they refuse to be converted. Esther is unaware of the Bishop's presence, and makes her entry. She then plays her scene with him, as if she thought he was the actor supposed to play the part of Ahasuerus. Touched by her beauty and religious faith, the Bishop gives the Jews the right to stay in Carpentras and preserve their own religion. The choir and chapter come to fetch their Bishop, moved by disapproval of a mass-conversion that would deprive them of real material advantages, and they express astonishment at finding their Cardinal-Bishop in such an incongruous setting. They move away, singing an anthem, while the Jews intone a hymn of gratitude. 'The masquerade ends in a sermon', says the producer, and the curtain falls.

Lunel treats this subject very freely, constantly mingling the Old Testament with the New. Dramatic scenes are immediately followed by scenes of comedy, and this made me hesitate a long time before deciding how to treat them. I wrote *Esther de Carpentras* in 1925 at Paris, Aix and Malines. It was first produced on the radio in 1937 under the direction of Manuel Rosenthal, then in 1938 it was transferred to the Opéra-Comique to accompany a revival of *Le Pauvre Matelot*, produced by Cocteau with décors by Monnin, and a ballet based on the *Suite provençale* (décors by André Marchand). Roger Désormière conducted the performance. I had hoped that Jean Hugo would do the décors for *Esther*, since he had appeared to be interested a few years previously, and had even done some sketches at the time of our conversation at Aix, but now he had lost these, and by the time the opera was produced he preferred to devote himself to painting rather than the theatre. His place was taken by Nora Auric.

Chapter Twenty-Three

The Death of Erik Satie

Throughout his life, Satie never knew the meaning of compromise, courageously overcoming the miseries of man's lot and drawing his strength from his own inner resources. He was very forthright in character and, as he detested certain critics, he could not bear the idea that his friends should keep company with them. When therefore he found out at Monte Carlo that Poulenc and Auric had made friends with Louis Laloy, whom he regarded as his oldest enemy, he behaved as if it were a personal affront. No doubt this slight misunderstanding would have blown over if Auric had not published an unfortunate article entitled: 'Adieu, Satie', criticizing the music of *Relâche* (a ballet presented by the Ballets Suédois) and explaining his reasons for breaking with its composer. He seemed to have forgotten the preface to *Parade*, in which he had written: 'Some well-informed critics, enamoured of audacities now grown familiar and of the fantasies that made us smile yesterday, pointed to the inexperience of musicians whose lack of charm and of originality they felt obliged to denounce. Meanwhile, Art pursues its path, from which no man can make it turn aside.' Satie was especially fond of Auric, and was very hurt by his attitude. The breach between them widened.

After the first night of *Relâche*, Satie fell seriously ill; cirrhosis of the liver was diagnosed. He got into the habit of coming to Paris every day after this, lunching with Braque, Derain, or myself. He ate only very light meals, sitting right up against the fire-place with his umbrella and overcoat, and his hat pulled down over his eyes. In this posture he would remain silent and unmoving until the time came to catch his train for Arcueil. We did not think it right that he should travel every day like this, and we were so insistent that he finally decided to settle in Paris. He tried to get into the Hôtel Istria in Montparnasse, but they could only promise him a room at a later date. Meanwhile, he found a room at the Grand Hôtel, thanks to the intervention of Jean Wiéner, whose father had once been manager of that hotel. Still wearing his hat and coat and clutching his umbrella, he would spend his days sitting in a large armchair, gazing at himself in a mirror and operating the bolt on his door by a complicated arrangement of strings which he himself had contrived. He was so irritated by the telephone that we avoided ringing him up, but often went to see him. His room was quiet and comfortable, but Satie refused to stay there, and in spite of the noisy company of painters and students, he installed himself in the Hôtel Istria as soon as a room became available. His state had worsened to such an extent that the doctors ordered him to bed. Poor Satie! He had never been ill before, and everything gave rise to dramas, from taking medicine to having his temperature read. Several times we asked him whether he had any relatives whom he wished to see, or to be informed of his illness but his deliberately evasive answers precluded further discussion of the matter. Yet it was becoming necessary to take some serious decisions. When the doctor insisted that he should be taken to hospital, the Comte de Beaumont, who had endowed a ward at the Hôpital Saint-Joseph, used his influence to obtain for him a private room. Satie asked Madeleine to pack his suitcase. As she knew he was liable to fly into inexplicable rages if things were not placed exactly in the way that he wanted them, she asked Braque to stand between them so that Satie might not be able to watch how she packed his case. We accompanied our friend in the ambulance as far as the little room from which he was never to emerge again alive. . . . The nun who put away his personal possessions soon realized that she had no ordinary patient to deal with: Satie's only toilet accessories were a scrubbing-brush and a piece of pumice-stone, with which no doubt he used to rub his skin.

Despite his intolerable sufferings, he still retained his own characteristic brand of wit. When Maritain brought a priest to see him, he described him to us next day as 'looking like a Modigliani, black on a blue background'. When Monsieur Lerolle came to see him about publishing *Relâche*, he insisted on being paid at once: 'You never need money so much as when you're in hospital,' he remarked slyly. Hardly had Lerolle paid over the money, than he hid the banknotes between the sheets of old newspapers piled up on his suitcase, together with all sorts of papers and bits of string. Satie refused to allow anything to be thrown away and loved to accumulate all kinds of odds and ends. At the beginning of his illness, we had brought him several dozen handkerchiefs. Yet, when Valentine Hugo asked him what he would like, he said: 'I've seen some lovely handkerchiefs in the draper's next to the Hôtel Istria, I should like to have some of them', and when at his request, Madeleine went to fetch a bundle of laundry from his concierge at Arcueil, she was dumbfounded to discover that it contained eighty-nine handkerchiefs. . . .

As soon as Poulenc heard of his illness, he asked me to beg Satie to see him. Satie was touched by this, but refused, saying, 'No, no, I would rather not see him; they said goodbye to me, and now that I am ill, I prefer to take them at their word. One must stick to one's guns to the last.' Several of his friends were at his side until his death, among them Brancusi, Wiéner, Désormière and Caby. The latter was a young composer who had introduced himself to Satie after the performance of *Relâche*. He cared for him with intense devotion, patiently putting up with the sick man's often unjustified rages. For six months, Madeleine and I went to see him every day. When we left him at the end of April to go to Aix, where we were to be married, we feared we should never see him alive again. After a visit to the Middle East from which I returned in very poor health, Madeleine was so alarmed by Satie's condition that she insisted on my going to see him next day in spite of my own feeble state. Alas, we found only an empty bed. . . .

Our poor friend's death created a series of administrative problems, some of which seemed insoluble. To avoid a pauper's grave for him, the law required that a member of his family should be present before the funeral took place: so his brother had to be found at once, at all costs. The news of Satie's death was announced by the Agence Havas in all the provincial and foreign newspapers. That is how his brother Conrad and his nephews came to hear about it. They went to the hospital, where they were given my address. They then came to see me, to ask for details of their relative's illness and death. Conrad Satie proved to be a charming man: he was sincerely grieved at not having been able to look after his brother, whom he loved dearly, and with whom he had quarrelled for family reasons that were really quite unimportant. . . . At the funeral, we were astonished to see an aged composer, Alexandre Georges, of whom Satie had never spoken, yet they must have been great friends in former days for the old man to have gone to the trouble of coming as far as Arcueil for the funeral. Satie had been so much one of us that we tended to forget that he had taken part in the activities of several generations, including the Rosicrucians, Sâr Péladan, Debussy and Ravel. . . .

Conrad Satie did not know the address of his married sister in Buenos Aires. In such a case, the law requires that seals be affixed on the deceased's property and a public sale held. Before this took place, Conrad obtained permission to take away all his brother's personal papers and correspondence. (He had kept all his letters, as well as the rought drafts of his own replies, even the most insignificant.) Conrad was an exceptionally disinterested and tactful man, and his first thought was for making his brother's work as widely known as possible. He packed into the suitcase, bearing the initials 'E.S.', that Satie had bought for Monte Carlo, all the little manuscript albums and separate sheets of music that he could find. He brought them to me, for me to sort out and publish what was worthy of being saved from oblivion. This was a labour of love for me: Rouart-Lerolle agreed to publish *Ogives, Les Préludes* and *La Messe des pauvres*. Universal-Edition accepted *Jack-in-the-Box* and *Geneviève de Brabant*, and bought the copyright of the ballet *Mercure* from the Comte de Beaumont, who owned the manuscript.

Conrad asked Désormière, Wiéner, Caby and ourselves to help him go through his brother's effects before the public sale. A narrow corridor, with a washbasin in it, led to the bedroom into which Satie had never allowed anyone, not even his concierge, to penetrate. It was with a feeling akin to awe that we approached it now. What a shock we had on opening the door! It seemed impossible that Satie had lived in such poverty. This man, whose faultlessly clean and correct dress made him look rather like a model civil servant, had literally *nothing* worth a shilling to his name: a wretched bed, a table covered with the most unlikely objects, one chair and a half-empty wardrobe in which there were a dozen old-fashioned corduroy suits, brand-new and absolutely identical. In each corner of the room there were piles of old newspapers, old hats and walking sticks. On the ancient, broken-down piano with its pedals tied up with string, there was a parcel whose postmark proved that it had been delivered several years before: he had merely torn a corner of the paper to see what it contained — a little picture, some New Year's present no doubt. On the piano we found gifts bearing witness to a precious friendship, the *édition de luxe* of Debussy's *Poèmes de Baudelaire*, and *Estampes* and *Images*, with affectionate dedications like: 'To Erik Satie, the gentle medieval musician' or 'To the famous contrapuntist Erik Satie.' Behind the piano, we found an exercise book containing *Jack-in-the-Box* and *Geneviève de Brabant* that Satie thought he had lost on a bus. With his characteristic meticulous care, he had arranged in an old cigar-box more than four thousand little pieces of paper on which he had made curious drawings and written extravagant inscriptions. They spoke of enchanted shores, pools and marshes in the time of Charlemagne. There were frequent allusions to a demon or magician who inhabited a 'cast-iron castle in the Gothic style'. He had also very carefully traced tiny plans of an imaginary Arcueil, in which the Rue du Diable stood near the Place Notre-Dame. Had we not also seen chalked up on the gate of the house opposite (by whom?): 'This house is haunted by the devil'. . . .

On the day of the sale, Satie's friends decided to buy everything personal that had belonged to him. Déso stood beside the auctioneer and while forcing up the bidding, also kept an eye open for anything likely to be of interest to us. Thus, the Comte de Beaumont acquired the big portrait of Satie playing the organ — a painting in the style of a stained-glass window — by Antoine de la Rochefoucauld; Braque bought the portrait by Desboutins and the old piano; I came home laden with all sorts of souvenirs: walking-sticks, drawings in red ink, no doubt representing the characters in the ballet *Uspud*; scrawls of what looked like plain-chant, illuminated and framed, and a large painting which when cleaned turned out to be our friend's portrait by Zuloaga.

In homage to Satie, Diaghilev organized a performance of *Parade, Mercure* (by kind permission of the Comte de Beaumont) and *Jack-in-the-Box* orchestrated by me and with décors by Derain. The Comte de Beaumont got Déso to conduct a concert of works by Satie at which the first performance of *Geneviève de Brabant*, orchestrated by Déso himself, was given. Ortiz designed puppets for this show. Conrad Satie had the delicate attention of offering Déso and me legal documents ceding all rights in these two works to us.

A year after Satie's death, a memorial tablet was placed on the wretched building he had inhabited at Arcueil; speeches were made by the Mayor, a communist Deputy, and Robert Caby, while I spoke in the name of all French musicians. Afterwards a concert was held in the Mairie. The programme bore a reproduction of a drawing by Caby of Satie on his death-bed. Viñes played, and I accompanied Marya Freund in *Socrate*. The last words in that work now assumed for me their real meaning as never before: 'Such, Echecrates, was the manner of our friend's parting, the wisest and most just of all men.' Just, Satie certainly had been, but chiefly towards himself, which is so much rarer.

Conrad presented me with all his brother's manuscripts. When the international situation deteriorated beyond remedy in 1939, I deposited them at the Bibliothèque Nationale, with the request that Monsieur Julien Cain, the Curator, should exhibit them at the Conservatoire the following winter. This prospect would have tickled Satie, who had always been scorned and ignored by that official institution. The War prevented this project from being carried out, however. I was able to exhibit at Mills College, the Boston Symphony and the Chicago Arts Club, the two or three manuscripts that I had bought from him in his lifetime and still had in my possession; exercises in counterpoint and fugue, with corrections by his teachers at the Schola, Roussel, d'Indy and Séryex, as well as some music-hall songs that I had also kept, composed by Satie when he used to play the piano at the Chat Noir. I was glad to have this opportunity of paying homage, even so far afield as in America, to the memory of my old friend and master, whose fierce independence and proud hatred of compromise I so often recall.

Chapter Twenty-Four

Travels

Francis Poulenc came to our wedding, for which Paul Claudel and my brother-in-law Etienne Milhaud acted as witnesses. The simple ceremony took place very quietly in the Synagogue of Aix-en-Provence. Madeleine and I had long since planned our honeymoon; we intended to spend a few weeks in Palestine. We sailed on a ship that was due to call at many ports: the first was Naples. We went to Pompeii along a dusty road full of pot-holes, with lorries, farm-carts, donkey-carts and flocks of sheep and goats milling in all directions. I still wonder how we got back alive. In Malta we were conveyed in a lift up to the town carved out of solid rock. The women wear huge double hoods, spread out like wings, to protect themselves from the sea breezes. The solidly built church of the Knights of Malta and the Governor's rococo palace form a lively contrast with the narrow streets lined with English shops and tea-rooms in which it was delightful, after the rather rough crossing, to sit down to cups of hot tea with toast. We stopped for two days at the Piraeus. A motley crowd jostled around the harbour, in which the fishing-boats were anchored so thickly that they formed a forest of masts. A kind of electric railway took us to Athens. I loved the tiny chapels, lit by innumerable tapers, constantly renewed by the piety of the worshippers. Through the half-open doors, I caught a glimpse of the ikons glittering with gold. The perfume of incense hung over the whole town, mingling with the smell of olive oil, which is equally characteristic of Mediterranean towns. There are very few sculptures in the Museum, but all are choice specimens. And now, at last, the Acropolis! How small and familiar it seemed to me! Viewed from a distance the buildings seemed to stand like everyday objects on a tray, and this accentuated their character of intimacy. They seemed so much smaller than the mental image I had formed of them from reproductions, as if they had been built on an ordinary scale, accessible to the human heart, in spite of their absolute perfection.

We were looking forward to our arrival in Constantinople, but just at the entry to the Dardanelles the weather turned bad, and the celebrated Golden Horn looked as grey as a Norwegian fjord through the fog and the rain. We stayed a week in Constantinople. The political reformation had just begun, and we saw the first signs of the emancipation of women: the abolition of the veil had been enthusiastically welcomed, especially by the older women. Naturally we visited the Mosque of St Sophia and the Cemetery of Eyoub where the graves are a disorderly huddle of vertical stones among the tapering trunks of the cypresses. We drove along the banks of the Bosphorus as far as the beginning of the Black Sea, whose name seems justified by the dark hue of its waters. The Asiatic shore of the Bosphorus is bordered with luxurious villas, the summer residences of the wealthy and of the Diplomatic Corps, whereas the European side is more popular in character. Some cousins of my mother, the Guido Friedmans, lived in Constantinople, and offered to take us round in order to avoid the monotony of the usual sightseeing tours. In their company we visited little native restaurants, with dishes on the menus familiar to me from childhood, but I was fascinated by the desserts: rose-petal jam, loukoums, pistachio nuts covered in sugar, honey-cakes made of puff-pastry. We heard some Turkish music; the instruments played in unison, *almost*. By listening very attentively, I could always detect, in one or other of them, a slight variant, so slight as to be barely perceptible. We often strolled in the Bazaar of Constantinople and were even nearly the victims of an amusing hoax. I wanted to give Madeleine an amber necklace, and although these were rather scarce, a merchant promised to get me one. He knew where there was a superb necklace; all that was needed was to persuade the owner to part with it. A day or two later he arranged a meeting with her; she was an old woman, apparently quite poor. A long conversation in Turkish ensued. She promised to bring the jewelry to the shop next day. It looked good to us, but we had too much experience of haggling not to be mistrustful of this little comedy. We asked the advice of a friend of our cousins, an expert in antiques, who declared the necklace to be modern and worthless. This rang down the curtain on the comedy, which is apparently traditionally played for the benefit of foreigners, and which had lasted several days.

In Beirut, we hired a little Ford. The brakes were held together by strings, and the motor leaked. Our driver only spoke Syrian but he brought along a friend to act as interpreter. They were lively young sparks, and treated their car with affectionate roughness. Lebanon, with its soft clear horizons, would be rather reminiscent of the American deserts, were it not for the occasional tuft of palms or a glimpse of Bedouin nomads, with their haughty, inscrutable faces, crossing the distances on their camels. After Lebanon, and Baalbek with its imposing ruins, Damascus nestling amid its greenery was a refreshing sight. The Bazaar is a real roofed-in town, so huge that you go round it on donkey-back. We bought candied apricots and all kinds of attractive trash, and even, although it was June, camel-hair cloaks like those worn by the shepherds, so Biblical in their silhouettes. When we left Damascus, our drivers seemed merrier than usual. Yet they had been playing cards all night and had lost all their money. In the middle of the mountains they stopped the car and showed us an acquisition of which they were very proud: a revolver loaded with two cartridges. They asked us to get out of the car to try out their weapon. Without enthusiasm, we complied. Our driver stood in front of a telegraph pole, fired off his gun at it at point-blank range, and then, laughing uproariously, got back into the car with his friend . . . the rest of the journey was uneventful.

On arrival in Beirut, I felt so ill that I went to bed. Madame Sarrail[1] very kindly sent round immediately a military doctor, who said I had amoebic dysentery. He gave me a series of injections of emetine to arrest the malady, prescribed bed for several days and forbade any further travel. To our great regret, we therefore had to abandon the principal goal of our journey, Palestine. Madeleine then began her life as a sick nurse, a role that has been too often hers. She bore it with unwearying devotion and exceptional good humour. We tried to go back to France direct, but all berths had long since been booked by Government officials going home on leave. Thanks to the influence of General Sarrail, we managed to get a cabin on a crowded boat bound for Egypt, where we hoped to catch an Italian vessel, the *Esperia*, a few days later. When we got to Alexandria, my health improved somewhat, and we were able to make a few excursions. In the train to Cairo we were gripped by the spell of this magical country as we watched the villages of beaten earth flashing by. There was always the same archaic system of irrigation, worked by patiently turning horses or oxen. For a long time we ran along the banks of the Nile, a marvellous river on which craft with black or salmon-coloured sails moved to and fro. We visited the Museum and the Citadel, as well as the Pyramids, whose amazing dimensions took my breath away. The Sphynx seemed so tame and so familiar that one expected it almost to eat out of one's hand. On the road to Sakkarah, among thickets of palms, monuments of antiquity merged with their natural surroundings.

The *Esperia* brought us back to Naples, where we found my friend Yvonne and her husband Illan de Casafuerte waiting to take us home with them. They owned a tremendous feudal castle in the Abruzzi, looking down on the ruined village of Balsorano, destroyed by an earthquake. The castle was absolutely typical of the historical buildings one visits but no one ever

[1] General Sarrail was High-Commissioner for Syria and Lebanon at the time.

inhabits, with its battlements, its fifty rooms, its enormous corridors and walls seven metres thick. Yet the Casafuertes had contrived to create a warm and intimate atmosphere; their children and dogs, and the constant visits paid by peasants bringing produce from their farms, made this imposing mansion a comfortable and animated dwelling. Besides, there was Balsorano's permanent guest, Monsieur Larrapidie. He was a real character; an aged violinist, deeply versed in the lore of the violin and the art of making stringed instruments. Claudel had made his acquaintance in Boston when he was French Vice-Consul. At that time, he used to take him out into the woods of Massachusetts and try, like some modern Orpheus, to charm the birds with his violin. When Claudel was appointed to China, Larrapidie went with him. He stayed in that country for a very long time, and even brought back an almost Oriental obsequiousness of manner that never left him thereafter. He met Casafuerte at the home of his niece Madame Lara during the 1914 war. Larrapidie was very unhappy because he had no apartment and was incapable of solving the problems of everyday living. He used to complain bitterly. Casafuerte, who was always impulsively generous, proposed that he should go and live at Balsorano. The next day Larrapidie rang him up: 'Where is this castle you were telling me about yesterday? I'm leaving for it tonight!' He stayed there for twenty years and finally died there.

I fell ill again during my stay in Balsorano. The peasant woman who brought me my meals, carried up all the furniture we required for our installation on her head. She would come near my bed every day with a murmur of: 'Speriamo, speriamo!' It was then that I began to write my seventh quartet. For us it will always be inextricably bound up with our memories of that journey. As soon as I felt a little better, my friends drove us in their car to Rome, where we were to take the train for Paris. When we stopped at a little village to fill up with petrol, we saw a lot of ancient bottles in the window of a café. Our collector's fever made us buy the lot: Garibaldis, Queens of Italy, Angels, Clocks and Acrobats. When we got to the Hotel Flora, we had them all taken up to our room, to the great dismay of the porter. He was somewhat mollified when we offered him the contents of the bottles. He speedily returned with an empty vase into which he poured all the contents of the bottles, regardless of the type of liqueur they contained: 'This will be a treat for the kids,' he said with a smile.

In 1926, cultural relations with Russia had been resumed. Monteux had had a great success there. Szigeti had been there twice and come back full of enthusiasm. His wife asked me if I should be interested in going. I gladly accepted. Reports on the U.S.S.R. were so contradictory that I was delighted to have the opportunity of judging for myself, as well as of being the first French composer to resume musical contact with the country. Wanda Szigeti immediately got in touch with the brother of the diplomat Krassine, who was to act as impresario for my tour. He arranged for me to conduct three concerts in Moscow and three in Leningrad. Jean Wiéner was to come with me as soloist.

We set out with Madeleine in March 1926. All went well as far as Berlin, but from then on it was impossible to make oneself understood. English was no good, nor were the two or three words of German that Jean knew. This was all the more embarrassing because we were passing through many different countries, and had to be continually changing money: from Esthonian marks to liths, and from liths to laths, etc. . . . . One day when we were vainly endeavouring to make ourselves understood, we heard some-one talking French. Jean rushed out into the corridor, and much to our surprise, threw himself into the arms of a strange passenger. He had found an old war-time friend, who was now Minister in Tallinn. As the train was stopping there for several hours, he invited us to lunch, and showed us the town and the Parliament, a very bold modern building erected on the foundations of a former prison in which Esthonian patriots were locked up before the country won its independence. He also took us out into the surrounding countryside to admire a famous view, but the car got stuck in the snow, and we had to run to catch the train.

Crossing the Soviet frontier in the middle of the night was quite impressive. A wooden arch covered with foliage bore a banner with the inscription in several languages: 'Workers of the world, welcome.' Soldiers in long great-coats supervized the customs formalities. Newspapers and books received individual attention, as a precaution against any attempt at capitalist infiltration. Leningrad seemed asleep on the banks of the Neva. Since the Government departments abandoned them, the red and green palaces appeared to have remained uninhabited. The sky was blue, and sun warm, and the thaw had set in. It was a curious sensation not to be able to read the name of a street or boulevard, but the Government made up for this deficiency by supplying a young musician to act as interpreter and go with us wherever we went, to help us in all our difficulties. Every day, the Commissar of Fine Arts responsible for cultural relations rang up to know what we should like to see at the theatre and reserved seats for us. All productions were most elaborate, and enthrallingly interesting. We had gone to the Opera the very day we arrived in Leningrad. The programme consisted of *Boris Godunov*. The brilliantly lit hall was crowded with men and women wearing overalls and dark clothes. Later on, we saw Prokoviev's *Love for Three Oranges* and *Russlan and Ludmilla*, a prodigious work by the great precursor Glinka which is unfortunately never given outside of Russia. The actors, as State employees, rehearsed for as long as might be required by the Director. Meyerhold invited us to a rehearsal of Gogol's *Revizor*. It was the hundredth rehearsal, and yet how many times he made them repeat the same gesture! In *Howl of China*, a political play, an important part was played by the supers. They represented Chinese coolies in a port. They had studied their parts so long that every move and gesture had its own significance, thus approximating to the art of choreography.

We were keenly interested by the Persymphans Orchestra. It played without a conductor. The musicians assembled in groups and were free to express opinions and criticisms during rehearsals. For the actual performance, attacks and entries were discreetly indicated by the leader. The experiment had been fully successful, but it had been a politically inspired effort, and a conductor would have obtained the same results, possibly a little faster. At all events, this demonstration of collective discipline was confined to the Persymphans.

Our concert was a great success, the players were docile and very understanding, and the audience was quite amazing. What love of music they showed! There were in Leningrad a number of musicians who had grouped themselves around the musical critic Glebov. They were all anxious to get to know new French works, and we met on a number of occasions. Popov, Kamiensky, Dechevov played their own compositions and those of their comrades. When Wiéner played them some syncopated music, they were amazed. Kamiensky, the 'giant with a heart of gold', who was an excellent pianist, tried vainly to imitate these new unfamiliar rhythms. We enjoyed the company of such unconventional and undeniably gifted young men. In Moscow, academic influences were much more in evidence, the youthful musicians were more argumentative and inclined to hair-splitting. They were full of curiosity and asked questions about all sorts of things: about Monsieur Poulenc's ideology, the origin of the 'Groupe des Six', and the percentage of sons of workers included in it. (Our reply, 'They are all sons of bourgeois,' must have been a great disappointment to them.) Generally speaking, the atmosphere seemed to us to be more formal and intellectual than in Leningrad. Nevertheless, a young man with dreamy eyes hidden behind enormous spectacles, came to show me a symphony which, in spite of its rather conventional form and construction, betrayed genuine gifts, and even had a certain quality of greatness, if it is remembered that its composer Shostakovitch was only eighteen at the time and still a pupil at the Conservatoire.

The latter was directed by Glazunov. I called on him, but he was cut off from the world by a veil of vodka fumes and was absolutely indifferent to human affairs. . . . The tradition established by Anton Rubinstein was still flourishing, and there was a marvellous school of piano playing. We heard several amazing sixteen-year-old virtuosos. I remember Kagan (I wonder what became of him?). Vladimir Horowitz, who arrived in Paris a few weeks later, is a brilliant example of Russian musical education at that time. We also watched pupils practising and saw very careful performances, including one representing the *Fair of Sorotchinski*, acted and produced entirely by students. These performances, instinctive with the purity and fire of youth, were most pleasing.

Of course, we visited all the museums. At Tsarskoye-Selo, a former servant of the Tsar showed us the mansion. He was living in an essentially bourgeois atmosphere reminiscent of the 1880's, surrounded by innumerable photographs and memories of his masters. Jean Wiéner was pulled up short at the sight of the Tsarevitch's toys; he would have liked to take them home to his own little boy. He missed his wife and family very much and seized the slightest opportunity of talking longingly about them. In Moscow, we queued up with peasants who had come from the most distant parts to see Lenin's tomb. Corridors draped in red led to a little room in which he lay in a glass coffin, exposed to the view of visitors. A former counsellor to the Soviet Embassy in Paris, escorted by an officer, managed to gain admission to the Kremlin for us. This was temporarily prohibited because of official meetings which were then going on. In this way we saw, among other things, a little chapel, which is just like a jewel.

Apart from ikons (of which we saw some superb examples in the Ikon Museum), there was never any real Russian school of painting, but in the museums there are magnificent collections. (Forty Rembrandts at the Hermitage, and many pictures by the Impressionists and from Picasso's 'Blue' period in the Chukin and Morosov collections.) The education of the masses was organized on a most remarkable scale; everywhere one saw groups escorted by specialist guides, who were giving talks on the exhibits.

The Russians led an arid and difficult existence. They were overcrowded, often several to a room; their clothes and furs were worn out; the food was poor, but the will to reconstruct their devastated country was manifest in all their actions. They lived austerely, rarely going out and never visiting dance-halls or cabarets. The intellectuals met in their clubs, to talk and smoke. One evening, however, we were invited to a so-called clandestine night-club — it would have been better described as one to which the authorities turned a blind eye. Our host turned up about two in the morning when we were preparing to leave. He persuaded us to stay, and we had a party at which our healths were drunk, and Jean's. Jean was persuaded to have a drink. . . .It was all very innocent and delightful. But the telephone kept ringing, and this did not fail to set us thinking.

One morning the official from the Ministry of Fine Arts, who asked me each day what I would like to do, proposed that I should choose between a visit to a factory, a hospital, or a school. No doubt he was disappointed to hear that I was no more interested in visiting a factory or a hospital in the U.S.S.R. than I should have been in my own country, but I said I should be glad to see a school.

The children greeted us by singing the Marseillaise and the Internationale, and to our great astonishment, we found every classroom adorned with banners bearing such inscriptions as 'Long live the Commune!' and a huge portrait of Louise Michel. It was customary to surround the pupils with objects illustrating the period of history which they were studying, and for the little Russians, Louise Michel was a legendary figure. In the school entrance there was a wall newspaper, edited and illustrated by the children, commenting on school business and the main political events.

Our parting from our young friends in Leningrad was a melancholy occasion. Sadly we wondered whether we should ever see one another again. For a journey to Soviet Russia was as rare an event as a visit to Western Europe for a Russian. This first contact had been so open-hearted and direct, and we had so many artistic interests in common that we should have liked to have kept up our friendship with these young musicians. Although the atmosphere was quite different from that elsewhere in Europe, one soon succumbed to its charm, and as once more we pulled up at the station of Tallinn, we felt uncomfortable, so deep had been the impression left by those few weeks. Luxurious shops and easy living now appeared to us to be an anachronism. Back in Paris we were assailed by questions, and the eternal: 'But of course they didn't really show you anything?' Good heavens, what did they show one in Belgium, England or Switzerland that was so outstanding?

No sooner had I got back to Paris than I found myself obliged to compose a new work for a tour in the United States. This had been organized by Robert Schmitz under the auspices of the Pro Musica Society, of which he was president, and whose aim was to spread the knowledge of contemporary music. There were branches of the Pro Musica throughout the country, so that our trip promised to be an interesting one. I beguiled the time by stringing together twelve extracts from *Salade*, images of characters from the Commedia dell'Arte that seemed all ready to take part in a carnival, so I grouped them together and called them *Le Carnaval d'Aix*.

Once again, I disappointed the American reporters by telling them I was no longer interested in jazz. It had now become official and won universal recognition. The Winn School of Popular Music had even published three methods: 'How to play Jazz and the Blues', in which syncopation was analyzed, I might even say dissected. The various ways of assimilating jazz were taught, as well as jazz style for the piano, and improvisation; its freedom within a rigid rhythmic framework, all the breaks and passing discords, the broken harmonies, arpeggios, trills and ornaments, the variations and cadences which can return *ad lib.* in a sort of highly fantastic counterpoint. You could also find instructions on playing the trombone, including the principal types of glissando and the way to make the sound quiver by a rapid little to-and-fro movement of the slide, and there were clarinet manuals exploiting all the new technical possibilities opened up by jazz. Even in Harlem, the charm had been broken for me. White men, snobs in search of exotic colour and sightseers curious to hear Negro music had penetrated to even the most secluded corners. That is why I gave up going.

I played my *Ballade* with Walter Damrosch at one of the series of concerts of contemporary music promoted by him under the title: 'Pleasant and Unpleasant Music'. Before each piece, the old maestro addressed the audience and asked them to classify the music as pleasant or unpleasant. I regarded this procedure as definitely 'unpleasant', whatever the verdict of the audience might prove to be.

Before I started to play *Le Carnaval d'Aix* with the Philharmonic Orchestra of New York under Mengelberg, I suffered a slight contretemps, for a piece of chewing-gum had got stuck to the sole of my shoe just as I came on the stage. I played the *Carnaval* again at Boston with Koussevitzky, who engaged me to play it with him again in Paris, where he was in the habit of conducting a few concerts every spring and presenting new works. It was in this way that I came to hear Aaron Copland's *Music for the Theatre*, which first roused my admiration for its composer.

This was a perid of prosperity in the United States. Welt-Mignon, a pianola firm, gave me a profitable contract, as did Baldwin's, whose pianos I had always used. Sales of mechanical pianos had been considerably boosted during recent years, for they enabled all the details of an orchestral score, which it was impossible to render on an ordinary piano, to be given. The Pleyela company had obtained exclusive rights from Stravinsky to publish all his works in pianola rolls. He had been given a studio for this purpose in the Pleydel building and throughout one winter, he himself played 'pleyelized' versions of his works so as to ensure the correct reading, and supervised the perforation of the rolls, which was all done by hand, as well as all the musical details to be added to this preliminary version. Jean Wiéner and I recorded a piano duet of my *Boeuf sur le toit*. Welt-Mignon was less bold than Pleyela. He asked me to play a few *Saudades* and some of Mendelssohn's *Songs without Words*. As I was no virtuoso, I considered it absurd to play works other than my own, but I was told that was just what the public would like to hear: Mendelssohn interpreted by a contemporary composer. . . . Personally, I think it was merely a way of getting me to play one *Saudades* the less! In any case, it did not matter, for the firm went bankrupt before the recording was published. The development of the radio and the gramophone rapidly cut across that of mechanical music, and all these experiments came to nothing.

Gieseking and Casella were staying at the same hotel as we were, and we often saw one another. Casella several times invited us to his room to hear his latest compositions, never failing to say: 'I think it is my best work!' We had lunch with Charles Ives, a pioneer of American music. He received few visitors, and worked unremittingly. Schmitz, who had taken me to see him, knew his compositions well; they were hard to play (and almost unreadable in manuscript), but bore the imprint of an extremely original personality.

We spent my holidays in Birminghàm, Alabama, with Jeanne Herscher who was teaching in the Conservatoire there. She was interested in the local folklore, and a Negro pastor assisted her in her research. In her company, we attended a religious service in a little Negro church that was all hung with white draperies and decorated for the Christmas celebrations. The church was packed. We were the only white folk and occupied places reserved for us by the pastor. The sermon began in an extraordinary way, reminiscent of those recordings of Negro sermons like: 'The black train of Death is coming, you must have your ticket in your hand!' The preacher's voice rose to a sort of melopaeic chant, now wheedling and now violent, but always awe-inspiring. The congregation responded by cries of 'Lord!' or 'Amen', which rang out all over the church. There was a sort of undertone of excitement — when it reached its paroxysm, the preacher suddenly lowered his voice, and gradually the fervour subsided. Then the sermon continued and the preacher spoke of the relations between white folk and coloured folk: 'Why are we so ill-treated? And yet the white folk entrust us with their dearest possession, their children!'. . . . The tide of his eloquence began to swell once more. His lyrical outbursts had an astonishing effect, the cries of the congregation following the inflections of his voice as a shadow follows the body that casts it. Those who fell into trances were immediately looked after by persons specially designated for the purpose. When the pastor judged that he had had a sufficient effect on his hearers, he brought his sermon to an end in a quieter and calmer voice. He asked his aged mother, a former slave, to stand, and then he introduced us to the congregation as French people who were friends of the Negro. We felt that the crowd was so inflamed with passion and so exalted that at the slightest signal they would even have lynched us, if this had been suggested to them (if such a thing were possible). Next day we were to have witnessed a baptism of two thousand Negroes in the waters of the Mississippi, but the ceremony was unfortunately postponed owing to rain. . . .

In New Orleans, the gulf between Whites and Blacks was even deeper, and their ways of life lay quite apart: the coloured folk had to use special staircases, and reserved seats in the buses and trains. Any white doctor who treated a Negro was irrevocably compromised in the sight of his clients. We were refused admission to a little Negro theatre where an operetta was being given. They apologized for not being able to let us in, but the laws were rigid. However, as we insisted, they fetched the manager, to whom we explained that we were French musicians, whereupon he invited us to watch the show from his office, in which there was a little window overlooking the stage.

We stopped for one day at the Grand Canyon, which impressed us enormously. From the plateau itself, we looked down on a huge abyss whose rocky walls were coloured as vividly as any picture postcard. We visited Portland, Denver, Chicago, Saint-Paul, Minneapolis and Montreal. Wherever we went, we met admirers and supporters of Robert Schmitz. On our return to the United States thirteen years later, we found that most of the branches of the Pro Musica no longer existed, which was a great pity, for Robert Schmitz had been a real pioneer of contemporary music. In addition to my visit, he organized similar tours by Roussel, Ravel, Honegger and Tansman.

Although it was tiring, the journey was tremendously interesting. Very often, we reached a town just in time for the concert and left immediately afterwards. Several consecutive nights were spent in the train. So it was a joy to be able to stay for a few days in Los Angeles. The lady President of the Pro Musica was waiting for us, and immediately asked us what our plans were. These were quite simple: we wanted to walk as far as the Pacific, upon which we had never set eyes before. She offered to take us there in a car and when we declined she became so insistent that we finally gave way. It was a good thing that we did, for we certainly covered more than 45 kilometres before she pointed to a greyish expanse of water and said: 'There it is!' It was nightfall already. . . . We did not even have the courage to get out of the car. When she brought us back to our hotel, she invited us to a Hollywood première. The prospect was tempting, but as it was due to take place an hour's drive away from Los Angeles we declined.

A day or two later, we visited De Mille's film studio, where he was producing the *Life of Christ*. He appeared before us in the midst of his apostles in a black and white landscape mounted on movable platforms. Mary Pickford and Douglas Fairbanks, then at the height of their fame, asked us to tea. They were delightfully informal. With all the exuberance of a child, he told us about the tennis match he had just been umpiring. She asked Madeleine, with the utmost naturalness, to take off her shoes in order to compare their heights.

Next, we spent a few days at Santa Barbara at the home of Henry Eichheim, a most pleasing composer who had lived for long periods in the Far East, and brought back many lovely old instruments. He lived with his mother, who was 96 years old (the same age as my grandmother Précile would have been had she lived). She was lively and full of animation. She thoughtfully placed a footstool under Madeleine's feet, much to the latter's confusion. She was afraid of dying, and had had a bed set up in the garden for fear of the slight earthquakes so common in that region.

We were not due to give a concert in San Francisco, but we wanted to go there. We arrived at night by ferry, and the spectacle was absolutely fairy-like. As we drank in the city's unusual atmosphere, I little dreamt that for several years we should live so near it.

Chapter Twenty-Five

Persistence of a Theme

While Jean Cocteau was spending a holiday at Le Piquey, he was greatly struck by a news item he read in the local paper: the son of some poor Rumanian peasants had been entrusted at an early age to relatives who were setting out to seek their fortune in America, and had had no further communication with his parents. He became a brilliantly successful student, and set out for Rumania to see his father and mother again. When he got to his native village, he had the idea of staying the night in his parents' house without letting them know who he was. They thought he was a wealthy foreigner and murdered him. Cocteau took this story as the basis of a libretto for an opera. His poetic version, written rapidly, without any crossings-out, appealed to me. Cocteau had meant it for Auric, but as the latter was very busy, he agreed to let me have it.

The plot of *Le Pauvre Matelot* is quite simple. A sailor's wife has been without news of her husband for several years. In spite of her father-in-law's efforts to persuade her to re-marry, she persistently refuses to do so. The husband returns unexpectedly, and goes first to a neighbour, who tells him of his wife's virtuous behaviour and poverty. The husband says he wants to 'see his happiness from the outside'. He passes himself off to his wife as a friend of her husband, tells her the poor fellow is still a prisoner, suffering from disease and the lack of money, and confides in her that he himself has been more fortunate: he says he is rich, and offers to spend the night at her house. She agrees, and kills him 'in order to rescue her husband'. The curtain falls before she has had time to realize her mistake and the crime she has committed.

Le Pauvre Matelot was composed at L'Enclos in 1926 and scored for a normal orchestra. It was produced in the following year at La Monnaie and the Opéra-Comique, but in very different ways. As it only lasted forty minutes, the Opéra-Comique put it on in conjunction with *Werther* or *Tosca*, which pleased neither the usual audience who were bored by modern music and were forced to put up with it in this way, nor the amateurs of contemporary music who had to wade through an opera by Puccini or Massenet. What was more, there was a strange trade union rule still observed in the opera-houses at that time, to the effect that any musician could get another, even if he had not previously taken part in rehearsals, to take his place at the performance. The substitute would often be sight reading the score, even on the first night. This custom, which might possibly be tolerable in the case of a piece from the repertory, was sheer madness in the case of new work. Thus for the first performance of *Le Pauvre Matelot*, I was favoured with no less than seventeen completely new players. Naturally the result was catastrophic. Understandably enough, the public and my friends to whom the work was unknown, held me responsible for the cacophony, whose origin they were not in a position to suspect. Since on the other hand, the Brussels production of *Le Pauvre Matelot* was faultless, one of my composer friends who had attended the first night performance in Paris, asked me in all innocence whether I had not re-orchestrated my score for the Théâtre de la Monnaie. . . . All misunderstandings were obviated in Brussels by including *Le Pauvre Matelot* in the same programme as Honegger's *Antigone*, and the fact that both librettos had been written by Cocteau conferred a very special unity on the whole entertainment.

Further performances were given at the Opéra-Comique, but the malaise persisted. One evening when I was up 'in the gods', the man next to me said with a heavy suburban accent: 'There's a pillar in my way, do you mind if I squeeze up closer to you?' All through the performance of *Le Pauvre Matelot* he was jammed tightly against my side, following very closely, frowning and breathing heavily. When the curtain fell, my neighbour leapt to his feet, muttering: 'Horrible! horrible!' and stalked out.

Le Pauvre Matelot was my most widely performed opera. Written for four singers, with no change of scenery and plain modern costumes, it is easy to produce. It ran for three consecutive years at the Opera on the Republikplatz, Berlin and was revived in Berlin immediately after the war. . . . It was also shown in more than twenty German cities as well as Vienna, Salzburg and Prague.

I conducted it myself in Barcelona, with Bathori and singers I had brought from Paris. Although it was snowing, which was quite an event in Barcelona, Bathori was tireless in going from shops to exhibitions and from museums to churches. The theatre was icy cold, we all wore several sweaters, and my singers were even able to keep them on on stage, fortunately for them! The show was given in a concert-hall. The walls were adorned with modern-style muses whose florid vulgarity was one of the secrets of the beginning of the century. The rudimentary scenery was barely lit, and the props non-existent. A makeshift curtain had been rigged up for the occasion, and as it was to be operated by one solitary stage-hand perched in the flies who could not be informed in any other way; Madeleine, who was prompting the singers, had to pull a cord attached to his foot, whereupon the curtain would hurtle down — I can still hear the frightful din it made — and send clouds of dust through the hall. There was no pit for the orchestra, so that the musicians sat in the stalls, and I conducted from the midst of the audience.

I was asked by Scherchen to score *Le Pauvre Matelot* for thirteen instruments. He wanted to put it on at the same time as *L'Histoire du soldat*. The first performance was given in Geneva. Ramuz produced *L'Histoire du soldat*, and Cocteau took the part of the Narrator with his clear voice, so luminous and distinct. He was also responsible for the mise-en-scène of *Le Pauvre Matelot*. (It was used again for the revival in Paris in 1937). It was a highly simplified kind of improvisation, owing something to the slow-motion technique of the cinema: two benches, a few screens, actors in jerseys, with their faces daubed with violent colours as in the Chinese theatre, to catch the light. Scherchen produced these two works in Turin and Florence. The 'Vienna Studio' troupe also produced *Le Pauvre Matelot* in Vienna and Salzburg. Fritz Reiner conducted it in Philadelphia and New York. It was played in Paris and Rome after the Liberation, and later in England in Chester and London and over the radio.

During our travels in the United States in 1927, when we had been running through a collection of old French-Canadian songs, we had noticed *Le Funeste Retour*, which described how a cabin-boy went to spend his shore leave with his mother, who had not seen him for a long time, and murdered him. It is strange how this theme is constantly recurring in literature and folklore. Albert Camus took a similar situation as a basis for his *Le Malentendu*, and in *L'Etranger* he relates a similar adventure:

Between my palliasse and the boards of my bed I had found an old scrap of newspaper, yellow and transparent and almost stuck to the cloth. The first part of one of the stories on it was missing, but the events it described must have taken place in Czechoslovakia. A man had set out from his village in Czechoslovakia to seek his fortune. Twenty-five years later, rich and accompanied by his wife and child, he had returned. His mother and sister were running a hotel in his native village. As a surprise for them, he left his wife and child in another inn, and had gone to see his mother, who failed to recognize him when he came in. As a joke, he decided to book a room for the night, and in doing so let them see that he had money. During the night, his mother and sister murdered him with a hammer to steal his money, and then threw the body into the river. In the morning, his wife had arrived and unintentionally revealed the identity of the traveller. The mother hanged herself, and the sister threw herself into the well. I must have read this story thousands of times. In one way it sounded highly unlikely, in another it was quite plausible. At all events, I thought the traveller had been asking for trouble, and one should never play silly tricks of that kind.

After reading this passage, I wondered whether the theme of *Le Funeste retour* was not destined to live on like those of Greek tragedy.

Chapter Twenty-Six

Miniature Opera and Grand Opera

Between 1922 and 1932, Paul Hindemith was organizing concerts of contemporary music, first at Donaueschingen under the patronage of the Prince of Fürstenberg, and then in Baden-Baden under the auspices of the municipal authorities, and finally in 1930 in Berlin. Hindemith was absolutely his own master, and tried out all kinds of musical experiments. In 1927 he asked me to compose an opera, which had to be as short as possible. Henri Hoppenot wrote a libretto for me, on the subject of *L'Enlèvement d'Europe*, off-handed, poetic, and slightly ironic in its treatment, and containing all the essential elements on a miniature scale. It was produced in conjunction with *Die Prinzessin auf der Erbst* by Toch, lasting one hour, Kurt Weill's *Mahagonny* lasting thirty minutes, and Hindemith's *Hin und Zurück*, lasting fourteen minutes. Emil Hertzka, the managing director of Universal-Edition, did not consider the publication of my work to be a commercial proposition: 'What an idea, an opera that only lasts nine minutes!' 'Now,' said he, 'if you would only write me a trilogy. . . .' The idea appealed to me. Once more I had recourse to Henri Hoppenot, who in spite of his official duties (at that time he occupied a post in Berlin), dashed off two more librettos of the same kind as the previous one: *L'Abandon d'Ariane* and *La Délivrance de Thésée*. The three operas together lasted twenty-seven minutes. The trilogy was immediately produced at the Operas of Wiesbaden and Budapest, and I did a recording for Columbia. I have never been able to understand why the firm did not make more publicity of the fact that each opera only occupied one disc.

In the following year, various cantatas and works written for the radio were produced at Baden-Baden. Scherchen conducted my cantate, *Le*

Retour de l'enfant prodigue. Hindemith took an active interest in the development of contemporary music for amateurs, and wrote works especially for them. In the course of a concert given in the forest, ancient music as well as his cantata *Frau Musica* was sung by peasants.

Another year, they put on music specially written for the cinema, and on this occasion I wrote a score to accompany a film of Cavalcanti's called *La P'tite Lilie*. I recorded it in Berlin a few weeks before the Festival. Hindemith's concerts and classes took up so much of his time (he was composition teacher in the Berlin Hochschule) that he was caught unprepared and right up to the last moment was feverishly composing his pieces for the Festival. I shall always see him scribbling furiously and passing each page as he finished it to two of his students who immediately transcribed it on a pianola roll. It was a score for an imaginative film by Richter called *Vormittagspuck*. For an animated cartoon, *Felix the Cat*, he used a synchronizing apparatus invented by a German engineer, Robert Blum. By means of this it was possible to run off the film at the same time as a reel of similar size bearing two staves on which the music was written, so that the music could follow the slightest movement of the picture. During the performance, the musical score was thrown on the conductor's desk at the same time as the images were projected on to the screen. In this way the conductor was able to synchronize his playing exactly with the film. Hindemith proposed that I should experiment with this apparatus, and having nothing better to do, I accepted: I got hold of the newsreel of the week, and using the Blum machine, I wrote a suite of short pieces for a small orchestra. Among the French visitors to the Festival that year were André Gide, Marc Allégret, Marie-Laure and Charles de Noailles, and Annie and Jean Dalsace.

Diaghilev came to Baden-Baden for a few days to try and persuade Hindemith to write a ballet for him. He was accompanied by a young eighteen-year-old composer, Igor Markevitch, whose work already bore the stamp of originality and maturity, and evident signs of mastery. It was painful to see how ill Diaghilev looked, and we were scarcely surprised to hear the news of his death a few weeks later. This fulfilled the prediction by a gypsy that he would die on the water: in fact his friends accompanied his corpse to the cemetery in Venice in gondolas.

The festivals in Baden-Baden were more to my liking than those given by the International Society for Contemporary Music. The latter performed great services, but as it was more catholic in its tastes, it had to open its doors too wide. There were I.S.C.M. committees in every country; works were submitted to these, and a choice was made, then the final programme for the festival was fixed by an international jury. Each year it took place in a different city (Salzburg, Zürich, Siena, Barcelona, Frankfurt, Liége, Paris, Warsaw, London). A large number of musicians, chiefly from Central Europe, attended these festivals, as well as those of Baden-Baden, but in the latter case the atmosphere was more intimate, and the programmes, thanks to Hindemith's exacting standards and judicious choice, were of unquestionable aesthetic value. During the war the American section of the I.S.C.M. organized an international festival to be held in the University of California at Berkeley, only a few kilometres from the college where I was teaching. I was a member of the jury.

There was a very active section at Basle, which had often commissioned works, including Bartók's Sonata for two pianos and percussion, and Roussel's *Sérénade*. In 1946, I was asked to compose a work for them, and wrote a group of six *a cappella* settings of some lovely poems by Jean Cassou: *Sonnets composés au secret*.

We went to stay for a few weeks in 1927 with Emil Hertzka, for whom we had a great affection. He had a house in the suburbs of Vienna, at Grinzing, a charming place famous for its little inns buried deep in flowers, where, as in the days of Beethoven and Schubert, whose mighty ghosts seem never very far away, you sit and drink new wine to the strains of Viennese waltzes. Audrey Parr, whose husband was now Secretary to the British Legation in Budapest, invited us there for a week at Easter. How delightful it was to explore the city, and the countryside dazzling with flowers, in Audrey's ancient Rolls-Royce! We all went to call on Bartók, with whom I had some slight acquaintance and who had recently been rather ill. I was an admirer of his music and knew that he had made long stays in remote districts of Transylvania and the Carpathians, where by dint of patience and unremitting effort he had succeeded in getting the peasants and mountaineers to sing him their songs, all of which he had recorded. Bartók's servant refused us admittance to his house. We explained to her at great length who we were, but the door remained bolted. We were so insistent that we finally attracted Bartók's attention, and he allowed us to come in. I begged him to play us some of his recordings. He put one or two waxed rolls on a gramophone which emitted nasal sounds through a copper horn. There was an extraordinary lilt to these dance tunes and songs sung to the accompaniment of the cimbalom and the violin.

On our return to Grinzing, I composed *L'Enlèvement d'Europe* and the polka for *L'Eventail de Jeanne*. The latter was intended for Jeanne Dubost, a charming friend of ours, for performance in her drawing-room where musicians, artists and left-wing politicians regularly foregathered. She used to organize musical evenings in honour of foreign artists and occasionally offered her friends some curiosity or other. One summer's evening the Russian Oboukov sang, or rather wailed, one of his mystical cantatas, greatly to the alarm of the passers-by who had gathered in front of the open ground-floor windows. Another time, it was a Red Indian chief who uttered his war-cries as he strode up and down her exquisite drawing-room. Her husband did not take any great interest in these artistic functions. He had little or no sympathy for her 'mountebank friends'. Most of them did not even know him, so that they were amazed to see this unknown gentleman always arriving very late and the butler hastening to serve him. On the day when the Redskin was there, Monsieur Dubost came in just as the former was planting an enormous feather in Madame Dubost's hair. A little later, he made her a discreet sign that she should take it out, but she exclaimed: 'But it's wonderful, darling, it's just as if he had given me the Légion d'Honneur!' As a token of our thanks for all she had done for us, Auric, Delannoy, Ferroud, Ibert, Roland-Manuel, Poulenc, Ravel, Roussel, Florent Schmitt and I decided to give her a surprise. We each wrote a little dance, and had them performed in her drawing-room by pupils from the Opéra. My Polka was danced by little Toumanova, who was then eight. Marie Laurencin, who was one of Jeanne's personal friends, did the décor as well as the organdie costumes and plumed headdresses. It was such an enchanting show that Monsieur Rouché decided to put it on at the Opéra. I was afraid that our works written for a drawing-room would be lost in a theatre, and besides, I had composed so many works that had never been performed at the Opéra that it hurt my pride to make my bow there with a little polka, dashed off one morning in May, in Vienna. So I remained on my high horse, and refused either to attend the rehearsals or the performance.

It was also during my stay in Vienna that I first made a start on *Maximilien*. A series of extraordinary coincidences had induced me to choose this subject. On the boat coming back from the United States in 1927, I borrowed a book from the ship's library containing an account of the Mexican expedition by a Belgian officer who had taken part in it. I was greatly interested to read his descriptions of the forests and mountains and of the works of art that remain to bear witness to the marvellous Aztec civilization, but what caught my fancy more than anything else was the details of the expedition, for I had never studied the history of that period. My notions of the Mexican War were confined to Manet's paintings of *The Execution of Maximilian*, or some relic piously preserved by friends in honour of an ancestor who, like the Douanier Rousseau, had fought beside the Belgians and Austrians who had vainly striven to shore up the already crumbling empire of Maximilian. I was immediately struck by the ordinary, timorous character of this member of the Habsburgs, thrown into a tragic adventure by the boundless ambition of his wife, Charlotte, and the political scheming of Napoleon III, combining to force upon him an improvised throne in a country which was so utterly unknown to him that he had no inkling of the extent of the revolutionary movement that was to raise part of the country up in arms against him. I told Madeleine how interesting it would be to write a historical opera based on the character of Maximilian. Hardly had I got back to Paris than I saw the newly published memoirs of Comte Corti in the window of the bookshop opposite my house. I hastened to buy the book, which was full of details concerning Maximilian and Charlotte. A few days later I was conducting a concert in Brussels when the papers announced the death of the King of Belgium's aunt, the former Empress Charlotte, who had been living in retirement in a château in Belgium ever since her reason had given way during her voyage to Europe at the time of the dramatic events preceding the tragedy of Queretaro. The weekly papers were full of photographs and illustrations; my material was collecting without any assistance from myself. More and more the subject occupied the foreground of my thoughts; so when Emil Hertzka found me deep in one of the volumes of the Memoirs and asked me what I was reading, I told him I feared he would find out only too soon, for it was very possible that an opera would come of it. Far from discouraging me, Hertzka recommended me to read Werfel's play, *Juárez und Maximilian*, which was then having enormous success in Germany and Central Europe. I knew Werfel slightly, having met him in the company of Frau Mahler, whom he later married. I got in touch with him immediately. As he spoke only German, and I was unable to do so, our interview was a very brief one, but my luck still held good, and the very next day he sent me a French translation of his play that he had just received. I read this and decided that with a few alterations it could be used as a basis for a libretto. We worked in collaboration. Dr Hoffman, a specialist in translations for musical purposes, wrote a libretto under his direction, and Lunel agreed to make a free adaptation of the German text. He preserved the order of the scenes and the broad dramatic outline, but pruned the text and enlivened the dialogue by interpolating arias and duets on traditional operatic lines.

I wrote straight away to Mexico to the writer Alfonso Reyes whom I had met in Paris as Mexican Minister, to ask him to send me some folk-tunes and soldiers' songs dating from the time of Maximilian. The Mexican Minister of Education sent me a political song, a popular chorus 'Mama Carlotta', and a collection of songs. There was one beauty, which I used as a song for soldiers mounting guard at night.

I was just going to make a start on *Maximilien* when I received a letter from Claudel asking me to go and see him at once. I knew he wanted to show me the first part of *Christophe Colomb*, which had long been on the stocks. Sert had been the first to ask Claudel to write him a brief scenario for a choreographic entertainment on music by Manuel de Falla, to be given at the Court of Alfonso XIII, King of Spain, but Claudel had refused to treat such an enormous subject in a few lines. Some years later, Sert suggested this subject to Reinhardt for a show, or a film to be made in Hollywood, with music by Richard Strauss. The idea appealed to Claudel, who suggested having me as a composer, on the strength of our having worked together so often. We motored out to the Château de Brangues in the Isère where Claudel was spending the holidays with his family. While croquet was being played on the lawn, and picnics planned, and the merry cries of children resounded on all sides, far away from all this activity, Claudel sat in his big library at work. It was to that room he took me to read me his new play. I immediately realized the possibilities it opened up for me, with its myriad intermingling strands of lyrical and epic inspiration. A week or two later, Claudel left for Washington. He had several interviews with Reinhardt, and the telegrams I received led me to suppose that the project would be carried out. I therefore set to work and had finished the first part of *Christophe Colomb* when Claudel and Reinhardt fell out as a result of differences of opinion on artistic matters. I finished the composition of my opera the following summer and showed it to the Director of the Berlin Staatsoper during my brief stay in that city for the recording of *La P'tite Lilie*. He decided to produce it the following year and to start rehearsals at once.

When Madeleine had recovered from the long illness that succeeded the birth of Daniel, we set out for Berlin to attend the last rehearsals for *Christophe Colomb*. Altogether there were one hundred rehearsals for the choral parts and twenty-five for the orchestra. . . . The perfection of the production exceeded my dearest dreams. Our stay in Berlin was very pleasant. There were many French people there at the time, and we used to run into one another at the Embassy, at Monsieur de Margerie's home, or at Monsieur and Madame André Maurois', or Jean Paulhan and his wife's, or at Henri Bernstein's. André Gide was staying at the same hotel that we were. He used to love to go to the Zoo, especially in the languorous early spring season which disturbed the animals in exactly the same way as human beings. Much to Madeleine's joy, he took us there, and together we visited a crocodile farm where twelve hundred of these creatures, of all sizes, seemed to have adopted an immovable position regardless of the awakening of Nature.

After a concert I conducted for the Berlin Radio, we had dinner with Hindemith's brother-in-law, Hans Flesch, who confided in us his anxiety concerning the political situation and his fears for the future. Unfortunately, he was right, for he was one of the first victims of the Nazis. We saw a lot of the Hindemiths, for Paul had no engagements at the time. We decided to attend the first night of my opera together, and I asked for a little box on the side in order to be able to see without being seen. The management ignored my request and put us right in the centre of the theatre, in the box formerly reserved for the Kaiser. It was a remarkable performance, and Kleiber's conducting was superb. The mise-en-scène was particularly clever: the curtain had been suppressed and the stage prolonged on either side of the orchestral pit throughout the whole length of the theatre, so that the choir could sing without impeding the action on the stage. At the back of the stage was a cinema screen; the idea of the intrusion of the film was to intensify the scenic effects. When Christopher Columbus is reading Marco Polo's Travels, blurred images of tropical landscapes flit across the screen as in a dream; in the scene when Columbus takes leave of his family, the same actors enact the episode in a different setting, thus duplicating, and therefore reinforcing, the effect; when Columbus interrogates a sailor concerning a piece of wreckage found near the Azores, the same scene is thrown on the screen, immensely magnified, in a way that seems to prolong its mystery into an inner universe opening out from our own. The technical resources of the Staatsoper were able to cope with rapid shifts of scene, which was just as well, since there were twenty-seven tableaux.

Christophe Colomb was an enormous success and ran for two years. Thereafter, it was given in the form of an oratorio, which can be done quite easily, since each scene is linked to the next by the Narrator. I owe the first French production of this work to Pierre Monteux, who put it on in Nantes with the excellent Town Choir under its leader Madame Le Meignan. Conducting a choir calls for great tenacity of purpose, and Madame Le Meignan had plenty of that: when the Town Council refused to let her go on rehearsing in one of the rooms of the former castle of the Dukes of Brittany, as her funds did not permit the hiring of premises, she threatened to hold her rehearsals on the public highway. They knew her and realized that this was no idle threat. It was deemed wiser to restore the use of the château. . . .

A few months later, *Christophe Colomb* was conducted by Manuel Rosenthal on the French Radio, with the Raugel Choral Society. I myself conducted it in London, where it was sung in English. It was given in Czech in Prague, and in Flemish and French on the Belgian radio.

Certain prominent personages expressed astonishment that my work should have been given its first performances in Germany. I have always submitted my works to the Opéra, in spite of the hardly encouraging reception they were given. Was I not told, concerning *Les Euménides*: 'What an idea to choose such a subject!' I thought that Aeschylus had already won his laurels. . . . Be that as it may, the fact that *Christophe Colomb* had been produced in Germany and not in France excited a good deal of comment, and a question was even asked in Parliament. As a result of this little incident, the Opéra was determined to produce one of my works, no matter which. I had just completed *Maximilien*, and this was accepted.

For a State-owned theatre, the subject of *Maximilien* was rather a delicate one. While rehearsals were going on, therefore, the Ministry of Fine Arts judged it wise to submit the libretto to the Belgian Embassy (because of the Empress Charlotte), the Austrian Legation (because of the fact that Maximilian had been a Habsburg) and finally to the Mexican Legation. Fortified with the approval of the representatives of the three countries in question, I imagined that I should now be left in peace, when suddenly I received a letter from the grandson of Marshal Bazaine requesting an interview with me. He was a very tall man, extremely solemn, and his anxiety was really touching. He was afraid that the presence of Bazaine on the stage of the Opéra might provoke a demonstration. I endeavoured to persuade him that no one could possibly have any such idea, since his grandfather had been utterly above suspicion during the Mexican expedition. To reassure him, I showed him the libretto, and he asked for a slight alteration in it. He was afraid of the disagreeable juxtaposition upon the stage of Lazaine and López, the officer who was ultimately to betray Maximilian. I was able to set his mind at rest by substituting another officer for López in this short scene.

In treating a fairly recent historical subject, I ran the risk of encountering people who had actually known the originals of my drama. After the first performance I received a call from Colonel Hans, who had remained at the Emperor's side at Queretaro up to the time of his execution.

In spite of his great age, he had an astonishing memory, and his recollections were circumstantial. He criticized the colour and shape of the beard worn by the actor playing the part of General Mejía, on the grounds that they did not conform with the original. We saw a lot of him, and it was most fascinating to hear him relate so many intimate details concerning the characters I had tried to re-create. Then General Malleterre's daughter, who had been called Charlotte in memory of the Empress, asked me for seats in order to re-live the moments of her childhood, when she had so often heard her father tell the tangled story of all these events. I also learned that the widow of the Republican General Porfirio Diaz, Juárez's right-hand man and successor, had attended one of the performances, at which she had no doubt seen her husband as he might have been at the time of their betrothal. . . . The performances of *Maximilien* were excellent, and Pedro Pruna's décors and costumes brought out the character of the work in the most tasteful fashion imaginable. Although the Press seemed to have grasped the meaning of the work, it really let itself go this time. I was abused, torn to tatters and dragged in the dust.

Les Choëphores was produced on the stage in Belgium. Claudel was Ambassador there at the time and was invited to supervise the production. For the costumes and décors, he called on his faithful collaborator Audrey Parr, who, as for *L'Homme et son désir* did her best to translate in her sketches the exact ideas he endeavoured to express to her in words. The part of Clytemnestra was taken by Madame Ida Rubinstein, and that of Orestes by Jean Marchat. The roles of Electra and Orestes were both spoken and sung, the singers and actors alternating with one another. The spoken choruses were delivered by 'Les Renaudins' under Madeleine Renaud-Thévenet whose interpretation followed Claudel's own idea of what he had been trying to convey so closely that this was the start of a very fruitful collaboration between them.

Apart from *Les Euménides*, which in any case is exceptionally difficult to perform, all my works for the theatre have been produced. The Finale of *Les Euménides* was given by Louis de Vocht and the admirable Caecilia Choir at a concert in Antwerp in 1927. The audience was gripped by the triple chorus of the voices of Athene, the Eumenides and the people of Athens, and made no attempt to conceal the depth of emotion it roused: carried away with enthusiasm, a dense crowd besieged the car of Monsieur Fester, President of the Concert Society, in which I was seated, and ran after us for a very long way. I was deeply moved. Some of my Parisian friends had attended the concert and decided to form a guarantee fund to ensure a repetition of it in Paris with the same performers. The programme had also included *Les Choëphores* with Claire Croiza magnificently playing the speaking role. The same success was repeated in Paris. Like the Belgian audience, the Parisians appeared chiefly impressed by the exaltation and power of the voices under the electrifying direction of de Vocht, whose fervour and enthusiasm had a superhuman effect.

It was after this performance that Columbia made recordings of extracts from *Les Choëphores* and of the Processional that conclues the Finale of *Les Euménides*. These records did a great deal to make my music more widely known. The work was never performed in the United States, and yet I found that, thanks to record-collections in the various universities and colleges, it was well known to most music-lovers.

Chapter Twenty-Seven

Visits

Visit to Manuel de Falla

We had become great friends with Jeanne Fernandez, whose combination of charm, high spirits, kindness and courage we found particularly attractive; she had got into the habit of visiting Aix regularly, and had bought a little house there called 'Le Couffin'. She came there during the holidays and was often joined by her son Ramon. As he had given a series of lectures in Madrid that had been extremely favourably received, he asked me whether I should like to go there. It was an opportunity to take Madeleine to a country I loved and to renew contacts with Spanish musicians. Ramon put me in touch with the University of Madrid. The aristocracy of Madrid took an interest in the intellectual functions held at the University City, which was to become the last bastion of freedom during the fighting around Madrid.

In Madrid I came into contact once more with Ernesto Halffter and Adolfo Salazar, who included among his gifts as a composer and writer on music a positive talent for the role of guide. With unaffected simplicity and light-hearted solicitude, he shepherded us everywhere, from the cafés in the Puerta del Sol where we sat dipping doughnuts dripping with oil in cups of thick chocolate flavoured with cinnamon, to the *terrasses* of the big cafés on the main streets where at cocktail time we regaled ourselves with *percebes* that looked like the feet of some kind of marine elephant. He took me to see Gustavo Pittaluga, the son of the famous surgeon, who was a very sick man at the time, and whom we were destined to meet again in Paris a few years later on the first stage of his exile, which finally brought him to the United States.

In addition to the lectures I gave in Madrid, I conducted some of my works, and played *Le Carnaval d'Aix* under the direction of Fernandez

Arbós. Together with Arthur Rubinstein, this eminent musician was one of the most entertaining characters I have ever met. . . . . Chance brought them together on one occasion in Paris, when each sought to out-do the other in wit and petulance. It was a duel, using anecdotes instead of swords. . . . During the same stay in Madrid, I was asked to repeat my lecture in Bilbao a week or two later. This gave us time for a visit to Granada and Seville.

It was a cold and rain-drenched day for our arrival in Granada. Muffled in a long overcoat, with a thick scarf over his face, Manuel de Falla was waiting for us at the station. This was a most touching attention, especially as I knew his own health to be delicate. He took us to our hotel. From the balcony of our bedroom we could look out over the forests that cover the hill of the Alhambra. When the rain stopped, an intoxicating scent of jasmin invaded the room, and a hundred thousand nightingales burst into frantic song across that sea of fragrant green leaf. The silhouette of Charles the Fifth's unfinished palace stood out against this background of interwoven flower-scent and bird-song. Next morning, Manuel de Falla came to fetch us to show us the Alhambra and the Generalife. These gems of architecture are located in such a marvellous landscape that we were torn between our admiration for the arabesques that adorn the walls, and enthusiasm for the astonishing loveliness which we glimpsed through every casement. Falla took us to his home at Antequeruela Alta for lunch, looking over a hillside inhabited by gypsies, who dwelt in caves carved from the living rock. As we passed by, children and old men came running with outstretched hands. On all sides, typical gypsy women appeared, wearing voluminous skirts and long shawls, with a carnation stuck in their hair above the huge combs. Guitars were playing, and their chords merged with the words sung by exquisite, husky voices practising the *canto hondo*, and a delicious odour of saffron, tomato and garlic hung over the scene. . . . All three of us went on foot, under a sun as fierce as molten lead. The only living thing we met was a cart or two raising clouds of dust that compelled Falla to cover his mouth with a large handkerchief and hide in the bushes until the air had cleared again. Falla had a charming white house where he lived with his sister. They gave us a delicious meal of different kinds of pancakes, made with cheese, fish and jam. We lingered long over our meal, chatting rather drowsily because of the heat from the brazier that warmed our feet, in spite of the precocious spring weather. Then Falla showed us the room where he worked and where he had been composing the *Atlantide*. When I was starting on *Christophe Colomb*, he had written to tell me that Columbus was to be one of the minor characters in his own next work. He had warned me in case I should be annoyed that we were both introducing the same character in our works. I answered that it was not of the slightest importance, since Columbus was the central figure in my opera. These circumstances, and the fact that I was such a great admirer of his work, induced me to dedicate *Christophe Colomb* to him. After lunch, we went for a long ride in a carriage, and then took our leave. I was keenly sorry not to be able to return Falla's delightful hospitality when some years later he and his sister came to Aix unexpectedly, the day before we left for Portugal.

Our favourite way of passing time in Seville was to stroll along the little streets too narrow for vehicles to pass through. There are picturesque shops, and clubs for men. Behind a huge bay-window on the ground-floor, you can see them drinking and playing cards as if they were sitting in a shop-window. We visited the Cathedral where Columbus's log-book is preserved. Looking down from the top of La Giralda between the spires, you can see the whole city and the Guadalquivir outspread at your feet.

In Bilbao, I gave my lecture to a very likeable group of young artists. The charming Basque city was split into two opposing camps: those who liked chocolate with cinnamon, and those who preferred it without. Happy days, when the only subject of discord was the taste for one particular spice!

Visit to Francis Jammes

I had not seen Jammes for a very long time, and I wanted him to meet Madeleine. In 1928, we decided to go home via the Basque country. The Jammes family had left Orthez, where they had lived for so many years, as a result of an extraordinary chain of circumstances: poetry did not provide them with enough to live on, for they had a lot of children; Ginette Jammes was ill, and the doctors had ordered her to a spa; and they had been given notice by the owner to quit the house they lived in. So they were passing through a very difficult time, when Jammes made a novena, and his prayers were granted. On the very ninth day, the postman brought a letter from a solicitor informing him that he was to inherit the fortune of an aged spinster recently deceased who wished to leave her property to a good Catholic with a large family, thus disinheriting the rightful heir, an unmarried nephew or cousin, who was a free-thinker. In this way the poet came into possession of a beautiful house and several farms in the heart of the Basque country.

It was there I went to see them and found them as friendly and affectionate as ever. There were now seven children around their grandmother, Jammes's mother, who also lived with them. Bernadette, the eldest, acted as her father's secretary. They gave us a lovely room adorned with ancient engravings, most prominent of all being a little frame containing the medal awarded to Ginette's father during the Mexican expedition. Jammes was in good health, working hard and taking an interest in all the affairs of the village. He loved to go for walks through the countryside with its blue horizons, but he was a little homesick for his native Béarn.

We used to get up late, to the sound of all the familiar noises that mingled with the hum of conversation, little disputes about a mislaid newspaper, comments on the mail from Paris, and the indignation of the servant who could not get used to hearing sermons in the Basque language at the local church. . . . It was all such a hubbub that Jammes would have to leave his study where he had been endeavouring to concentrate, and shout in stentorian tones: 'Be quiet, you'll wake the Milhauds!'

After dining with the Abbé Dibildos, Director of the Ecole Stanilas, Madeleine and I did our best to play my score of *Christophe Colomb*. It was after hearing this that Jammes wrote a little account of it that was published in three numbers of *Le Divan*. One Sunday, we squeezed the entire Jammes family into our little car to go and see *'les trognons'* (apple-cores or cabbage-stumps) — Jammes's nickname for his two youngest girls who were boarders at a Convent in Fuenterrabia. We stopped for lunch at Hendaye, where Jammes ordered an impressive quantity of oysters and wood-pigeons, those delicious birds the hunting of which he describes in one of his books. As we left the dining-room of the hotel, an old gentleman with an owl-like profile bowed to him. It was Miguel de Unamuno, who softened the bitterness of exile by living just across the frontier, and from the balcony of his bedroom could gaze at his native land.

Hardly had we crossed the frontier than Jammes waxed lyrical. . . . Trees, houses, old women playing cards in front of their hovels, all seemed to him as marvellous as if he had landed in a distant island, for the whole of our friend's universe was circumscribed within a very small space, no more than a few hours travelling time between one part of it and the next. Homeland: the Béarn; land of exile: the Basque country; the borderland of romance: the Spanish frontier. . . . A universe filled with wonder for the purest of poets.

Visit to Francis Planté

On leaving Hasparren, we stopped at Mont-de-Marsan because I wanted to pay homage to the oldest living French pianist. It was thrilling to meet one of the greatest virtuosos of the nineteenth century, a living witness to a period of music so remote from our own. Planté lived on a magnificent estate. In spite of his age, he was very active and still, year after year, indulged in his favourite sport of hunting. Every morning in bed, he had the latest works of contemporary pianoforte music brought to him, and amused himself by annotating and fingering them. He gave me the pleasant surprise of letting me hear him play one of my works, using his own fingering. He was the very incarnation of a pianist, and especially marvellous at interpreting his beloved romantics which required special qualities of precision, elegance and subtlety in the use of the pedals. Here his technical mastery was particularly superb. He would comment on them as he played: 'Pretty modulation . . . lovely passage . . . Bravo! Bravo! Bravo! Chopin!' He talked of Liszt, and 'young Wagner' whom he had known. Planté did not play at concerts any more, except for local charities. When he had completed his programme, he still kept on playing, murmuring: 'Bravo! Bravo! What do you think of this tune? Adorable!'

Our parting from him was rather melancholy. With a plaid shawl round his shoulders, he came as far as the car with us. The sunlight was gilding the trees, whose yellowing leaves already spoke of autumn.

Chapter Twenty-Eight

Under the Shadow of Illness

For the past few years, my health had been getting steadily worse; recurring attacks of rheumatism confined me to bed for weeks at a time and racked me with atrocious pain. During these periods of illness my dear Madeleine was also a prisoner, nursing my sickness and giving me moral strength through her unconquerable optimism, unalterable good humour and patience, and her infinite devotion. How often she spent the night in an armchair, seeking in every way possible to bring me relief. . . . During the lengthy convalescence that succeeds each of my attacks, the use of my legs only gradually returns. Soon I could only go about in a car, for even a few moments' walking sufficed to bring on a relapse or even a violent attack. How often I had to cancel a tour or a concert! Like Offenbach, whose life I had just been reading, the outcome of all my plans depended on chance, and like him, too, I often attended rehearsals leaning on two sticks and wrapped in a shawl.

During the night of February 8th 1930, I dragged myself to the drawing-room on my crutches while Madeleine was in labour in the bedroom: our son Daniel was born next day. He spent his first night beside my couch in the drawing-room. Every now and again, he would utter a little cry, as shrill as a cricket's chirp. The first gift that greeted his arrival was a rattle that Sauguet brought, and then a marvellous flowering almond from Picasso, which we had transplanted in the courtyard. Was this a gift from the fairy that presides over the art of painting to mark the destiny of our child?

When we came back from Berlin, we sent Daniel off to Aix with his nurse Marinette, a charming girl from the Béarn, while I went to Vittel to take the waters. What a dismal time that was! Twenty-one consecutive days of rain spent under the galleries, waiting for the hour when I should swallow a glass of water. How slowly the days dragged by! Fortunately, we met Ambroise Vollard and Marie Dormoy, and very soon her gaiety and Vollard's highly original personality lightened our gloomy horizon. There was a whole 'Ubu' side to his character that captivated us. He had known so many painters that he never ran out of anecdotes or personal memories. He took us for rides in his car, and we attended together a show in the Théâtre du Peuple at Bussang, where a very interesting experiment in decentralization was being carried out, with performances organized by the workers. We kept in touch with Vollard in Paris: it was quite impressive to sit at lunch with a gentleman beneath a portrait of himself in the costume of a toreador, painted by Cézanne.

For a number of years, I had been having homoeopathic treatment, for this was the only thing that seemed to do me any good. The waters of Vittel had aggravated my condition, so we decided to go to Lausanne to consult Dr Nebel, one of the most famous homoeopaths in Europe. He was an amazing character, who examined his patients by means of a pendulum, and was able to base his diagnosis on a photograph. But although this wonderful doctor detected the cause of illnesses by such mysterious means, the astonishing cures he effected were due to his medical science. Dr Nebel made no attempt to conceal from me the gravity of my condition, but the treatment he prescribed soon began to do me good. For several years running, he sent me to Ragatz and then to Cauterets for homoeopathic treatment: to the amazement of the other patients, I only swallowed a few mouthfuls of water and took baths lasting two minutes. . . . Sometimes it became necessary to have recourse to more mysterious aids to rid myself completely of my painful attacks. In 1934 I was bed-ridden, with pains in the feet, the knees and the right arm. The months were slipping by, and nothing was doing me any good. I was trying all kinds of treatment without success. I was slightly feverish and incapable of working or writing. My only distraction was to receive the visits of one or two faithful friends. Then I started to throw shadows on the wall by my bed, using the light from my bedside lamp. Patiently, for hours, I tried to make profiles and portraits, and by dint of practice, I managed to move my fingers independently of one another to an unusual extent. By slight alterations in the position of the various joints, I achieved some likenesses that were well-nigh perfect. This was a wonderful source of distraction for me: my collection included Sauguet, Poulenc, Satie, Hindemith, Prokofiev, Cocteau, Marguerite Long, the Princesse de Polignac, the Comte de Beaumont, etc. I regret not having had photographs taken of these silhouettes, for I never managed to do them again, once I was cured. I was out of practice, my fingers were as rusty as those of a pianist who had not been working hard enough. This distriction, however, was doing nothing to cure my illness, which still went on. At my cousins, the Allatinis, I had met a Dr Feral. He had done my mother a lot of good, releasing her from a most rigorous diet she had been following for years. Dr Feral had studied in Vienna, and also with witch-doctors in Abyssinia. He could not practise in Paris, for he was a foreigner. He had set up a beauty parlour on the Left Bank, and earned a living in this way. He would only give medical attention to one or two friends, and came to see me. My feet looked to him as if they were dead. He gave me some magnetic treatment through the blankets themselves. His fingers exuded a gentle warmth that tired me tremendously. He did not lose heart, although my feet were still terribly swollen. He told me of a treatment he would like me to follow, but could not himself prescribe because he was not recognized as a doctor in France. He brought a dark, silent, bearded physician to see me. They had a mysterious colloquy, as a result of which they decided that it would be premature to administer this treatment, and the laying on of hands was resumed at more frequent intervals. A few weeks later, another consultation took place, as serious as if it had been a question of amputating my legs, and the doctors decided to apply cotton wool and court plaster to my feet in alternate layers.

After swaddling them in huge woollen socks, they recommended me to keep on all this paraphernalia for two days. Next day, when Madeleine came in after stepping out for a moment, she was astonished to see me standing up, leaning on my crutches; two days later, I left for Brussels to see the performances of *L'Annonce faite à Marie*, for which I had written the incidental music.

Dr Soulié de Moran practised acupuncture; a Far Eastern medical method of the greatest antiquity. It consisted of superficial applications to the skin, never enough to draw blood, of needles of gold, silver or other metals, at points corresponding by reflex action to some tonic effect. The treatment was not at all painful. I tried it: it was successful every other time. It should not be inferred that I am always ready to submit to any outlandish treatment. I have always been afraid of healers whose gifts were not supported by medical knowledge, and who might therefore do more harm than good. Nevertheless, my last adventure deserves to be related. At the beginning of the war, I was rather ill, and had had several relapses. *Medée* was being produced at the Opéra in May, but as I could not even slide from my bed on to an armchair, I had very reluctantly to abandon the idea of attending the performance. A day or two before the first performance, Daniel came into our room very early in the morning, followed by an air-raid warden who wanted to summons us for a chink of light showing from a second-floor window. Yet all the windows had been painted with blue paint. . . . What we had not bargained for was that Daniel would scrawl all over them with his finger, 'Down with Hitler!' and 'Long live France!' I tried to excuse myself, but the warden would not listen; he asked me why I was in bed. I explained to him in a few words that I was ill, and that this was preventing me from going to Paris to see my opera. 'So no more,' said he, 'Don't worry, you shall go to Paris!' And without another word, he threw his helmet into a corner of the room and started to lay on hands. He was no liar: two days later, I was able to set out.

In California, during the longest attack I ever had to endure, when I started to write down these Memoirs, how often have I regretted that some Chinese magician has not come and offered me relief. . . .

Chapter Twenty-Nine

Congresses, Festivals, the 'Sérénade' and the 'Triton'

Although I take little interest in the sort of speeches made at musical congresses, I like to attend these functions because they provide an opportunity for seeing other countries. In September 1931, the Portuguese Government organized a Critic's Congress, to which I was invited, as well as Bernard Shaw, who refused, and Pirandello, who accepted. I was not required to take part in the discussions, nor in the work of the Congress. I was merely asked to conduct one of my own works at a concert to be given in Lisbon. I have very rarely had any contact with critics, and this was an opportunity for me to meet some of the men who had been dragging my name in the mud for years. I was tickled by the prospect, for I never take any notice of unfavourable criticism. I was delighted to find that my old enemy Robert Kemp was a charming man — provided you kept him off the subject of music, and that he had very extensive literary tastes, as well as a fund of hgh spirits that helped to make the journey a most agreeable one. The organization of the Congress was in the able hands of Antonio Ferro, the Director of Portugal's propaganda services.

The whole country seemed to be out to greet us. One evening, we were offered a celebration by the inhabitants of one of the ancient popular quarters of Lisbon, Alfama, which looks down over the river. The narrow streets were hung with flags, and banners bearing the inscription: 'Long live Criticism!' (critics have never been fêted like this before — or since) stretched from one upper floor to another in this working-class district. Through the half-open doors of ancient palaces that had now fallen on evil days could be seen tables groaning with all kinds of dainties. They were like fairy-tale palaces temporarily abandoned by their inhabitants to make way for the members of the Congress. Fireworks exploded in all directions to express the charmingly childlike joy of the populace. I heard songs and refrains that I was to hear again a few days later in the excellent Portuguese film of *Maria del Mar* about life in a fishing village.

We stayed at Estoril, in the suburbs of Lisbon. We all went off in a boat to see a bull-fight, like those of the Camargue, to which we had been invited. The traditional picnic was a riotous affair. Lunch was served on the banks of the Tagus (near where we sat whole sheep and oxen were being roasted) and we were waited on by young peasant girls in gaily coloured costumes while guitarists accompanied the melancholy refrains of the *fados*. To finish off the proceedings, we saw a bull-fight in the courtyard of the farm. Riding an immensely valuable thoroughbred, the *torero* tries to remove the cockades and rings attached between the animal's horns. His movements have to be executed with speed and precision, if his horse is not to be wounded. In the north of the country, we were also received with banqueting and festivities. Pirandello took part in all these entertainments like the rest of us. He was reserved, silent and retiring, leaving everything to his secretary Colin, whose activity as a publicity agent left him little respite. He was particularly appreciative of a visit to the university city of Coimbra, where young students in their traditional black gowns grouped themselves around him in respect and veneration. . . . I was greatly impressed by the harbour of Oporto, where lorries and animals milled around in all directions. High above it stands the enormous iron bridges built by Eiffel and connecting the two upper parts of the town. The Critics' Congress concluded with an enormous reception. Our hostesses, most of them members of the nobility, had put on in our honour the superb traditional costumes handed down in their families for generations. The popular dances were more light-hearted than in the south, and the *viras* livelier than the *fados*. Later, I wrote a suite for the piano called *L'Automne* based on my memories of this lovely journey: *Septembre, Alfama* and *Adieu*. There is one melody in *Adieu* consisting of a *vira* in slow time, whose feelings sum up for me the whole of the little suite.

I have several times been invited to attend the musical festival held at Florence in May each year. It was pleasant to meet old friends and foreign composers, and our visits were usually very gay affairs. We would all lunch together in one of the little *trattorie*: Berg, Křenek, the Malipieros, Casella and his wife, and then go off on some excursion together. The formal inauguration of the Congress was held in the great hall of the Palazzo Vecchio, and presided over by one of the princes of the blood. Each speaker used his native language, their reports being immediately repeated in Italian by a genuine virtuoso of the art of translation, Madame Preobrajenska. The concerts organized by Labroca and conducted by

Vittorio Gui were highly polished performances. But what an audience! They were still hissing Debussy's *Nocturnes*. I saw some very remarkable theatrical performances. I also heard *Simone Boccanegra* for the first time. The festival of Il Maggio Fiorentino also engaged foreign producers. Copeau gave some Shakespeare in the Boboli Gardens, and a play about Savonarola on the Piazza del Palazzo Vecchio, on the very spot where its protagonist had been burnt.

The 1937 festival was particularly interesting, because it also included the celebrations in Cremona of the bi-centenary of Stradivarius. For this occasion, instruments had been brought from all the corners of the world, and the whole represented an exhibition of a unique character. Unfortunately the concert for strings was rather disappointing, either because the players were not accustomed to handling such sublime instruments, or because they were quite simply not sufficiently skilled. With the Collaers, I went as far as Mantua, where we visited the Gonzago Palace. The portraits of the illustrious Gonzago family form a collection of human faces of a quite uncommon ugliness. From the balcony of the room where Monteverdi's *Orfeo* was first given in 1607, we gazed for a long time out over the huge plains flooded from the marshes bordering the Po.

The last festival of Florence that I attended also happened to coincide with the visit of the Führer. There was still complete freedom of musical expression in Italy, and the absurd story of degenerate art had not yet been adopted. The festival therefore went off as usual, although everyone was a little nervous. Mussolini had given orders for the whole town to be cleaned; every roof had been painted, as well as the Ponte Vecchio. Fountains and lions of papier mâché were arrayed outside the station to impress Hitler on his arrival. German policemen were checking the identity of passers-by and searching all hotels. But a considerable section of Florentine society left the city on the day he arrived, as an overt demonstration of hostility. The Rietis took us in their car to Ravenna. . . .

The Festivals of Venice were held biennially and represented yet another heaven-sent opportunity of seeing my musician friends. The highly varied programmes included well-known works such as Verdi's Requiem given on the Piazza San Marco, as well as contemporary works conducted by their composers. In the little conductor's dressing-room at the San Carlo it was a normal sight to see Stravinsky's mackintosh and Constant Lambert's tweed overcoat hanging near my two walking-sticks modestly tucked away in a corner, while Pizzetti would be putting up a mirror, opening a silver toilet-case, and arranging flowers, his wife's photograph and a sheaf of telegrams. Rieti's delightful little chamber opera *Teresa nel Bosco* was given. The last time I visited Venice, Stravinsky conducted his *Capriccio* with his son as pianist, a happy collaboration; Markevitch presented his *Icare*; while I gave the first performacne of the *Suite provençale*. Unfortunately, either owing to the damp, or to the tiredness induced by the lack of cars, so that I was obliged to go everywhere on foot, not only to rehearsals but also to the Café Florian to savour their delicious *gelati*, my legs began to give me trouble, and I was afraid I was going to be bed-ridden again. As soon as my performance was over, therefore, Madeleine whisked me off to the hotel and started to pack our bags. After a few hours in the train, I felt considerably better.

There were in Paris two active chamber music societies, the Sérénade and the Triton. The latter had been founded by P.O. Ferroud, who was killed in a motor-car accident in Hungary. It had a very large selection committee, including foreign composers resident in France, such as Honegger, Mihalovici, Harsanyi, as well as many French composers. The programmes were highly eclectic, and many new works were performed. Madeleine gave Hindemith's *Hin und Zurück* in her own translation, as well as most of the other works by that composer. The orchestra conducted by Munch occupied a small corner of the platform. The tremendous efforts made by Hindemith to sponsor works designed for amateurs had inspired me to write my *Cantate pour louer le Seigneur*, written for chorus, solo voices and orchestra, and easy to play. The work was presented by the Abbé Caillet in the cloisters of the Cathedral of Saint-Sauveur at Aix-en-Provence. Durand started to publish under my direction a series called 'Music for the Family and for use in Schools'. Armand Lunel wrote the words for *Un petit peu de musique* and *Un petit peu d'exercice*, and René Chalupt provided me with a little play with twelve songs entitled *A propos de bottes*. These were all children's pieces. For several years I had been following with the greatest of interest the extraordinary results being obtained by Mademoiselle Pelliot by means of the Gédalge method, of which she was the principal exponent. When Hindemith's *Wir bauen eine Stadt* and my *Un petit peu de musique* were given at the Triton, I asked her to provide the children's choirs, and I was amazed to see the speed with which these children aged from eight to ten, drawn from elementary schools in the Bastille quarter, learned to sing and mime our playlets. The violins and cellos in the orchestra were selected from the pupils of private schools. In my score, as in Hindemith's, the music did not go beyond the first position.

The selection committee of La Sérénade, presided over by Yvonne de Casafuerte, was less catholic in its tastes than that of the Triton, and based on more clearly defined aesthetic standards. Its members were Auric, Poulenc, Markevitch, Nabokov, Rieti, Sauguet and myself. Thanks to the generosity of the Vicomtesse de Noailles, we were able to present Kurt Weill's *Mahagonny* and *Der Jasager*, for which the soloist Lotte Lenya, and the conductor Maurice Abravanel, came across from Germany, as well as a group of children, for *Der Jasager* was written specially for schools. I was lecturing in Holland at the time the concert was given and in the train that was bringing us back to Paris, I told Madeleine that we should no doubt find that the city had been taken by storm. Little did I know then how true this was, for the delirious enthusiasm aroused by these two works lasted for several days. The Montparnasse set used the concert as a pretext for political diatribes; it saw in it an expression of the moral bankruptcy and pessimism of our times. Smart society was as carried away as if it had been the first performance of Bach's *Passion*, in mentioning which I am merely repeating what was said to me by one of my friends, a lady somewhat infected by the captivating snobbishness which enabled the Sérénade to keep going. We also presented festivals of the works of Stravinsky, the first performance in France of the *Dumbarton Oaks Concerto*, Sauguet's *La Voyante* and Poulenc's *Bal Masqué*. The children's choir of the Armenian church, directed by Baron de Van, sang plain-chant as it was sung in the year one thousand A.D., accompanied by cymbals and castanets, amazing music whose tempi were extremely rapid. On one occasion, the Sérénade gave a concert at the Church of the Trinité, consisting of Satie's *Messe des Pauvres*, Sauguet's exquisite *Messe Pastorale* and works by Olivier Messiaen, the composer whose works enjoyed an enormous vogue after the Liberation.

Among the first performances which I gave the at Sérénade, I should like to mention *La Mort du tyran*, based on a text to which my attention had been drawn by Daniel Halévy. It was a passage by Lampride, translated by Diderot in his *Dissertation sur la poésie rythmique* and quoted as an example of rhythmic movement raised to the point of transport. In it the author depicted the outcry and imprecations of the Roman populace on the death of the Emperor Commodus and their hopeful cheers for his successr, Pertinax. I wrote this work in 1932 for voices, percussion and a few instruments capable of making themselves heard through the greatest possible tumult of sound: the piccolo, the clarinet and the tuba. When the dancer Alanova asked me for a work for choir and percussion, I offered her *La Mort du tyran*. She gave a choreographic interpretation of it at the Sérénade, under the direction of Désormière, together with the Gouverné choir, who were responsible for both the spoken parts and the singing. The orchestra was a small one, and the six percussion players each performed on several instruments. On this occasion, the dancing was only a pretext for the music. *La Mort du tyran* is essentially a work for the concert-hall. It was given in Brussels with a choir and the Renaudins. It was ideal to be able to entrust one of one's works to this group, so highly trained in the expression of the most violent dramatic feelings and using the most powerful elocution. Claudel was delighted with their work, and it was in co-operation with them that he arranged the spoken choruses that provide the off-stage noises in *L'Otage*, a kind of genuine verbal orchestration in which sentences uttered in high tones or in low stand out against a background of hammer-like repetitions of onomatopaeas and disjointed phrases. A recording of this was made, and used for the performance at the Comédié-Française.

The Sérénade had a little sister society in Rome called the Concerti di Primavera, organized by Rieti and a few other Italian musicians under the patronage of the Contessa Pecci Blunt. I was engaged by them on two occasions. In 1934, their programme included the Viola Concerto dedicated to Hindemith, and given its first performance by him at Amsterdam under the direction of Monteux, and repeated again in Rome. *Un petit peu de musique*, excellently translated by Rieti, was sung by children wearing the Balillas uniform. Hindemith and his wife stayed with the Labrocas, and often came to see us at Rieti's home. Hindemith would sit down at the piano, and as he had a phenomenal memory, would play whole operas by heart. One evening he was joined by Mimi Pecci and they sang together at the top of their voices choruses, duets and arias from one of Verdi's operas. The noise was deafening and the effect extremely comical, but as it was Good Friday, our neighbours were shocked and banged on the wall to make us be quiet. Fortunately they never knew that one of us was the niece of Pope Leo XIII. . . .

Our stay in Rome happened to coincide with the canonization of Don Bosco. We wanted very much to be present at the ceremony, but were unable to reserve any seats. Madame Charles Roux was good enough to offer us two in a little gallery. We arrived at Saint Peter's at 6 a.m. to find that eight hundred persons armed with invitations of the same kind as ours had already tried to get into the little gallery, which only held eighty. We did not abandon all hope, but sought out a suitable vantage point where I could lean against a balustrade. The multitude presented an unforgettable spectacle: sisters of charity, priests, peasants, women with their heads covered with black veils that were indistinguishable from their black clothing, were squeezed into every corner of the basilica, mercilessly jostling one another with their elbows. A Red Cross tent had been erected at the entrance to the cathedral. Once you had got inside the building, there was no way out. The congregation, having left home at the crack of dawn, relieved themselves with no heed for their neighbours, while others tranquilly ate the food they had been wise enough to bring with them. The arrival of the Pope's curule chair and the fan bearers caused tremendous excitement. The papal benediction, vibrant with spiritual power, was greeted by a surprising reaction on the part of the crowds. Instead of bowing their heads, or prostrating themselves with religious awe, they suddenly broke out into applause and cries of 'Viva il Pappa!' Losing all shreds of the most elementary self-control, a nun climbed up on to the platform against which I was leaning in order to get a better view of the proceedings, and literally climbed on my shoulders to reach a balustrade. Others were clinging to statues or perched on the holy-water stoups. At first I was taken aback by these demonstrations, but after a while I was rather touched by their spontaneous, childlike familiarity, as of children greeting their father.

I returned once more to Rome for the Concerti di Primavera, and Yvonne Astruc played the *Concertino de printemps* that I had composed for her in 1934. Jacques Ibert had just been appointed Director at the Villa Medici. Ably supported by his wife Rosette, he upheld the prestige of French art, a task which grew more and more difficult with each year that passed, in a most efficient and meritorious manner. Thereafter I never went back to Italy because of the racial legislation, and soon my music was banned in that country.

Chapter Thirty

Music for the Theatre and the Cinema

For a long time so-called symphonic composers were ostracized in film circles, and as a class rather looked down upon by film producers in search of composers capable of writing music that would be both popular in appeal and a commercial proposition. Gradually the serious musicians managed to win their way into the studios by putting on false noses, that is by disguising their music in a style calculated to earn the approval of film producers and directors. Once it had been proved that fine scores like Auric's music for *A nous la Liberté* or Honegger's for *Les Misérables* could win popular success, these musicians' reputations were established and their services were much sought after. The first round had been won. Soon Roland-Manuel, Ibert, Delannoy were writing music for the screen. While their scores contained all the simple elements needed to attract the general public, they remained personal works, stamped with their author's personality from the very first bars. French musicians are accustomed to orchestrate their own scores, a fact which helps to preserve the personal aspect of their works, contrary to what usually happens in Hollywood where there are professional orchestrators who churn out on a commercial scale musical pathos à la Wagner or Tchaikovsky.

Of all the 'symphonic' musicians I was no doubt the one who roused most mistrust, so the number of film scores I have written remains strictly limited. My first film was *Madame Bovary*, a film by Robert Aron, who, in spite of the intellectual qualities and undoubted culture of the producer Gallimard and the director Jean Renoir, was unable to spare me a rather inquisitorial visit from these gentlemen to hear what sort of music I was writing for their film. I believe that in spite of the scant courtesy with which they heard it out in silence, they must have felt reassured, for I never heard any more from them. My music was composed during a long illness, and I was still very unwell on the day for the recording. I had myself taken to the studio and remained in the sound cabin all day long, on the assumption that my presence would be of more use to the sound engineers than to Désormière, who had had a great deal of experience of the film industry.

It rarely happens that a score written for the cinema is also suitable for concert performance, for it is usually too fragmentary and too descriptive, solely adapted to the requirements of the screen (for purposes of illustration, scenes of bals musette, village bands, fairground scenes, etc). Nevertheless I managed to extract from the music for this film a piano suite suitable for amateurs called: *L'Album de Madame Bovary*.

Désormière, Honegger and I collaborated in *Cavalcade d'Amour*, which deals with the same subject at three different periods (Middle Ages, 1830 and 1930). I chose the first. Later on I used this music in a suite for wind quintet: *La Cheminée du Roi René*. Sometimes, but very seldom, a film out of the ordinary gives a composer the opportunity to make fewer concessions and ignore the commercial angle. This was the case for Cocteau and Auric's *Sang d'un poète*, which was commissioned by the Vicomte de Noailles. Some documentaries may also give an opportunity for more original scores: one or two of those written by Delannoy and Tailleferre were given concert performances. The only chance I ever had to do the like was for Malraux's *Espoir*. The film depicts a poignant episode from the war in Spain, and music was not required until shortly before the end of the film when the peasants are carrying home the bodies of the Republican airmen who had bombed the bridge of Teruel and crashed in the mountains. This very moving funeral procession lasted eleven minutes, and I wrote for it my *Cortège funèbre*, the first performance of which I gave on the C.B.S. Radio network in New York in July 1940 in memory of those killed during the War.

Music for the theatre involves highly complex problems which may be dealt with in widely differing, often contradictory, ways. When the producer plans the production of a new play, he attends to the function to be played by the music with the same minute care that he devotes to the lighting, and he often asks the composer to make alterations in the course of the actual rehearsals, so that the musician must be highly adaptable. But when the incidental music has been written with no view to immediate performance, as I had done for *Les Choëphores, Agamemnon* or *Protée*, it is quite another problem. Now it is the producer who must endeavour to conform wholly with the work previously completed by the authors.

Claudel has always imagined the role to be played by music in his various plays. It is an exciting experience to follow his lyrical outbursts as he tries to express the ideas he wants to convey. In the published version of

L'Annonce faite à Marie, very precise indications are given as to the musical accompaniment. Claudel never ceases to ponder over his plays. This is why there are several different versions of the same work. *Protée* was published in 1913, in two acts. Claudel added a third during a voyage to Japan. *La Jeunne Ville Violaine* was re-written and became *L'Annonce faite à Marie*. The fourth act was shortened and simplified not long before the 1939 war. At the first performances of *L'Annonce* a score composed by the Abbé Brun was played, but when a few years later a lavish production of the play was planned for the Théâtre Pigalle, Claudel asked me to produce a more elaborate score. He came to L'Enclos to see me and work out the general plan in my company. He wanted the music to intervene not only when the text called for it (fanfare and liturgical choruses) but also to provide a kind of enhancement of the sound of the poetry, sometimes by means of the repetition of fragmentary phrases or by offering a pretext for a song, or a sung commentary on the action, or for birdsong and a long melody celebrating noontide and the sweetness of summer. All this had to accompany the action of the play without in any way holding it up: the speech was to have a sort of musical shadow accompanying its every movement. The idea was fascinating, but Claudel was carried away by the interior flood of lyricism that swept him along like a kind of force of nature, and did not stop there. From Washington he sent me a lyrical commentary on every sentence in his opening scene, tremendously interesting but likely to make it last three times as long. I was therefore obliged to stick to the plans we had worked out in Aix. I scored my music for the instruments that are most suitable for the microphone (organ, piano, flute, clarinet, two saxophones, two Ondes Martenot and percussion) and for vocal quartet. Theoretically, the music was to be recorded for going on tour, but the theatre management changed hands and the project was abandoned. *L'Annonce* was produced at the Palais des Beaux-Arts in Brussels. The singers and orchestra were beautifully handled, but the actors were only amateurs. It was most interesting to see the scenes in which the effect of duplication was employed, the music and the singing proceeding indepenently of the action on the stage. It was a case of reinforcing the dramatic effect rather like the visual experiment that had been tried out in *Christophe Colomb* when a scene similar to the one depicted by the singers was thrown on to the screen. A series of performances of *L'Annonce faite à Marie* was given at the Théâtre du Parc. When Jouvet toured South America in 1942 he wrote to me asking for the score, but as my copy of it had stayed behind in France, I decided to write some new incidental music. I kept strictly to the stage directions in the printed text and composed a very different score, much less lyrical and having a quality of austerity that linked the play even more closely to medieval music. As soon as my work was completed, I sent it off to Jouvet, but I had not foreseen that in wartime an envelope containing music and words in Latin might arouse the censor's suspicions. It was held up long enough to guard against any dangerous eventuality, and reached Jouvet too late. He had been compelled in the meantime to ask an Italian refugee composer, Massarani, for his collaboration. I turned the new music for *L'Annonce* into nine Organ Preludes and five *Prières* for voices and organ based on Latin texts.

In 1933 André de Richaud asked me to collaborate with him in *Le Château des papes*, a new play for Dullin to open the season with. I did not know Richaud, but I had admired his play *Village*, the sheer movement of which was positively amazing. I had seen all of Dullin's productions, and his use of music had always been interesting and original. He exercised great care and discernment in his choice of musicians: Maxime Jacob for *Vôlez-vous jouer avec moa* by Achard, and Auric for *The Birds, Volpone* and *The Silent Woman*; for *Antigone* Honegger had written some enchanting fragments for oboe and harp, while Sauguet had composed music for Roger Ferdinand's *Irma*, Delannoy for *La Paix* and Ibert for *La Volupté de l'honneur*. It is not always easy to evoke and describe a character in a tiny phrase lasting only a few seconds. In *Le Château des papes* there were, in addition, choirs that had to sing between scenes and in isolated sentences. Dullin and Richaud had taken up their quarters in the Château de Lourmarin. The former came as far as Aix to give me his instructions. He had locked up de Richaud in the château, to make sure that he would work on the play instead of setting out in search of the liquid moonlight he writes about so much in his books. There was nothing hidebound about Dullin, no ready-made formulas, and although it was more expensive, he always preferred to use 'living' music rather than recordings. I scored my music for two pianos, one trumpet and an Ondes Martenot. I believe it was the first occasion on which this valuable instrument was tried out in the theatre, with its almost unlimited range from high to low, its tremendous power and soft tones just within the limit of the audible. An arrangement of loudspeakers in the body of the theatre and in the roof enabled the sound to be projected from several different points at once. My vocal quartets were sung by choirs of actor-singers, among whom was that charming Madame Limosin who a few months later perished in dramatic circumstances at sea with all her family. What a thrilling experience rehearsals at L'Atelier were! Dullin works from the living model. Disregarding what he has prepared in advance, he experiments directly, constantly altering and revising, rarely satisfied. For days he goes over the same passage. Changeable because ever aspiring to perfection, he makes the musician's work twice as hard. 'Don't you think it's a little long?' 'Yes, perhaps you're right,' you reply, and the scene is cut. Then the next day he will say: 'Don't you think it's a little weak to support the opening theme?' You alter it, or speed it up, and as likely as not, come back to what was suggested in the first place. This is excellent training for those who collaborate with him. Dullin is in agony, overcome with despair, passing without transition from tears to laughter: some trifling incident such as a clumsy move by one of the actors is enough to make him forget his worries and quickly recover his spirits and optimism. In the *Le Château des papes* there was one scene describing the Black Death which gave us enormous trouble. We worked on it all night, but next day Dullin had a sudden inspiration, which made him alter everything — *and he was right too*. All this preparatory work revived Madeleine's love of the stage. She had abandoned her dramatic studies in deference to her father's wishes, but now, by arrangement with Dullin, she attended his classes and those given by Madame Dullin and Lucien Arnaud. We did not like to be parted for long, however, and she only decided to go on the stage after the financial reverses that left her mother without resources.

For Dullin, I composed music for *Le Faiseur* and *Plutus*, very cleverly adapted by Simone Jolivet, and for *Julius Caesar*. The importance of the crowd scenes in the latter and of the battle sequence, raised difficult problems. We thought of mingling recorded sounds with those made by the actors themselves, and of then superimposing my score (for seven instruments) upon them. The mechanical aspect of these experiments seemed to us to be incompatible with a live performance, and the idea was abandoned. In fact a roll on the drum *sounds* more real in the theatre than a recording of actual sounds. It was as a sequel to these performances of *Julius Caesar* that I was asked by the Old Vic to write a score for Michel Saint-Denis's production of *Macbeth*. There too a preference was expressed for live music, but I was limited to five instruments. A young conductor deeply versed in the requirements of theatrical music showed remarkable adaptability, especially in the scene with the three witches, in which the music and the words must be absolutely synchronized.

For the translation of *Romeo and Juliet* by Jouve and Pitoëff, I wrote a suite for oboe, clarinet and bassoon based on themes from Corrette, a petit-maître of the eighteenth century, very freely handled both as regards harmony and melodic line. This *Suite d'après Corrette* was published and recorded. It was very pleasant to work with Pitoëff. With the manuscript open before us, we would pick out the passages in which music was required and work out the timing together. Then I composed my music, which corresponded exactly to the spoken text. In addition to *Romeo and Juliet*, I wrote for him music to René Lenormand's *La Folle du ciel*, using harp, Ondes Martenot and voice (my songs were sung with great charm and feeling by Ludmilla Pitoëff); *Amal* by Tagore and Gide; *La Première Famille* by Supervielle and Anouilh's *Voyageur sans bagages*. From the last-named, I extracted a Suite for piano, violin and clarinet. The smallest orchestra I ever used was undoubtedly for *Le Bal des voleurs* by Anouilh: it consisted of one single player, a clarinettist, who mingled with the actors on the stage — sometimes, it is true, he played the saxophone. . . .

I have only on one occasion worked for Jouvet, at the Comédie-Française in *Tricolore* by Kestringuez, and once too for Dopeau, in André Obey's *Le Trompeur de Séville*. Contrary to what Pitoëff and Dullin liked to do, these two producers used to have the music recorded. Whereas the fact that the players only had to be paid once made it possible to have a bigger orchestra, and thus obtain a greater variety of timbres, in my opinion there was no real substitute for *living* music. In the case of the fanfares for *Le Trompeur de Séville* I used one or two eighteenth-century themes that recurred later in the score from which I drew my *Suite provençale*. During the performances of Henriette Pascar's production of *The Golden Boy* there was a little incident. The plot is quite a simple one: a young violinist decides to abandon his career for that of a prize-fighter. At the end of Act I he plays the violin for the last time (I had written a little melody that had been recorded); then he sadly lays the instrument back in its case in front of his sorrowing parents. At the dress rehearsal, the sound of the violin was only heard some time after the violin had been put back in its case. The stage manager offered his apologies, and next day the music was on time, but unfortunately he lost his head and put on a piano record by mistake. The effect was startling!

Henriette Pascar had been responsible for some delightful plays for children, on subjects adapted by Charles Vildrac. I composed the music for *Le Médecin volant*, and later based the first and third pieces of *Scaramouche* on it. I also introduced in the middle of this suite the theme of the brief overture I wrote for Supervielle's *Bolivar* at the Comédie-Française. Although I had written a full score for this work, I did not use any part of it in the opera I was to compose later. I did, however, take from it the *Trois Chansons de négresse*.

In 1936 the Popular Front Government decided to celebrate its accession to power by a gala theatrical performance that would also be a patriotic and political pageant. They chose Romain Rolland's *Le Quatorze Juillet*, and commissioned music from Charles Koechlin, Albert Roussel, Honegger, Ibett, Auric, Daniel Lazarus and myself. My piece was intended to accompany the funeral procession for the burial of Necker. My orchestra consisted solely of wind instruments and brass, and was conducted by Désormière. I was unable to attend the performance owing to illness, but I was able to judge the popular enthusiasm aroused by the show when it was broadcast on July 14th. Later on I rescored this piece and called it *Introduction et marche funèbre*. A few months later another collective gala was given under Government auspices, on the central theme of Liberty. Numerous musicians and writers collaborated. The idea was a noble and moving one, but it was translated into reality in a lame and heterogeneous fashion, with no unity of effect. With the exception of one or two scenes, it was a failure, and terribly 'hammy'.

Nearly every year I went to Orange for the Fêtes. Whether it was a solemn and majestic opera by Gluck, or the sun-drenched music for *L'Arlésienne*, or Paul Mounet bawling out poetry, for me the effect was always unique of its kind. The theatre's acoustic qualities never failed to astonish me: a sigh or the most lightly breathed syllable could be clearly heard by eighteen thousand spectators. The orchestra was crystal clear in texture, with each instrument's line standing out, unblurred and stripped of extraneous sound. The city presented an amusing spectacle, hotels and boarding houses being taken by storm, and streets and cafés filled to overflowing. In the evening, a huge crowd streamed out silently, almost majestically, towards the theatre. There was a quite extraordinary atmosphere of quiet beauty and popular rejoicing. I had the great good fortune to be able to take part in it through my music for Valmy-Baisse's *Bertran de Born*, which included a ballet and songs, *Moyen Age fleuri*, for which I used eighteenth-century Provençal themes. The *Chansons de troubadour* were later taken from this work, other fragments of which were included in the finale of the *Suite provençale*. I thought the rehearsals in the Theatre of Orange even more beautiful than the actual performances, because of the sunlight and the golden glow of the stone. The stage was conventionally floodlit and stood out sharply against the nocturnal vault of the heavens, in which on these moonlight nights there glittered millions of stars. Some fragments of the *Suite provençale* were included in *La Coupe Enchantée* produced at the Orange Theatre by Pierre Bertin in the following year.

Among other of my works based on music for the theatre I should mention *Fragments dramatiques*, derived from the incidental music for Jean Mistler's *Le Conquérant*, produced at the Odéon.

During this period when my efforts were divided up between so many fragmentary works, I wrote two important works of a religious character. It is curious how often a chance encounter or an unexpected detail may lead to the creation of a considerable work. In 1936, at one of Madame Long's receptions, we met Madame Ida Rubinstein, and talked to her about the Ohel players from Palestine, who differed from all the other Jewish theatrical companies, usually strongly under Russian influences, and were playing at the Théâtre de l'Ambigu at that time. The primitive, rustic style of production, its savagery almost, and the authentic flavour of the acting, so delighted us that we had gone several times. Madame Ida Rubinstein asked to be allowed to accompany us. At the end of the evening, she asked me if I should be interested in writing her a work based on a Biblical theme. I suggested a collaboration with Claudel, and she enthusiastically agreed. I had worked with her before: since *Le Martyre de Saint-Sébastien*, she had appeared in one show after another (*Amphion* and *Sémiramis* by Valéry and Honegger, *Perséphone* by Gide and Stravinsky, and ballets by Auric, Sauguet, and Ibert). In 1938 she had commissioned me to orchestrate some waltzes by Schubert and Liszt for a ballet called *La Bien Aimée*, with décors by Benois. Although the subject was a simple one, it involved some ticklish problems in the situation arising when a young pianist throws a spell on those around him through his playing. What I had to do was to try and exceed the virtuosity of Schubert's waltzes, those adorable short pieces only a few bars long already made difficult enough in all conscience by Liszt's variations. I was only able to do this by means of the Pleyela. This was for me an amusing experiment from every point of view, for the mechanical rigidity of the Pleyela compelled the conductor to follow it as if it had been the most implacable soloist imaginable.

I stopped at Brangues to see Claudel, who at first refused point-blank to agree to a Biblical subject. What? Which one? No! He would not do it. Next morning at breakfast, Henri Claudel told me that his father had asked not to be disturbed, as he was working. About eleven o'clock, he came in with the completed scenario of *La Sagesse*, based on the Parable of the Wedding-Feast. A month or two later, Madame Ida Rubinstein asked me to approach Claudel for him to write a scenario on *Jeanne d'Arc* for Honegger. I caught him on his way through Paris to Brussels: 'What!' said he, 'another Joan of Arc? No, I won't.' The rhythm of the train must have touched off his imagination, for on arrival in Brussels, his plan for *Jeanne au bûcher* was already drawn up, and Madame Rubinstein received the precious manuscript a few days later.

La Sagesse and *Jeanne au bûcher* were to have been produced together at the Opéra, but the scheme was postponed several times. Honegger's oratorio was given in Basle, and later in Orléans for the Feast of Joan of Arc, an official occasion graced by the presence of representatives of the Government, the Church and the Army.

La Sagesse slumbered in Madame Rubinstein's archives until 1946, when within a few months of one another, Rosenthal and Collaer presented it on the French and Belgian radio respectively. The recordings of these two broadcasts were sent to me in California, to bear witness to the excellence of the performances.

My second Biblical work was *Le Cycle de la création* by Don Luigi Sturzo, the Italian priest who had been the leader of the Christian Democrat party and had left the country for his own safety after the murder of Matteoti. Several years before, he had asked me, through the intermediary of Emil Hertzka, whether I would be willing to set his text to music. He came to me from London, where he had taken refuge, accompanied by a group of producers who were interested in his work. He handed me the manuscript, on which he had noted the prosody of the Italian, to facilitate my work and avoid unnecessary errors. In spite of the incredible number of projects accepted for stage and screen, *Le Cycle de la création* has never been performed.

It has always been a source of regret to me that before the 1939 war there was never any serious move towards decentralization in France, especially if the success obtained by some provincial companies is remembered. In Marseilles there was a band of very talented young men, who were introducing the local audiences to a host of ancient and modern plays previously unknown to them.

Henri Fluchère, an *agrégé* in English and teacher in the Lycée of Marseilles, translated and adapted for them Elizabethan plays as well as *Murder in the Cathedral*. These enthusiastic young actors cheerfully faced all difficulties, turning them to their own advantage. I saw a performance of *The Beggar's Opera* in the Salons Pins at Marseilles that absolutely enchanted me. There was no real stage, merely a kind of platform at either end of the hall, like those provided for the orchestra in a ball-room. Their dimensions were so small that the scene-shifting took an unconscionable time, almost too long to be reasonable. Louis Ducreux produced his play by using the two platforms alternately, requesting the audience to turn their chairs round in order to see the scenes to be performed at the other end of the hall. I harmonized and orchestrated the melodies of *The Beggar's Opera* for him and later published a selection from them under the title *Le Carnaval de Londres*.

Another effort towards decentralization was that of the 'Compagnie des Quinze'. Michel Saint-Denis hoped to be able to enlarge its activities and produce plays in old market-places, châteaux, or the arenas suitable for play-acting such as abound in Provence. A house in the neighbourhood of Aix-en-Provence was turned into a scenery workshop and school of acting. Saint-Denis also hoped to interest Provençal artists in the enterprise. He asked Jean Giono for an adaptation of the *Odyssey* and wanted me to do the music for it. I had met Giono several times at Manosque. He had read me the manuscript of *Le Serpent d'etoiles*, which I had thought an admirable subject for a cantata. He had also told me how he came to write this book, which further added to my enthusiasm for it. While out walking he had come across a hill-top from which he had seen numerous flocks of sheep converging on one particular point. This had surprised him, for it was not the season of the *transhumance*, and he had learned that the shepherds were going off to their annual gathering, at which there would be an impromptu performance of a play. Giono had been intrigued and, borrowing an exercise book and a pen and ink from a little village girl, had had himself taken by cart to as near the rendezvous of the shepherds as it was possible to go. There were thirty thousand sheep surrounding a narrow space marked out by lanterns like will-o'-the-wisps. Speaking their patois, in which all the dialects of the Mediterranean were mingled as in a melting-pot of poetry, the shepherds enacted a pastoral drama on a cosmic theme. Giono had noted it down and translated it into French. He offered to take me to the Feast of the Shepherds on the following year, so that I might steep myself in the atmosphere of it before composing my music. He promised to inform me of the date by telegram. I waited in vain for some sign from him, and after writing several times, a telegram arrived to tell me that the Feast had taken place without his being informed. When I met Giono again, I had the distinct impression that he had been romancing, and he readily confessed that the cosmic drama had never existed outside his own imagination — and was none the worse for that!

All this artistic activity in Aix and its surroundings made me long even more to see the city become an important centre for musical and theatrical festivals. A university city where studious youth can labour and meditate amid its eighteenth-century buildings steeped in tradition and the amazing beauty of the surrounding countryside, made familiar through the landscapes painted by Cézanne, my native Aix seems peculiarly fitted to become the centre for a Mediterranean Festival. May I live to see that day!

Chapter Thirty-One

Around the Exhibition

In spite of the dificult period that followed the adoption of the Popular Front Government's social reforms (forty-hour week, holidays with pay, organized leisure) and the disturbances, strikes and factory occupations, preparations for the International Exhibition of 1937 went ahead and were eventually crowned with amazing success. Yet the mutter of sinister threats and portents was already to be heard. There was to be an Austrian pavilion, but the evil forces of the Anschluss were never very far away. Picasso's *Guernica* adorned the walls of the Spanish pavilion, but the Republic had been murdered. Opposite one another, the German and Soviet pavilions seemed to challenge one another to mortal combat. One evening as we watched the sun set behind the immense mass of flags of all the nations that fluttered above the Pont d'Iéna, Madeleine clutched my arm in anguish and whispered: 'This is the end of Europe!'

The arts were well represented. Great painters, both French and foreign, had produced panels and frescoes, while sculptors had been given an opportunity of showing off their prowess, and architects of demonstrating their new ideas. The national broadcasting system had a studio with walls of glass, so that the public could see all that was going on. The broadcasts were relayed over the whole exhibition by means of a system of loudspeakers, and music seemed to have found its natural home in space. One autumn evening I listened to the pure crystalline notes of one of Mozart's concertos, dropping at our feet like leaves from the trees. Another time, it was Debussy's *Nocturnes* that merged with the lights that twinkled in the peacefully moving waters of the Seine. But the Government did more than this to familiarize the public with music. It ordered some twenty-odd scores for the Festivals of Water and Light. The architects Beaudoin and Lodz invented a special device which made it possible to synchronize, to within one second of one another, the playing of fountains and firework displays. I was asked to write music for the *Fête de la lumière*. My score ended with a poem by Claudel specially written for the occasion. The rehearsals had a charm all of their own, the music merged with the passing scene and was not even noticed by the onlookers. But after dark, people watched and listened in perfect silence: sky-rockets and showers of coloured lights, tinted smoke-clouds and multi-coloured balloons mingled with the voice of Elena Fels, to which three singers responded, 'O blessed light!', and the changing play of fountains and lights.

The Musée de l'Homme had mustered all the most modern techniques for the presentation of the ethnographical collections previously dismally displayed in the antiquated Palais du Trocadéro. The Vicomte de Noailles and Henri Monnet asked me to write a cantata for the inauguration of the museum. Robert Desnos, who was as capable of writing genuine poetry as occasional verse, wrote the words for the *Cantate pour l'inauguration du musée de l'Homme*, which was performed before a tightly-packed crowd in the lecture-room of the museum.

Official ceremonies followed one another thick and fast, as if to add to the brilliance of that brilliant season. The Government decided to celebrate the seventy-fifth anniversary of Aristide Briand's birth by a ceremony at the Sorbonne, to which speakers from all countries would be invited. Anxiously I asked Marguerite Long, who had been deputed to commission a work from me, what singers and players would be available. 'The band of the Garde Republicaine or the Manécanterie des Petits Chanteurs à la Croix de Bois,' she replied. As Claudel had for so long worked under Briand and admired his policy, I got him to collaborate with me in a choral work. He selected a number of verses from the Bible, and together we wrote the *Cantate de la paix*.

The Abbé Maillet, founder of the Manécanterie, had his quarters in the heart of Belleville[1] and welcomed there any child who wished to sing. Although their musical gifts might be small, they were given special attention to try and develop whatever potentialities they might have. Even when the result was nil, at least the children had the benefit of healthy surroundings and benevolent care. Rehearsals were quite devoid of severity or constraint. The children did what they liked, sitting on the ground, or standing in a corner, with fingers in their noses or their feet on their neighbours' chairs, but always attentive to the words of the Abbé, whom they adored. Their voices were supported by a group of grown-ups for the bass and tenor parts, but what carried me away was the absolute purity of the

[1] One of the poorest quarters of Paris. (Translators' note.)

soloists' unbroken voices. I was amazed by the speed with which they learnt my music. . . . The Manécanterie included the *Cantate* in its repertoire, and the Petits Chanteurs à la Croix de Bois often sang it on tour, as well as in Paris. . . . The Abbé told me it was not unusual, when they were travelling, for one child to sing a bar or two from the *Cantate* and the others to join in the chorus and sing it right through to the end. Filled with enthusiasm for our young interpreters, Claudel and I wrote for them *Les Deux Cités*, the first performance of which was given by them at the Sérénade, and a few days later they sang it again at the church of Saint-Etienne-du-Mont during Holy Week. Later still I wrote the music for a documentary film on the Manécanterie.

I have always had a great liking for the cantata form. Through Francis Poulenc, I was asked by the Chanteurs de Lyon to compose one for them. I immediately made a start on the *Cantique du Rhône*. In 1937 I used fragments from the *Song of Songs* for a cantate to celebrate my parents' golden wedding. After a number of family parties and a tea for some of our friends and the women from my father's factory, some of whom had been with him for more than fifty years, I conducted a concert on the Marseilles Radio, in which my parents had the pleasant surprise of hearing the *Cantate nuptiale*.

Maguerite Long was accustomed to make her pupils learn contemporary music. (Had not Madeleine played Debussy's *Arabesque* to the composer in 1911?) She asked a group of musicians to compose some pianoforte pieces on the theme of the Exhibition and had them played by her pupils, among whom was the grand-daughter of the President of the Republic. . . . My modest contribution was played by an eight-year-old boy, Jean-Michel Damase, later to be a Prix de Rome.

Also at this time I composed a piano work which gave me enormous trouble. It was a suite for two pianos, to be played by Ida Jankelevitch and Marcelle Meyer. I took some passages from two sets of incidental music for the stage, and called the mixture *Scaramouche*. At once Deiss offered to publish it. I advised him against it, saying that no one would want to buy it. But he was an original character who only published works that he liked. He happened to like *Scaramouche* and insisted on having his way. In the event he was right, for while sales of printed music were everywhere encountering difficulties, several printings were made, and Deiss took a special delight in informing me: 'The Americans are asking for 500 copies and 1000 are being asked for elsewhere.'

When I left for the United States in 1940 his friendship for me was such that he let me know through my mother that he authorized me to have reprints made of any of my works published by him, so that his American agent was able to keep up sales. It was a real grief to me to learn of the death of my excellent friend. He was actively engaged in the Resistance and, on being captured during the occupation, he was beheaded.

During the Exhibition, various foreign companies succeeded one another at the Théâtre des Champs-Elysées. I saw a memorable performance of *The Doll's House* given by the Oslo Theatre Company. Why is Ibsen always played so slowly, as if to drive every syllable home like a nail? These Nowegian players were swift in speech and movement: Norah had all the careless freedom of a bird. At the Théâtre d'Essai, companies of young actors were given a chance to win their spurs. I wrote the incidental music for Webster's *Duchess of Malfi* in Ducreux's production, and for the *Hecuba* of Euripides, adapted by André de Richaud and produced by Marchat and Herrand. De Richaud had travelled widely in Greece and hoped to transport the whole production to the Theatre of Epidaurus. They sounded me on the subject, as well as Derain, who had already designed some lovely costumes and prepared plans for making use of the actual landscape in the décor, by hanging drapes from giant cactus plants.

In 1940, I visited the New York Exhibition, but I did not find the atmosphere that had so entranced me in Paris. I was particularly disappointed by the lighting displays, a pale imitation of our own. There was no contemporary music: the spectators were drenched in a flood of canned music. The day I went there it was nothing but Wagner!

Chapter Thirty-Two

The Pre-War Years

The idea of war was increasingly becoming an obsession: for years it had never been very far from our thoughts. I remember the anguish we felt when, on leaving the Chinese Theatre in New York in 1926 in the company of Copeau and Bourdet, we saw the headlines announcing the Italo-Albanian Treaty and the mobilization of our fleet. Next day it was forgotten, we could see the events in their proper proportion. How many fire-eating speeches had Mussolini made during the previous twenty years or so? From 1933 on, the obsession grew ever worse. I was present at a debate in the Chambre des Députés after the remilitarization of the Rhine. Protests were made against the violation of the treaty and the threats that had been uttered, but no action was taken. One evening when we arrived in Paris from Aix, our rest was disturbed by the news vendors, shouting the news of the murder of Dolfuss. Then came the Abyssinian crisis! The slaughter of Abyssinia before the very eyes of an impotent League of Nations whose sanctions were incapable of preventing the crimes of the monster in the Palazzo Venezia. The Anschluss! The murder of Austria! And no one said a word! The sinister sequence of events in the Sudetenland; the dismemberment of Czecho-slovakia after Munich, and the War in Spain, a dress rehearsal for the Axis troops! The murder of Republican Spain. . . . And yet life went on as before; it was still peacetime was it not? There was one's work to be done, one shut oneself up in it; what else was there to do in a world that had gone mad, and was caught in an iron grip that grew tighter day by day? One turn of the screw, each day one turn more. . . .

In 1938 the Pro Arte Concerts in Brussels and the Concerts run by Mrs Coolidge decided to celebrate their twentieth birthday together. They had both done yeoman service for music and had grounds for feeling pride in their achievement. In homage to them, I composed a cantate, in which I hoped to group together all our friends in a kind of Franco-Belgian family party. I chose some poems by a young Belgian poet, Maurice Carême, taken from his delightful volume entitled *Mère*. I called my work the *Cantate de l'enfant et de la mère*. In order that all our little band of friends might take part in this work, I wrote it for rhythmic recitation (so that Madeleine could join in too), piano (for Collaer), and quartet (for the faithful Pro Arte). I conducted the performance in the enormous concert-hall of the Palais des Beaux-Arts in Brussels on May 18th 1938. It must have looked like a flea-circus, for our soft music and tender, intimate poetry recital came after some bravura pieces executed by the military band of the Guides, in full dress uniform and energetically conducted by Arthur Prévost. The air still rang with the sublime din of wind and brass, through which the lightning of the cymbals seemed to flash above the thunder of the drums.

The State bought paintings and works of sculpture for its museums, it commissioned architects to erect official buildings, but it did nothing to help musicians. The Director of the Beaux-Arts, Georges Huysmans, ever a friend to artists, thought that it would be a good thing to encourage musicians by official patronage, for in difficult times like ours it no longer paid to write operas; taking a long time to write, and longer still to orchestrate, if they were ever played, of which the composer could never be sure, one of them could only be performed six times in a season because the subscribers would not want to see the same work more than once. In 1938, therefore, commissions were given for a three-act opera by Delannoy, a one-act opera by Henri Barrault, an operetta by Auric, a symphony by Elsa Barraine, and a cantate by Germaine Tailleferre. I was asked to do a ballet or opera in one act. I chose the opera. For a long time I had been wanting to depict the character of a jealous woman, whose passion would drive her to crime, as the inevitable conclusion of her exacting, boundless love. Medea seemed the ideal subject for such a theme. The previous summer, Madeleine had, for her own amusement, selected scenes from Euripides and Seneca. Thanks to her sense of the theatre and her knowledge of my predilections, she was able to write a libretto, reviving the character of Creusa, who occurs in Corneille's *Médée*, to serve as a foil by her innocence and sweetness to the violence of Medea herself. I composed by *Médée* during the summer of 1938.

A concert-promoter in the United States, Albert Morini, had often commissioned works from me for artists on his books (a series of duets with orchestral accompaniment; the *Fantaisie pastorale* for piano and orchestra; a dance, *L'Oiseau*, written for orchestra), and now he came to me in Paris to persuade me to conduct some of my works in America. I liked the idea, but it could not be carried out owing to the political situation. In view of my ill-health, I did not want to go without Madeleine, nor did I wish to leave Daniel behind, or make him interrupt his studies, so I put off my acceptance of Morini's proposition. In 1939, Hitler occupied Prague, and Czechoslovakia vanished into the silence of the European Chancelleries. This could not happen again, however, because France and England had given their guarantees to Poland, Greece and Rumania. Not only was war constantly in our thoughts, but in our imaginations too, for we could see two thousand bombers bombing Paris without any declaration of war. Madeleine said to me: 'You ought to send your manuscripts to Kurt Weill in America.' I only wish I had done so! Instead I sent them to my brother-in-law, who was a justice of the peace in a little Normandy town called Domfront that you would think to be the safest place in France. We also thought it would be wise to buy a little house on the outskirts of Paris in case of emergencies, but we set about it too late, for so many Parisians had the same idea that they invaded the agencies, buying up everything whatever the price quoted. All the agent could offer us was a little café in the heart of the country. It was a well-built little house, and it was fun arranging it to suit us. There was a big bedroom on the first floor, with one window looking out over the vast plain and the other on to the forest of Molière, where you can still occasionally meet a herd of deer. Although there was no practical means of transport available to get to Le Petit Séran, we finally bought it. Up to the time of writing, we have never had a chance to live in it.

A new star was rising in the theatrical firmament: Jean-Louis Barrault. The stage setting for *Autour d'une mère*, based on a story by Faulkner, was startling, though it owed something to the rather dated aesthetic ideas of the Ballets Jooss. I could find nothing wrong with Cervantes's *Numance*, with décors by André Masson. The play contained allusions that seemed made to fit the Spanish War. In April 1939, Barrault asked me for some music for an adaptation of Laforgue's version of *Hamlet*. I scored it for five instruments. Barrault made an unforgettable Hamlet, who had been imagined by Laforgue as representing absolute decadence.

The Opéra-Comique put on a most painstaking production of three of my works in one programme: *Esther de Carpentras*, with décors by Nora Auric, *Le Pauvre Matelot*, with a setting by Cocteau, and the *Suite provençale*, as a ballet with a décor by André Marchand.

Two new gramophone companies branched out magnificently in quite opposite directions. L'Oiseau-Lyre issued recordings of Couperin, Rameau and medieval music, with a few contemporary works such as Sauguet's *La Voyante* and my *Suite d'après Corrette*. Le Chant du Monde on the other hand published a vast collection of folk-music. This involved a two-fold problem: either it should be left intact, classified in the archives of a musical library, or it should be freely handled by a musician and incorporated in his own musical personality. Le Chant du Monde asked Koechlin, Auric, Jaubert, Delannoy, Honegger, Désormière, Hoérée, Loucheur, Sauveplane and myself to harmonize French songs (I dealt with four from Provence). The same firm also published an admirable series of songs for the Spanish Republican armies, with a most attractive harmonization and orchestration by Gustavo Pittaluga and Rodolfo Halffter, both refugees in Paris at the time.

For the past two years, we had been going to Les Mayens de Sion for a month before going to Aix. This enchanting part of Switzerland is in the canton of Valais, and dominates the valley and the twisting course of the Rhône. The hotel-keeper was pastry-cook, baker, grocer and café-keeper all rolled into one. The inhabitants of the chalets and the peasants all came to him to purchase their provisions and drink some Fendant wine or eat *la raclette*. We loved this spot, perhaps out of fellow-feeling for dwellers in the Rhône valley, and Madeleine had told the hotel proprietor: 'We shall come back every summer, unless something dreadful occurs. . . .' On the other bank of the river, the Hindemiths had been living in a little village between Sierre and Crans: they had finally decided to leave Germany, as Paul's music had now been banned and he himself was prohibited from teaching. Next door to them lived Blanche Honegger, who one afternoon played us the Concerto for violin and flute that I had composed for her and her father-in-law, Marcel Moyse. On our way back to Mayens, we made a little detour to visit the village on the hillside where Rilke lies buried. That summer I composed the *Quatrains valaisans* for *a cappella* choir, based on poems written in French by Rilke.

It was during this stay in Switzerland that Daniel's taste for painting first showed itself. On our way to Les Mayens de Sion by car, we had stopped in Geneva to visit the exhibition of paintings from the Prado which were provisionally housed there. It was a very hot day, and there was a dense crowd that prevented us from seeing the pictures properly. We were in a hurry to reach Mayens before nightfall, so we were dragging Daniel along behind us as we hurried through. A few days later, he expressed the desire to go back. We thought it was a childish caprice, and refused to go down to the plain again. He insisted, however, so one rainy day we took him back to the exhibition, and much to our surprise we found that he had remembered all the pictures he had seen during his previous visit. He asked us to buy a great many reproductions, which he himself selected with unfaltering sureness of what he wanted.

The day before we left for Aix, I had a telephone call from Paris from the manager of the Chicago Symphony Orchestra, asking me on behalf of Frederick Stock to compose a work for the fiftieth anniversary of the orchestra. When we arrived in Aix, Vladimir Golschmann came to see me to ask for a *Fanfare* for the sixtieth anniversary of the Saint-Louis orchestra. Morini's letters proposing a tour in the United States were growing more and more pressing. But the international situation was growing too dark for me to take such a decision. I fell ill into the bargain, and it was from my sick-bed that I heard on the wireless the news of the invasion of Poland, which led to the declaration of war by England and France.

Chapter Thirty-Three

The War

We decided to stay on at L'Enclos. Bedridden and incapable of working, I listened to the radio night and day. When I think back to that time now, it seems like some long, interminable period of waiting, in which the predominant feeling was one of impotence and frightful anguish, and of daily anxiety for all our friends who had been mobilized. The official communiqués, posted up in chalk on a blackboard outside the Sous-Préfecture during the 1914 war, had been replaced by the announcements read on the wireless, to which we never wearied of listening wherever we might happen to be. The accounts of the Polish campaign were terrifying. In even the remotest places you felt the shadow of an impending doom. Illusory hopes and wireless bulletins and still more waiting: that was the 'phoney war', when everyone said, 'The Germans would never do that to us!' or put their faith in the Maginot Line. The only enemy seemed to be the boredom that reigned in the front line. We were asked to supply packs of cards, draughts-boards and wireless sets for the troops. Why did they not rather give them arms? One captain wrote from the Maginot Line to the wife of a retired general whom he had asked for some games: 'It's your lotto sets that are winning the war!' At that very moment Poland was perishing beneath the onslaught of the motorized divisions and the dive bombers.

My parents went back to town at the end of the summer, but we stayed on at L'Enclos with my mother-in-law. In November I was able to crawl out of bed and come down to the little dining-room, which was the only room with any heating in it. I had had the piano brought in there from the drawing-room. I had no heart for work, and yet I had to deliver a work for the anniversary of the Chicago Orchestra. The idea that it would be the only

French work on the programme helped me to shake off my torpor, and I made a start on my First Symphony.

That winter we were never alone. Many friends came to spend a few days with us: Hélène Hoppenot, Francis Poulenc, Rieti and his wife; while still others dropped in on their way back from Paris. Madeleine had the idea of organizing a little theatrical company to give performances in hospitals and barracks, and this was easily done by roping in two of the young Paliards, Jane Bathori, Andrée Tainsy and Jacques Denoel, one of her pupils, aged seventeen, who had come from Lorient at the age of fourteen to attend her classes at the Schola Cantorum and was now spending the winter at Aix in order to go on with his studies. Thus the house was transformed into a place for rehearsals. A deputation of nursing orderlies from the hospital at the Ecole Normale, and one of their number who was also a Dominican, came and asked Madeleine to produce a play they had written about their hospital. In it they made amusing references to their inaction, and poked gentle fun at some of their comrades. The principal authors, an active member of the Marseilles tramway workers' union and a cinema operator from Joinville, supervized the rehearsals, after which one of the orderlies who had been a steward with the Messageries Maritimes ceremoniously served coffee. It was a great pleasure for us to be in daily contact with so many good souls. Friends who had been mobilized had noticed, like ourselves, that the excessive bustle of the life we had been living in Paris had made us forget the gaiety and generosity of workers and peasants.

Once my symphony was finished, the ice had been broken, and I went on composing. Since the foundation of the Synagogue in Aix-en-Provence in 1840, when a speech of which I still possessed a copy had been given by my great-grandfather, first my grandfather and then my father himself had acted as bursar for it, and I wished to compose a cantata to celebrate its centenary. As Aix was the last refuge of the Comtadin sect, I set to music three of the prayers in their liturgy, selected and translated by Armand Lunel: the prayer for the souls of the victims of persecution, one for the day of reclusion, and one for the Pope (as temporal lord). In each I incorporated a fragment from the great mystical poem by Gabirol, translated by Mardochée Venture who had published, at the end of the eighteenth century, prayer-books for the use of French Jews. I also composed a suite called *Le Voyage d'été*, melodies on poems by Camille Paliard in praise of holidays in pre-war days.

The Paliards were friends of my mother who often came to see us at L'Enclos. Jacques Paliard was a professor of philosophy at the University of Aix. Camille wrote poetry, and poetry was for her a natural and habitual form of expression. Sometimes we would visit them. In their drawing-room reigned an atmosphere of enchantment, through which could be faintly discerned the bells of the near-by convent and bugle-calls from the barracks. The Paliard children talked and Boudou the dog gambolled around us, as we lingered to chat and read verse beside the stove that had gone out and on which, Heaven only knows why, there always stood a flat-iron. . . .

Near Aix, in the Camp des Milles, there was an internment camp for enemy nationals and some refugees well known to be anti-nazis were soon released. This was the case for Ernst Erich Noth, whose lovely novel *Le Désert*, written directly in his adopted language, French, had just been published by the N.R.F.

In October my *Médée* was produced, together with Richard Strauss's *Daphne*, by the Flemish Opera Company of Antwerp. Was this an illusory gesture on behalf of a neutrality that did not make sense? One of the performances of *Médée* was broadcast. We huddled around the set, listening to my opera, and after each aria there was a news bulletin, preceded by the inevitable: 'At the third stroke the time will be exactly. . . .'

In February we received a brief visit from Dom Clément (Maxime Jacob) who was now a nursing-orderly and had come to spend his leave with us. He had not changed, but his eyes had a purer, happier look. I asked him what his impressions of military life were. 'I feel like a civilian again,' he answered, slipping his tie underneath his collar. He played me some of his music, in which religious and secular inspiration alternated, lively and touching songs of a popular character being followed by peaceful and austere religious chants. During his stay there was an admirable perform-ance of *Christophe Colomb* in Flemish on the Brussels Radio. We listened to it with him at my parents' house, Le Bras d'Or.

I had a relapse in March. I had taken to my bed again and should have seen nothing of the Provençal spring had not Madeleine brought some sprays of almond blossom into my room. Weeks went by; the date of the first performance of my *Médée* at the Opera drew near, but I felt sure I would be unable to undertake the journey. This was when I received the visit from the wonder-working air raid warden which I have described elsewhere. Two days after his treatment I was able to go off in the car with Marcelle Carmona and Madeleine. We had a serious breakdown along the way and had to continue our journey by train. Contrary to all our anticipations, I reached Paris in time for the last rehearsal. The Opéra had made a remark-able effort. The score had been minutely revised by Gaubert, and Marisa Ferrer gave a wonderfully powerful and grandiose performance in the part of Medea. I had persuaded Monsieur Rouché to let Dullin prepare the stage-setting. Dullin had been keen to tackle the problems of an operatic production, but he had soon been disheartened by the insuperable difficulties he had to contend with. In particular, the chorus were a thorn in his flesh. Finally he found an admirable solution. He arranged them in rows on either side of the stage like a human wall, while dancers expressed the emotions of the characters. Masson's scenery, and Dullin's absolutely unconventional production, made the show a most memorable one. I have often thought of this last gift to me from the Opéra in Paris, on the eve of the great disaster. . . . The first night was as elegant an occasion as any pre-war gala performance, but the muffled sound of anti-aircraft firing could be heard. Next day we had news of the invasion of Holland. Hélène Hoppenot implored me to go back to Aix, and insisted that we should leave by road. I took a taxi to Lyons, where we picked up our little Fiat. Madeleine, Marcelle Carmona and I gazed at the countryside, torn between sadness and wonder. Never had it seemed more beautiful or more sublime. . . .

The days that followed passed swift and slow, and implacably the Battle of France was fought. All the roads were jammed with refugees, all of whom seemed to be wanting to get to Aix, both those from Holland and the north fleeing before the Germans, and those coming from the south and abandoning the coastal areas for fear of the Italians. The fall of Paris, the advance of the Germans, Marshal Pétain's decision to stop the fighting, came to rend our hearts as we sat in a little bistro in the Vieux-Port at Marseilles. All round us people wept in despair. On our way back to Aix we met an uninterrupted line of lorries carrying away the men of the R.A.F.

I had had too many contacts with German, Austrian, Czech and Italian refugees not to have a very good idea of what an occupation would mean. I realized clearly that the capitulation would prepare the soil for Fascism and its abominable train of monstrous persecutions. Madeleine proposed that we should leave the country. I was powerless, incapable of running away, or even hiding if need be, but such a decision was a bitter pill to swallow. . . . When one of our young friends, who was later to become a very gallant member of the Resistance, said to Madeleine, who was confiding in him how much she was worried: 'All we've got to do is to drop England and sign a fifty-year pact with Germany!' she realized the full horror of our situation and set to work immediately to organize our departure. Already all the Consulates were besieged by a tightly-packed crowd of British citizens trying by every means possible to get out of France. At Cook's, where we booked seats on the Clipper, we met the Werfels who were in despair because they had been refused visas because of their nationality — they were Czechs. In desperation, they took a taxi for Bordeaux, where they hoped to get their papers. Sadly, and with foreboding, we took our leave of them. . . . For us, however, everything went off well. I had in my possession all my correspondence with my manager, and pre-war newspaper articles announcing my symphony, so that the American visa was granted immediately. As for the Portuguese visa, the official at the Consulate was kind enough to give it to me without even telegraphing to his Government. At the last moment the driver who had undertaken to take us to the frontier, refused to go. Madeleine loaded up the little Fiat, and we said goodbye to our relatives. We set out in an exceptionally violent thunderstorm. We were stopped several times along the way for our papers to be examined. The road-blocks grew more and more numerous, because the Minister of the Interior had just put a ban on all movements by road. We had to explain our position, show our passports and our tickets for the Clipper.

Some soldiers were hard to convince, the Senegalese for example. We drove on till late at night, and when we came to a square in Narbonne the black-out was solid — you could not see an inch in front of your nose. Madeleine asked a passer-by the way to an hotel. 'You won't be able to find room anywhere, dearie,' said a woman's voice. 'You'd better come home with me!' The good woman was a market-gardener, who gave us her bed, made us some coffee and insisted on giving us breakfast before we left. We carried away with us a warm memory of her open-hearted hospitality.

At Cerbère, we left the car in a garage and crossed the frontier. We were searched by young Phalangists, wearing scornful and triumphant expressions on their faces. We nearly missed the train, because they insisted on weighing every tube in our stock of homoeopathic remedies and looked up every name in the dictionary. . . . The trains were not running regularly, and there was only a limited number of seats. We should have preferred to book through to Lisbon, but were not allowed to do so. The tickets were only issued by sections, and no one was able to give us even an approximate idea of what the total cost would be. We travelled third class, with good-hearted peasants who marvelled at Daniel, who never stopped drawing. They all insisted on sharing their food with us. We reached Madrid about midnight, and suddenly, to our horror, noticed that Daniel had disappeared. Panic-stricken, Madeleine ran off to find the entrance of the station, but there were several of these. She came back to me, and I went on shouting his name at the top of my voice. This is what saved the lad. He heard me and found his way back to us. Half asleep, he had been following a lady whom he took to be his mother. . . . We stayed two days at a little hotel, to wait for the train to Lisbon. It was at that oment that we learnt that we should not be allowed to take any Spanish money out of the country. We therefore decided to spend all our pesetas, much to Daniel's amazement, for he had never had so many presents before in his life. . . . We booked sleepers, and what a relief it was to cross the Portuguese frontier!. . . . The officials were kindly and sympathetic. At Lisbon, we rushed to the Clipper Office, but our tickets were no longer valid. They had been paid for in Marseilles, and the franc had lost its value. We had no means of making up the difference in price, having only brought out the sum authorized by the Government, namely twelve thousand francs for the three of us. We had not even enough money to book a passage by boat. While we waited on events, we moved into a little hotel. I wrote letters to Kurt Weill, to my manager, to Mrs Reis, to Pierre Monteux and Mrs Coolidge. I told them where we had got to, and these good friends set about organizing a future for me in America. . . . Antonio Ferro the Minister of Propaganda, let us know that the Portuguese Government would be responsible for all our expenses while we stayed in Lisbon. Ernesto Halffter, Falla's favourite pupil, together with his Portuguese wife, came to see us with offers of assistance. I conducted a concert on the wireless, organized by Freitas Branco. I played *La Cantate de la mère et de l'enfant*, recited by Madeleine. I also gave a lecture on Poetry and Music at the Conservatoire which several of our friends attended.

The Baronne de Goldschmidt-Rothschild, who had managed to escape from France accompanied by her children in a little car into which she had packed some of the pictures from her amazing collection — works by Van Gogh, Manet, Cézanne, Cranach — was in Estoril at the time, and told me how disappointed she had been when the bank had refused to let her send some money to her gardener in Toulon. I saw in this a way of salvation for us. I got my father to send the money, and she paid me, so in that way I was able to leave.

On board the *Excambion*, I was handed a telegram from Mills College offering me a teaching post.[1] It was only now, after the wrench of departure, that I realized that I was entering on a new phase in my existence. I should find few copies of my orchestral works in America. Deiss was the only publisher engraving my scores and had sent copies regularly to his agent Elkan-Vogel in Philadelphia. The agent for Universal-Edition would not have many of my works in stock. . . . I should have to start work afresh to cope with any demands that might be made by concert societies. Lying in a deck-chair beside my wife and son, I felt how privileged I was to be able to be working with them at my side and I can never be grateful enough to Providence for not having parted me from them at that time of ordeal. . . .

That was a gloomy crossing. There were a few Frenchmen on board: Jules Romains and his wife, Robert de Saint-Jean, Lévy-Strauss, the Duviviers, and the American writer who is such a Frenchman at heart, Julian Green. Like ourselves, all were filled with inconsolable grief. . . . I remember now the desperate, profound sadness that fell upon us on that 14th July 1940 when we foregathered in my cabin. . . .

When we arrived in New York next day, my faithful friends Kurt Weill and his wife, Lotte Lenya, were standing at the quayside to greet us.

[1] My name had been put forward by my friends, Pierre Monteux, Robert Schmitz and the members of the Pro Arte Quartet.

Chapter Thirty-Four

The United States 1940–1947

As we only had a few suitcases, the Customs formalities were soon over. We had lunch with Claire Reis. This delightful friend, the foundress and director of the League of Composers, was doing her best to get me lectures and concert-bookings, and had gathered together in my honour all the most eminent journalists. In the afternoon, we went with Kurt Weill about a hundred miles by car to see Dr Thaddeus Ames, Treasurer of the League of Composers, who had written to me in Lisbon as soon as he heard I had arrived there: 'As you are travelling with your child, I think you would like to have a few days with your family in the country before doing anything else!' We had eagerly and gratefully accepted his invitation. We met him, accompanied by his sons, half-way to Old Lyme, in Connecticut. They took us to their lovely house, filled with antique furniture and old trinkets, where Mrs Ames was waiting to receive us with open arms.

Summer was scorching, the countryside green, and the great rivers were near at hand. Our hosts were devoting their holidays to various forms of sport. Slowly we re-adapted ourselves to the blessings of peace. After a few days of most welcome relaxation, we settled in New York in a little hotel opposite the one where Elsie Rieti was staying: Vittorio was due to arrive from France in August, and we decided to wait for him, before going to California. Exile strengthened the bonds of friendship that already united us, and a comparable friendship sprang up now between our children that never ceased to grow stronger. Although Fabio was a little older than Daniel, they got on well together, having a taste and talent for painting in common. We took nearly all our meals in the hotel, where we had a tiny kitchenette with a little refrigerator and an electric cooker at the bottom of a cupboard in the entrance-hall. Whenever we went out together, people would hear us talking French, and would stop us to ask us questions on the events that filled them with consternation, and would immediately tell us of their sympathy for us and of the anxiety they felt.

I got into touch straight away with the agents of my publishers to know which of my works they had in stock. The result was rather discouraging! Heugel had no representative in the United States. The Associated Music Publishers, who were the agents for Universal-Edition and for Eschig, only had the scores and parts of the *Saudades do Brasil, Sérénade* and *La Création du monde*. Elkań-Vogel of Philadelphia had copies of all my works published by Deiss, who had always taken the precaution of sending them to him as soon as they came out. As Deiss had the good sense to write to my mother from the occupied Zone to say that I had his approval in advance for any decisions I might reach with regard to my works published by him, and that I could have reprints made if I so desired, I was able to have several new editions of *Scaramouche* printed.

On August 4th, I conducted my *Cortège funèbre*, the score of which I happened to have with me. The parts were prepared by the Columbia Broadcasting System which always remained faithful to me and gave me an engagement every time I passed through New York.

The Ballet Theatre, which in 1939 had given performances of *La Création du monde* under the title of *Black Ritual*, with Negro dancers and choreography by Agnes de Mille, was playing in the open-air stadium at the time. We went there one evening on an invitation by Alexander Smallens, who conducted the orchestra and was thinking of commissioning me to compose a ballet for them. Daniel was now ten and on the threshold of a new existence, and we could not leave him alone in the hotel, so he accompanied us wherever we went. They were giving *Giselle*, and Daniel, who had never seen any ballets before, suddenly exlaimed: 'But mummy, I didn't know they had such fun in cemeteries!' Smallens's plan succeeded; he introduced me to the Director of the company, Richard Pleasant, who asked me next day to write *The Man of Midian*, based on the life of Moses. I composed this music on arrival in California, and the ballet went into rehearsal straight away. Financial complications arose, however, and the company changed hands. Under the new management, the choreographic rights were kept independent of the musical side, and the ballet was never produced. Pierre Monteux gave the first concert performance under the title of *Opus Americanum No. 2*, for it was the second work I had written in the United States, the first being my Tenth Quartet, or *Birthday Quartet*, which I had completed in New York, and which had been asked for by Mrs Coolidge, to be played on October 30th 1940, at the annual concert she gave in Washington to celebrate her birthday.

As railway tickets to California for the three of us would have cost the same as a second-hand car, we bought a Ford, which is still with us, and travelled to Oakland by road. Our first stop was at the home of the dancer Ruth Page, to discuss a project for a ballet, which was only put into effect a few years later: *The Bells*, on the poem by Edgar Allan Poe. The lovely bungalow in which Ruth used to spend the summers stands on the banks of Lake Michigan, a few miles from Chicago. We took advantage of the opportunity to go and see the museum in that city, which is absolutely marvellous. Our journey out through the Middle West continued uneventfully, through the corn-growing districts, with the huge farmsteads set in the midst of unending fields of maize. This way of travelling was a great novelty for us. We spent the nights in the open country or on the outskirts of cities in what were called 'Motels' or 'cabins': little bungalows, very comfortably furnished, consisting of one or two bedrooms with a shower, and a garage. We used to pay the proprietor on arrival, so that we could set out early without having to wake him, and we endeavoured to cover as much distance as possible before the sun was high. The mountains of Wyoming were like a beneficent oasis, and the desert plateau horizons reminded us of the Lebanon, or of certain landscapes by Salvador Dalí. Then we crossed the Great Desert, where the heat was stifling. For eighty miles we were dazzled by the glittering of the salt crystals that cover this huge area which starts as soon as you leave the capital of the Mormons and runs parallel to the Great Salt Lake, with its heavy sluggish waters across which the railway runs on a viaduct, like a road through the midst of the waters. As we left the desert, we came to the same treeless mountains as before, with curiously shaped rocky pinnacles like huge pre-Columbian sculptures, of ochreous hues; and then there were another three hundred miles of near-desert country to cross. How often during this long journey I should have been filled with panic, if it had not been for the numbers of cars we met! After passing over some wooded sierras, we had the first glimpse of the fertile Californian plains, stretching away as far as the eye could see to the dim line of yellowish hills on the horizon. Later I came to know that these hills turn green with the very first autumnal rains.

Once more my destiny in the United States was bound up with that of Robert Schmitz and his wife, for they lived quite near the college, where their daughter Monica was completing her studies. They very kindly offered us their hospitality until we could find somewhere to live, which was no easy matter. First we rented the house of one of the professors, who was on leave of absence at the time, and then after his return a cottage which we had to leave because we adopted a dog. Our third dwelling was very pleasant, but too far from the college during the summer school; so we settled for six weeks in a diminutive bungalow, before moving on to the house which the college had built for us and where we are still. It stands on a little height from which we can catch a far-off glimpse of the bay and is surrounded by all kinds of trees, mimosas, palms, camellias, magnolias, and all the varieties of plants that grow in the warm temperate zone. The animals have no fear of man, for they are protected on the campus, and whole tribes of partridges, hares and squirrels wander across our lawn. There are innumerable birds, big robins, jays as blue as those of Europe are black, and above all myriads of humming-birds with vibrant wings and frantically hurried flight, the metallic red of their throats flashing in the sunlight like summer lightning. We lived in this garden of enchantment, but with our ears glued to the radio, for our hearts remained attached to our native shores, and our thoughts were ever with those who had to live in the midst of the tragedy that had engulfed our world.

Mills College is a foundation for girls, with seven or eight hundred students. It grew in numbers and fame thanks to the outstanding personality of its great President, Dr Aurelia Reinhart, whose successor, Dr Lynn White, a distinguished medievalist, has carried on its humanistic traditions.

I knew America well, but this was my first experience as a teacher. American colleges have an atmosphere that is all their own. They are like little islands, set apart in time and space, where young people eager for learning may find all that they need: libraries, often crammed with priceless treasures, laboratories, an open-air Greek amphitheatre, a theatre, a concert-hall, an exhibition gallery, studios for sculpture, pottery, photography, weaving, an elaborate swimming-pool, tennis-courts, stables, an observatory.

American musical education is very different from ours. Whereas in France absolute specialization is required, and music can only be studied in the Conservatoire or other specialized schools, here music forms part of general cultural studies and is even taught to very young children. They are given classes in musical appreciation and the history of music, with gramophone illustrations: every school has a large collection of gramophone records. . . . The children play in the band or a little orchestra, or else they sing in the school choir. This syllabus continues right up to the college or university, at which stage the student may, if he so desires, specialize in music. At Mills College, four years are normally required to obtain the degree of Bachelor of Arts, and during this time the girls study harmony, counterpoint (up to four-part) and orchestration. They study Bach's chorales until they are able to compose variations on extended chorales. They follow lectures on the history of music (symphonic music, chamber music, etc) including a year's course on Bach alone. They learn to read and conduct an orchestral score. Finally, they are allowed to compose and study, in absolute liberty, every possible form of musical expression. In addition, they play in the orchestra or sing in the choir and have to be capable of giving an instrumental recital (piano, violin, flute, etc), or a recital of song, before their course is completed. After graduating, they may if they so desire stay on a year or two to prepare their Master's degree, the course for which includes the study of fugue form, the composition of a large-scale work, or a thesis on some musical subject. . . . For these advanced courses, some young men are admitted to Mills College, and since the war, in accordance with the 'G.I. Bill of Rights', I have had a number of ex-soldiers studying with me. American women students are usually extremely gifted, but I can never get over the surprise of seeing with what ease, at the opening of the session, when asked to compose something, they carry out the exercise, and after only a few lessons are writing songs, little pieces or even a whole sonata movement. They are self-confident, and free from all complexes and inhibitions. They do not look upon composition as something solemn or momentous, but rather as a subject like any other; not reserved for exceptional beings, but something to be done with greater or less success, and always with ease and gusto. Each year my girls take part in two public concerts: in the spring it is a ballet, composed, danced and produced by themselves, then later there are two concerts of works composed in class (suites for piano and other instruments, songs, chamber music works, chorales, etc).

I have some excellent colleagues here in Mills, and I get on very well with the members of my department. My 'chairman', Luther Marchant, has always shown great understanding and made all my tasks easier. He teaches singing and organizes the school concerts. Moreover, he is entrusted with the often delicate mission of collecting donations for the concerts, the library or the scholarship fund. Another teacher, Marguerite Prall, has the secret of opening up before her pupils the whole vast field of musical knowledge without filling them with dismay. Before the girls come to my class, they are thoroughly grounded in their preparatory studies by young composer-teachers. In 1940 it was Arthur Berger who was responsible for this work and, when he left to become the music critic of the New York *Sun*, for three years Charles Jones taught advanced harmony, counterpoint up to four-part and preliminary work on Bach's Chorales. His successor, Howard Brubeck, is a young Californian who took his M.A. at Mills in 1940 and has stayed on as my assistant. These two young composers have been invited by Monteux to conduct their works with the San Francisco Symphony Orchestra.

I teach right through the summer, so that I have little in the way of holidays. The summer school lasts six weeks and those who take it are teachers and students of all ages who want to cram into their course as much as possible. An excellent resident quartet gives twelve concerts of classical and modern quartets, and each year plays the whole series of Beethoven's quartets. Quite apart from the fact that I like writing quartets, it is the excellence of these players that has led me to compose four quartets since I have been in America. During the summer session, the departments of dancing, dramatic art and music give classes similar to those given during the year, except that they take place every day and work is carried on at high pressure. The remainder of the session is devoted to Hispanic studies in the Casa Panamericana and the study of French in the Maison Française. There are teachers and assistants teaching literature, grammar, style, conversation and diction. I believe that Mills College is the only school in the United States to engage a French writer for the summer session. Jules Romains and Pierre de Lanux were there before the war. In 1940, after the collapse of France, there was an alarming falling-off in the numbers of those wishing to study our language. American students tend to be highly impulsive, and political events may lead to explosive reactions on the cultural plane. This was the period of the 'good neighbour policy', when French was abandoned in favour of Spanish. It speaks volumes for the strength of character of President Reinhart that the 1941 Summer School was placed resolutely under the sign of French culture through the engagement of Fernand Léger, André Maurois and myself. Maurois's classes were highly popular, and he spent another summer at Mills. In 1944, it was Julian Green's turn. He had just published his first book to be written in English, and it was moving to note that in it he had evoked his memories of his childhood in Paris. René Bellé, who is a professor in Los Angeles, came several years running: his naturally lovable character and his enormous culture endeared him to us, and I am especially grateful to him for the interest he took in Daniel, in whom he awakened a real love for our literature.

Madeleine has taught every year in the Maison Française and also given classes on diction and literature in the College throughout the year. She produces French plays, a task which involves complicated problems, for none of her actresses has studied dramatic art and they are handicapped still more by the fact that they are speaking in a foreign tongue. Nevertheless, by dint of much patient rehearsal and hard work, the performances are excellent. She has produced plays by Molière, Regnard, Labiche, Supervielle, Vildrac and others, with music by Lully, or scores specially composed by Brubeck, Jones and Livingstone Gherart. Life is hard for Madeleine here: there are no servants in the United States except at wages higher than the salaries of University professors, aside from the fact that they must be fed and housed. I admire my American colleagues who lend a hand with the housework. Madeleine has to cope with it all unaided: cleaning, buying provisions, cooking and washing-up — and we have a constant stream of visitors. She also acts as chauffeur for me and has to snatch a few moments here and there for her own work and reading. You see that the title of the little piano suite I wrote for her, *La Muse ménagère*, is no fanciful allusion. As for Daniel, he attended school here in America, but soon realized that painting was his true vocation. In the beginning he was greatly aided by the presence of Corrado Cagli, who instructed him in the rudiments of the art.

Elsie and Fabio Rieti came to stay a month or two in Berkeley. From childhood on, in Italy, Paris and New York, Fabio too had been trained by Cagli. This was one more link between the two lads, and when Corrado joined up, Fabio as the elder was able to help Daniel a great deal. We also found some of our family here in Berkeley, for our cousins, Georges Valabrègue and his wife, left France with their three children at the same time as ourselves, and have settled here. It was only by chance that I found how our destinies had run on parallel courses. Ever since then they have become for us the symbol of the 'family', come to lunch on Sundays and join us on feastdays.

We love going to San Francisco, which is only thirty-five minutes away. From the gigantic bridge connecting the city with Oakland, you can see the lovely hills faintly traced against the horizon, their colours constantly varying with the changes in the transparency of the atmosphere. San Francisco is full of character. From the tops of its steep hills you can always catch a glimpse of some new corner of the bay: Chinatown, or the Italian quarter with its innumerable *pizzicherie*, or even the new quarters with the white apartment houses piled up like a child's bricks, high above the Pacific, all with a personality of their own.

We are often invited to San Francisco, where we have a number of charming friends who are always ready to welcome us. How many times we have been invited to one or other of the operas or concerts during the season by Mrs Sydney Ehrman, or Mrs I.W. Hellman, Mrs M. Koshland, Mrs S. Stern and their charming daughters. Our old friends the Monteux spend twenty weeks of the year in San Francisco, and it was a great joy to meet them again, at the other side of the world. Pierre Monteux has succeeded in forging the San Francisco Symphony Orchestra into an admirable ensemble by his brilliant conducting over the past twelve years, and I was able to judge for myself of its excellence when I conducted my First Symphony. Monteux gave several of my works, expecially my Second Symphonic Suite (*'Protée'*), which he has recorded. Many soloists, meteors flashing across our country horizon and lighting up our Western seclusion, pause at Mills to have a meal with us: Casadesus, Francescatti, Thibaud, Rubinstein — and their fleeting visits conjure up memories of Paris and Provence. . . .

Apart from the Symphony Orchestra, there are no local musical resources in San Francisco; visiting companies bring us the New York successes of a year or two before. The Ballets Russes give performances of their latest creations and new scores, not always under the best of conditions owing to the vast amount of travelling they have to do and the limited time for rehearsals: but it is always a joy to see them and applaud the works of Stravinsky or Copland, the scenery by Dalí or Eugène Berman, whose painting every day acquires new greatness, wringing tragic expression from all the pomp of baroque and the distress of suffering humanity, in a sublime amalgam of tattered clothes and crumbling palaces. For six weeks in the year, the Opera of San Francisco engages some of the stars from the Metropolitan in New York to sing and play their usual repertoire, to which the subscribers greedily listen two or three times a week. In this way we had the pleasure of meeting once more Lili Djanel, Singher, Herta Glatz who sang *Le Pauvre Matelot* with the Salzburg company in the United States, and above all dear Lily Pons for whom I wrote *Quatre chansons de Ronsard* with orchestral accompaniment — she has sung them so often, and recorded them, with her husband André Kostyelanetz conducting. There are several museums in San Francisco, and we are great friends of the curator of the Museum of Modern Art, Grace Morley. This gifted woman is always ready to offer one of the rooms in the museum for some function connected with French culture. Chamber music recitals are also given there. I have always loved listening to music in picture galleries. What lovely performances were given by the Budapest Quartet amid Alexander Calder's Mobiles and Lurçat's tapestries! We shall see Grace Morley when we go back to Paris, for she has just been appointed to the American section of UNESCO.

At least once a year we visit Los Angeles. This is a city, or rather a vast expanse of country, peopled by a whole *world* of artists, writers and musicians from every country all living great distances apart. Some of them have been attracted rather by the climate than by the proximity of the film studios. Schoenberg has bought a house there, to live out his old age, surrounded by the happy din made by his two little boys, whom even the gentleness of their mother and sister is powerless to subdue. The Stravinskys live here too. Igor is now composing the masterpieces of his maturity and Vera tends the flowers and fruit-trees, and with her peaceful smile welcomes the old friends who drop in nearly every evening to see them: Catherine d'Erlanger, the Sokolovs, Eugène Berman, the Tansmans and their two adorable little girls, refugees since 1942. We always stay with Sacha. Colette has been doing much the same as Madeleine here. Since they went back to France, some months ahead of us, we have missed their delightful hospitality, and feel a little lost when we got to Hollywood.

The world of the cinema is a world apart, and I know very few film producers, except René Clair, whose marvellous imagination finds difficulty in sprouting as luxuriantly as his friends would like in the Hollywood jungle. I do not think I should ever have written any film music here, had it not been for a chance conversation with Norma Rathner, a young American lady attached to the State Department during the war, who was just back from Paris where she had been very friendly with the Désormières. She suggested me as a composer to her friend Albert Lewin, who was making a film of *Bel-Ami*. He liked the idea, as did his musical director, Rudolf Polk, who rang me up immediately. I stayed in Hollywood for five weeks, writing my score. Although in Hollywood most of the orchestrations are not done by the composers but by musicians specially employed for the purpose, I was given the right to score my own music, conduct it, and be present at the dubbing. I have kept an excellent memory of that film: there were no upsets or snags, everything passed off in an atmosphere of mutual confidence and friendliness. Albert Lewin is a highly cultured man, and what is even rarer in those circles, genuinely modest. In the evenings I went to see the Stravinskys or George Antheil, to recover from my exertions. Since the days of his *Ballet mécanique* the latter had developed enough to write huge symphonic frescoes or even cowboy songs for the films. I also sometimes went to see Erich Zeizl, an old Austrian pupil of mine who had fled from his country at the time of the Anschluss, and I spent some delightful evenings with Toumanova, my little dancer in *L'Eventail de Jeanne*, who had since become a great star! I greatly relished these quiet moments after the arduous work of the day, and feeling so remote from the bustle of excitement that usually swirls in the wake of the Kings and Queens of the Cinema. The first signs of financial success with them inevitably consist of a luxurious swimming-pool and a picture by Renoir without which their houses would not be complete.

The entry of the United States into the war did not have much immediate effect on the life of the college; the students waited until they had completed their studies before joining up. The war made itself felt but slowly; yet in spite of our remoteness it still kept creeping in. Is it fair to criticize a farmer of Iowa or Texas for not realizing the significance of Hitler's threat to the rest of the world? How many Frenchmen had understood the meaning of the fighting in Spain at the very frontier of their own country? The attack launched by the Mikado's aircraft precipitated events. We ought to thank him for that!

As the college had a month's holiday at Christmas, I took advantage of this to go and give some concerts in the East and get in touch with my friends again. I used to stay regularly in Chicago to lecture at the Arts Club and give some concerts. I conducted the Chicago Symphony Orchestra three times, twice in my First Symphony which I had written for the 50th anniversary of the orchestra and again for *Opus Americanum No. 2*, and the *Suite française*. I myself played my Second Piano Concerto which I had composed at the request of my manager that I should have one of my own works to play, that is, one written for a soloist who was not a real virtuoso. The parts of the old war horses I had previously used for this purpose, the *Ballade* and *Le Carnaval d'Aix*, were not in America. I nearly always stayed with my friend Bobsy Goodspeed whose house was a rendezvous for all artists and writers passing through Chicago. When I arrived in the United States, Golschmann had asked me to orchestrate two extracts from *La Sultane* by Couperin. I conducted them with his orchestra in Saint Louis and also gave a concert in Cincinnati, where I spent a week with Lucien Wulsin, the proprietor of the

Baldwin piano firm whose instruments I use in this country. In his house there reigned a delightful, homely atmosphere, and all his children spoke French fluently. His mother had lived in France for a long time. In 1940 I conducted in Boston the *Cortège funèbre*, the *Suite provençale* and the *Fantaisie pastorale*, for which the soloist was Stell Andersen, the pianist for whom I had written it. In 1946 I conducted the Second Symphony which I had composed at the request of the Koussevitzky Foundation in memory of Madame Koussevitzky. This distinguished conductor had been with the Boston Symphony Orchestra, regarded throughout the world as one of the best in the United States, for the past 25 years. Musicians such as he show extraordinary adaptability when dealing with new works and a quite unusual spirit of understanding and co-operation. Every summer Koussevitzky devotes the whole of his time to the Berkshire Music Centre founded by himself, where he organizes very large festivals and runs a school of music which is especially famous for its classes in conducting. This school always invites some foreign composer to come and share the teaching with Aaron Copland. Hindemith, Martinu, Honegger have gone there and I hope to go there myself when I return from France.

Shortly after the landings in North Africa, Henri Hoppenot, who represented the Algiers Committee in Washington, was placed in charge of the operations for the liberation of the Antilles. He went there on a warship, was acclaimed by the Gaullist population and received the capitulation of Admiral Robert. In local folklore, the name of Hoppenot is now honoured like that of an angel of deliverance. The Governor sent me some musical material which he thought might interest me and some popular melodies which I used in *La Libération des Antilles*. I could not resist using the popular songs which included works like: 'Mawning,. Massa Minister Hoppenot. . .' I used the same material in *Le Bal martiniquais* for two pianos, which I later arranged for orchestra. While Henri Hoppenot was engaged in these operations, his wife, Hélène, had come to spend a few weeks at our house, and I met Henri again in 1944 when I went to Washington to conduct a concert there. Another great joy was to meet Saint-John Perse again. Since the Armistice he had been engaged in a modest post in the Library of Congress, occasionally publishing, from the height of his lofty exile, a few noble poems.

I went to stay in New York with Marion and Pierre Claudel and was greatly touched by the affectionate greeting they gave me. In their apartment all was orderly and peaceful, and they had four lovely little girls. I wrote some piano pieces for the two elder girls, Violaine and Dominique, and made them promise to play them to me when I came again, but I did not get back to New York until 1946, for I fell seriously ill on my return to Mills.

A few weeks later I heard the news of my mother's death. I had always been haunted by the idea that I should not be at my parents' side when they died, but I had never imagined that 6,000 miles and insuperable obstacles would lie between us. When my father had died in 1942 at the age of 89, the thought that my mother was all alone in her ordeal had been unbearable to me, but I had consoled myself by remembering that she had tended my father's illness with loving devotion and that right up to the end his faithful doctor, Dr Charpin, and two devoted servants, Emmanuel and Suzanne Lhinarès, had been with him. It was also a consolation to know that he had been able to stay at home, whereas so many Frenchmen had been torn from their families. Up to the invasion of the unoccupied zone, my mother had written regularly. Thereafter she had to endure the presence in her house of 70 Germans, and nightly visits from the Gestapo. In 1943, when it became necessary for Jews to hide, she took refuge with her nurse in Dr Roman's clinic, opposite Le Bras d'Or. It was there that she passed away, without pain but completely alone. In spite of the Occupation, she had gone on writing to me and many of her letters, forwarded by friends in Lausanne, Buenos Aires and Tangier, reached me during the war; others were held up by innumerable censors and I only received them long afterwards. This was a real miracle, as if my mother had been still alive. . . .

The day after her death there was a real house-to-house search in Aix and once again the Lhinarès proved their devoted friendship. For several weeks they sheltered my mother-in-law at the risk of their own lives, and then took her to the home of one of their relatives in the mountains, where she was able to wait for the end of the war in the company of my Aunt Amélie Milhaud and her daughter Marcelle Carmona, who played a very active part in the Resistance.

Throughout my illness, which lasted several months, I continued teaching, my pupils coming to me in my bedroom. I was suffering from such a great deficiency of calcium that the doctors thought I should never be able to walk again. When I finally managed to crawl out of bed, there followed a prolonged period of re-education in the use of my limbs, during which I used crutches and an invalid chair. A friend of mine, the famous surgeon Dr Eloesser, who is a great music lover and proves it by tending musicians with disinterested care, prescribed penicillin, which was a new remedy still reserved for the Armed Forces. Gradually my pains left me and I was once again able to lead a normal life, although my health remained very delicate and I was unable to get by without a car. This is what delayed my return to France for so long. I did not undertake any more journeys alone, except to Laramie in Wyoming. Allan Wilman, who teaches music in the University of Laramie, had organized a series of annual concerts of contemporary music, the first of which he had reserved for me. I was to conduct my 'cello Concerto, played by Wetzel, a Belgian soloist. As there were not enough students to form an orchestra, many of them having been called up, Allan Wilman recruited his players from schools often very remote from Laramie, had them over for several week-ends for rehearsals and lodged them in the college for the week before the concert. Thus my orchestra consisted wholly of young people, filled with an abundance of goodwill and enthusiasm. How it warmed one's heart to see them!

On my way back to California by train I heard the news of Germany's capitulation. Already, ever since the liberation, I had been losing the feeling of exile. Contact with France had been re-established and we knew we should be able to go home again. What had largely contributed, throughout the occupation, to our sense of loneliness there in California had been that, in spite of the affection of our American friends, news from Europe and the clandestine visits by members of the Resistance went no further than New York or Washington. Unfortunately, the first letters to reach us from Europe brought news of bereavement: the death of my young nephew Jean Milhaud, and more than twenty near or distant cousins in the German extermination camps. Then we received news of friends who had miraculously survived, letters still warm with affection and fidelity. Rosenthal conducted the first performance of *La Sagesse* in Paris, and almost at the same time, Collaer conducted it in Brussels. A long succession of writers engaged on missions to the United States came to us here in California and gave us details of the occupation and of the Resistance movement. Sartre visited war plants with a group of journalists and stopped for a few hours in San Francisco. What a joy it was to hear news by word of mouth of all our friends!. . . Louise Weiss spent a few days with us; Duhamel, Thimerais, Vercors gave lectures, the latter creating a great impression by his humane and lofty ideas, although *Le Silence de la Mer*, the first literary manifestation of the Resistance, had distinctly puzzled American opinion. Charles Trenet, a very vivacious singer-poet, brought us the rather crazy songs which everybody in Paris was humming.

Thanks to the tenacity, organizing genius and unwearying devotion of Anne Logan Upton, Head of the American Relief for France, the Théâtre de la Mode came to San Francisco and had a real success. When Yves Baudrier came it was as if the whole family of musicians had been reunited. How glad we were to see him, though only for such a fleeting visit. He played us his own records made by his comrades. Already, a few weeks before, Jacques Scheffer had played us Poulenc's songs sung by Bernac, a record of Eluard reciting one of his poems, a heart-rending commentary on the liberation of Paris and the bells of Notre-Dame . . . all this gradually helped us to feel back home in France.

The San Francisco Conference renewed our contacts with many friends and acquaintances, whom we greeted with a stream of questions after having been so long cut off from our compatriots. Violaine Hoppenot, whom we had last seen the day we left Lisbon, had now become a thin, emaciated girl with an expression in her eyes which was both piercing and remote, reminding one of the glorious years she had spent in the Resistance movement. With her came a throng of young diplomats and journalists, from the silent Beuve-Méry to the young hopefuls of the Quai d'Orsay and the Press. They fell into the pleasing habit of calling regularly on us. These young people were joined by Professor Etienne Gilson, who was perhaps the youngest of them through his mental alertness, and high spirits and enthusiasm. Young authors were engaged to come to the Maison Française in Mills, and Georges Magnane was the first to tell us about the poets of the Resistance and about existentialism. Then came Claude Roy, whose youthful genius and ardour brought us a bright ray of French sunlight. Others who had played an active part in the Resistance also helped us to understand the spirit of the new France; we were particularly friendly with Rosine Bernheim, a young heroine from Vercors, who had been deported to Ravensbruck. This year we are expecting to see Henri Troyat, whose novels and biographies have been published in English and have aroused very keen interest.

Daniel has made some good friends in California, but it is especially in New York that he found friends and teachers to help him in his work. The first exhibition held by Corrado Cagli after his return from Europe, where he took part in the Normandy landings, the liberation of Paris, the battle of the Ardennes and the invasion of Germany right up to the junction with the Red Army near Leipzig, consisted of a series of impressive drawings done on the spot, of the freeing of Buchenwald, the wreckage of the Rhine bridges and the shooting of spies. These scenes from the great tragedy were depicted with that sure technique which links Cagli's art directly to the Masters of the Italian Renaissance. Corrado has a studio near Fabio's, and supervizes his young friends' development with affectionate care.

The last two years we have left Daniel alone in New York for part of the winter. I conducted a few concerts there during the Christmas holidays. In 1946, it was the New York Philharmonic Orchestra in the *Suite française* and *Le Bal martiniquais*. Since my illness I conduct sitting down, which does not inconvenience the players but detracts from the enjoyment of the public. I gave a performance of my *Two Marches* and *L'Introduction* and *Marche funèbre* on the Columbia Broadcasting network, and the *Saudades do Brasil* with the flexible and vivacious C.B.S. orchestra. In 1947 with the same orchestra I made a recording of my First Symphony. A few days later Madeleine took part in *Perséphone*, conducted by Stravinsky. In spite of material difficulties, Claire Reis, supported in her efforts by various American composers, went on giving concerts of contemporary music. The League of Composers devoted two concerts to my work, one in 1941 when I played the *Cantate de l'enfant et de la mère*, and the other this year when I selected a programme of cantatas: *Les Amours de Ronsard, Les Adages, Pan et Syrinx,* and the *Cantate pour l'inauguration du musée de l'Homme,* because music of this kind is rarely heard in the United States. Apart from the soprano, the tenor and Madeleine, the players and singers were all pupils of the Juilliard School, where the concert was repeated. It was at this point that the tragic accident occurred to Francis Salabert, who was flying to attend one of my concerts. He had just taken over the business of poor dear Deiss. Peacetime tragedies were following hard on the griefs of the war. On the other hand, a fortunate chance threw us into contact with Philippe Heugel who, with his brother François, was to play an active part in his father's publishing firm. He had come to the United States to learn at first hand the problems with which publishing had to contend in this country.

I was already well acquainted with the music of Aaron Copland, Roger Sessions and Walter Piston, but I am glad to be able to say that my stay in the United States has enabled me to get to know their work even better. What strikes one immediately in Copland's work is the feeling for the soil of his own country: the wide plains with their soft colourings, where the cowboy sings his nostalgic songs in which, even when the violin throbs and leaps to keep up with the pounding dance rhythms, there is always a tremendous sadness, an underlying distress, which nevertheless does not prevent them from conveying the sense of sturdiness, strength and sun-drenched movement. His ballet *Rodeo* gives perfect expression to this truly national art. His recent symphony, written for the Koussevitzky Foundation, has more grandeur and a deeper lyricism, but the melancholy simplicity of its themes are a direct expression of his own delicate sadness and sensitive heart. Roger Sessions's music is less direct and more complex; thoroughly thought out. Recently he carried out in the University of California at Berkeley, where he is a teacher, an experiment which seems to justify my impression. He composed an Opera called *The Trial of Lucullus*, using a libretto by Brecht. The work contains pages of extreme beauty but it is extremely difficult both to grasp and to perform. It was written, orchestrated and rehearsed and performed in less than five months! The singers and the players were all students. In the same programme Charles Cushing conducted an excellent performance of *L'Histoire du Soldat*. He is a young composer who studied in Paris with Nadia Boulanger and has a profound knowledge of contemporary music. I have often had occasion to consult his library, and we always get a hearty welcome at his house. On the other side of the continent, Walter Piston trains young men at Harvard. Like Roger Sessions he is reserved in character and immensely cultured. Of his recent works, I greatly admired his Third Symphony and his Sonata for harpsichord and piano, in which there are great qualities of zest and movement, dignity and economy in the handling of the dramatic element, and an excellent sense of proportion. Finally Virgil Thomson, who collaborated with Gertrude Stein, is the real American disciple of Erik Satie and divides his time between New York and Paris to the great benefit of cultural relations between the two countries. I should also like to mention the sturdy, harsh music of Carlos Chavez who often comes from his native Mexico to conduct in the United States. It is thanks to him that I went to Mexico to give a concert. He has trained a flexible yet disciplined orchestra there which is astonishingly skilful in playing contemporary music. What other musical ensemble could give, as this one has done, within a single period of six weeks, festivals of Stravinsky, Hindemith and Milhaud conducted by the composers themselves? We were all three delighted by our trip to Mexico. Hardly had we crossed the frontier than we were overwhelmed by the truly Latin atmosphere in which we found ourselves. Deep down inside ourselves, we discovered a past to which the revelation of the great monuments of pre-Columbian art, the churches and convents where Baroque art has run riot, the tumult of the big Indian markets, the appearance of the villages and above all the gentle charm of the landscape, were all closely linked. Carlos Prieto made it easy for us to see all these marvels: he is an industrialist who loves music, as do all his family, and he placed a car at our disposal. His sister is a composer, and he asked me to write a piece dedicated to him. In response to this request I wrote a Trio for strings.

I should not like to end this chapter without enumerating all the 'notes with music' composed by me during my stay in America: three ballets: *Man of Midian (Opus Americanum No. 2); Jeux de printemps* for the 80th birthday of Mrs Coolidge, played in the Library of Congress with choreography by Martha Graham; and *The Bells*, based on the poem by Edgar Allan Poe, produced in Chicago by Ruth Page and revived by the Ballets Russes de Monte Carlo. One opera, *Bolivar*, on a libretto after Supervielle — the subject of Bolívar suited me admirably because I wanted a libretto crammed full of action, with a masculine hero. Moreover, the central idea of the play was that of liberation and freedom, which in 1943 occupied my every thought. I had already written some incidental music for this play when it was performed at the Comédie-Française but I did not use any of this old material now. The text also had to be slightly altered to make it a suitable libretto for an opera. Supervielle, who was in Montevideo, sent me some 'airs' with which the action might be interspersed, and Madeleine prepared a libretto, keeping as close as possible to the poet's beautiful words. The only alteration she made was in the ending when the dying Bolívar sees in a vision his young wife dead. Before this scene, she inserted an aria for Bolívar writing his will in exile, and for this she used the actual words of his will.

I composed four string quartets: the Tenth ('Birthday Quartet') dedicated to Mrs Coolidge; the Eleventh, for the 25th anniversary of the League of Composers; the Twelfth dedicated to the memory of Fauré, for the centenary of his birth; the Thirteenth dedicated to Madeleine, because 13 has always been our lucky number. (I composed this in my hotel bedroom in Mexico.) In addition, I produced a few short chamber works: a Sonatina for two violins, composed for my pupils in a railway carriage at the same time as a Trio which I offered to my wife and my son in memory of a trip to the East. For Germain Prévost, I composed two Sonatas for viola and piano and, because he loves friends, youthful faces and music, *Quatre Visages* for viola and piano (*La Californienne, la Wisconsinienne, la Bruxelloise, la Parisienne*). For Alexander Schneider and Ralph Kirkpatrick, I wrote a Sonata for harpsichord and violin. Some virtuosos wish to make sure of being allowed to give the first performance of a new concerto, and for this reason I have usually had a fair number of orders in executing which I have granted the soloist exclusive rights in each particular work for a period of twelve months. I composed a concerto for two pianos for Vronsky and Babin, who gave the work its first performance in Pittsburg with Fritz Reiner; a clarinet concerto for Benny Goodman, which he never played although he performed the transcription of *Scaramouche* which I had made for him in 1941 from the saxophone version; 'Cello Concerto No. 2 for Edmond Kurtz, which was given its first performance by the New York Philharmonic under Rodzinsky; Violin Concerto No. 2 for Arthur Le Blanc, a Canadian violinist; and Piano Concerto No. 3 for Emile Baume. I also received some orders of a rather special kind: the prodigious musician Larry Adler, who is capable of playing the mouth-organ with one hand, and accompanying himself on the piano with the other, asked me to compose for him a *Suite* for harmonica and orchestra, which he played for the first time in Paris. Fearing, however, that the Suite might never be played again, once the soloist's exclusive rights had lapsed, I wrote another version for violin and orchestra, which was often played by Francescatti. Naturally the two versions are completely different, in view of the nature of the instruments for which each is written. I also wrote a Concerto for Marimba, in which I used the vibraphone as well. Jack Connor, who is going to play it at Saint Louis under the direction of Golschmann, is capable of playing the two instruments alternately or simultaneously.

When a publisher asked me for an easy piece suitable for a school 'band', I composed my *Suite française*, utilizing folk-tunes from Normandy, Brittany, the Ile-de-France, Alsace-Lorraine and Provence in order to familiarize students with the songs of the regions where the Allied armies were fighting for the liberation of my country. I made a symphonic version of the *Suite française* of which I have often given concert performances. After the first performance of this Suite by the famous Goldman Band, Shirmer commissioned me to write a piece for the same type of orchestra. I wrote *Two Marches: In Memoriam* (in memory of Pearl Harbour) and *Gloria Victoribus*. I composed *Le Bal martiniquais* for two pianos (there is also an orchestral version of this work), and Gaby and Robert Casadesus made a recording of it. For the two pianists, Gold and Fisdale, I composed *Carnaval à la Nouvelle-Orléans* using French tunes from Louisiana. I also composed a few songs: *Rêves, Cinq Prières, Poèmes de Supervielle, Chants de Misère*, by Camille Paliard, and *Six Sonnets écrits au secret* by Cassou, for *a cappella* choir. Of all the poems written about the Resistance, these sonnets are the ones I find most moving, for although born of cirumstance, they have the same quality of permanence as the most beautiful examples of classical poetry.

Although my first two symphonies were composed for American Musical Societies (Chicago Symphony Orchestra and the Koussevitzky Foundation), my third and fourth were commissioned in France. Henri Barraud, Director of Radiodiffusion Française, asked me to write a *Te Deum*, which I composed in the form of a choral symphony. It consists of four movements, one of which is for choirs singing without words, and a finale based on the words of the *Te Deum*. I have just received a letter from the French Minister of Education, asking me for a piece of music to celebrate the centenary of the Revolution of 1848. I shall write my Fourth Symphony on the boat perhaps; for the time for my journey is drawing near, and we have already booked our passage on a Norwegian cargo steamer sailing via the Panama Canal.

I am going to see my friends again. Some of them have done their best to preserve all the mementoes of my past: Roger Désormière has rescued my piano and pictures, and, an even greater service, paid the rent for my apartment all through the occupation; Honegger and Sauguet stored all my papers and some music; Poulenc kept all my works published by Deiss as soon as he heard the news of our poor publisher's arrest; Paul Bertrand succeeded, not without difficulty, in recovering the trunkful of manuscripts which I had sent to my brother-in-law in Domfront, representing the labour of thirty years. And in Aix, too, devoted friends have looked after all my mother's silverware and jewelry. The Germans looted both our houses: Le Bras d'Or was successively occupied by the Italians, the Germans, the F.F.I., the Americans and the band of the French Air Force. L'Enclos was turned into a hospital and according to all acounts is in a pitiful state: but the walls are still standing, and that is better than nothing at all. . . .

As soon as the summer school ends on August 13th, we shall set sail. I shall leave behind me seven long years of life in America, for which I shall always be grateful to that great country. I shall return again, in order not to abandon the work I have started here, but already in imagination I can feel the emotion that will well up in my heart as I see the shores of my long-lost homeland looming above the horizon.

Chapter Thirty-Five

Between Two Continents

Our ship was a Norwegian freighter, which we boarded at Alameda, not far from Mills. We crossed the bay at nightfall and went under the huge arches of bridges all sparkling with lights; a sight of unexpected grandeur. We kept quite close to the coast, for our first and only stop was Los Angeles.

After a short visit to some friends and to Stravinsky, who played us the first Act of *The Rake's Progress* which he was in the middle of, we set sail in earnest. The ship was small, but comfortable. There were only twelve passengers, all elderly, and they left us in peace.

The illness of a stewardess forced us to stop at a port in Guatemala. We weren't allowed to disembark, so I had to gaze at the magnificent forests from afar. How badly I wanted to journey into that jungle! As it turned out, engine trouble caused a five-day stop in Panama, and so once again we were able to breathe in the atmosphere of a tropical city. The country is quite small, you can get from one ocean to the other in a few hours, going right through the forest and over the mountains without ever seeing the canal. Once, coming back from an outing, we got out of the car to enjoy the view at the edge of the forest. It was dusk, and I heard the extraordinary night-sounds that had made such an impression on me thirty years before, in the forests of Brazil.

Going through the canal was very interesting. The ship moved very slowly and was held up at numerous locks, then it crossed a large lake and reached the Atlantic. After that there were no further incidents, and the weather was magnificent. Our enforced leisure allowed us to read and work. Daniel wrote an essay on the poetry and philosophy of Lao-Tzu, and I worked on my Fourth Symphony, commissioned by the French Government for the anniversary of the 1848 Revolution.

One evening the radio picked up the first European stations, and the next day we saw the French coast. However, we had to restrain our impatience because the ship had to call first at Rotterdam then Antwerp.

Collaer and his wife, together with Franz André, were waiting for us in Rotterdam. This was our first contact with friends from whom we had been separated for so long, and very moving it was. It was also our first exposure to the ravages of war, the city centre was nothing but a vast no-man's-land! We stayed with the Collaers near Brussels and were greatly tempted to take the train for Paris, but we had brought so much food and furniture with us we had to go back on board to make sure they passed through the customs safely at Le Havre.

During our brief stay, the Belgian Radio invited me to give my first European concert since the war. I conducted *Protée*. Madeleine admitted that each time she heard this piece it inevitably aroused memories of the scandal it had provoked on the occasion of its first performance. Nothing of the sort now! One old lady even murmured to her companion, at the end, 'not bad!' How times change!

We rejoined our boat at Antwerp. For a long time we sailed through narrow little canals with land on each side and everywhere we saw boats that seemed to be lying in meadows.

At Le Havre four figures were waving as we came into port: Annie Dalsace, Jane Bathori and Andrée Tainsy, and with them Madeleine's young pupil Jacques Denoël. It was against the rules to receive visitors on board. Undeterred, we held long conversations by shouting back and forth until the captain took pity on us and authorized our friends to spend the evening with us. The following morning we disembarked. My brother-in-law Étienne, his wife and their son Georges had all come to meet us. It was very moving seeing them again, and very upsetting, too; their eldest son, Jean, had died while being deported: he was only 16. Everywhere we saw signs of war; Le Havre destroyed, whole areas of Rouen devastated. France and the French people meant all the more to us because of it.

We soon fell back into our old ways; it seemed impossible that we could have been away for so long. The moment Daniel got back he climbed on his bicycle and went off to ride round Paris. After the few days necessary for Madeleine to get us settled in our apartment, which was completely empty, we went to Aix-en-Provence.

It was a great shock for me to be in Aix without my parents, who had both died during the Occupation without my being there to look after and comfort them, that all at once my health declined, and I became very ill. This illness — one of the most severe of my life — obliged Madeleine to resume the duties of a night nurse. Nothing helped me, and I was in terrible pain. From my sickbed I heard the concert that I was supposed to have conducted. Roger Désormière had taken my place at the podium for the first European performance of my Second Symphony and the première of the Third *(Te Deum)*, with chorus, which the Radio had commissioned from me to commemorate the victory. Once again, I was given the opportunity to marvel at the ability of this incomparable conductor.

In January I returned to Paris by train and ambulance. I had just been appointed Professor of Composition at the Conservatoire, where my predecessor, Henri Busser, considerately agreed to continue his classes until I was able to take over. I was determined to keep on working, despite my physical condition. I was, however, obliged to cancel several concerts and recordings of my work, but where the rest of my activities — teaching and composing — were concerned, I tried to fulfil my commitments. I would therefore receive my students in my bedroom and conduct my classes from my bed. It would have been impossible for me to stand up for so long a period of time. On those occasions when I was obliged to go out, I had to call upon the services of an ambulance. I was able, in this way, to attend the final rehearsals for a ballet which I had just composed to a libretto by Jean Genet, *'Adame Miroir*. This was presented with great care and taste by Roland Petit's Nouveaux Ballets. A sailor, relentlessly pursued by his own double, loses himself in a labyrinth of mirrors — beautifully designed by Delvaux — until he suddenly finds himself in the presence of Death. It was also only through medical attention that I was able to sit on the stage at the Théâtre des Champs-Elysées to conduct my Fourth Symphony. The concert was to celebrate the centenary of the 1848 Revolution. Désormière had chosen some tremendous works to complete the programme: Beethoven's Fantasy for piano, chorus and orchestra and Berlioz's superb *Symphonie funèbre et triomphale*. A few days later, I went to the Opéra-Comique where my ballet *Jeux de printemps* was staged with sets by Lucien Coutaud.

But it was also time for me to start thinking about returning to the United States. Daniel had left us to study painting in Rome. I had classes on composition to teach at Tanglewood. Honegger had taught there the year before. He had lived in a small chalet in Lenox, where he had fallen so ill that his life lay in the balance for several days. I think that the chalet's charming landladies must have had a very poor impression of the constitution of Parisian composers, seeing that my own health was also impaired. Thanks, however, to my wheelchair I was able to take full advantage of the facilities at Tanglewood. During the time I was there, due to Serge Koussevitzky's promptings, there was a music festival involving the Boston Symphony Orchestra, master classes and a whole series of concerts and conferences.

Our summer ended in California, at the Music Academy of the West, where I was appointed honorary director. This school sits high upon a hill, a short distance from Santa Barbara. Our terrace overlooked groves of lemon trees which spread out towards the Pacific. This summer school was smaller than that at Tanglewood, but no less interesting. For a period of three weeks, Schoenberg, Roy Harris and myself taught courses in composition. That three such different composers were to be shown work by the students meant that the classes were really only of use to those who were already well advanced in their studies; since for a far less experienced student, the judgement of such diverse teachers could only have caused confusion, even though all three of us preached the need for a solid grounding in basic technique.

In September we returned to our house at Mills College. Teaching and work began at once. I wrote *Kentuckiana* for the Louisville Orchestra: an overture in the French style based on twenty Kentucky airs. I prepared a score for *Jeu de Robin et de Marion* for the Juilliard School. When I had completed these commissions, I turned to a rather special project. At the première of my Fourth Symphony in Paris, one of my friends had given me a small music notebook exquisitely bound in green leather and dating from around 1848. Each page contained eight staves. Nothing had been written in it. No young girl had written out her sentimental melodies for guitar accompaniment there. I conceived the idea of using the book to compose two quartets that could be played separately, but which when played simultaneously, would form a third work, an octet different from the two component quartets. Naturally the execution of this work required the cooperation of two quartets, but when Columbia expressed a desire to make a record of the work, the Budapest Quartet chose to record the Octet themselves. This wasn't easy. After having made separate recordings of the Fourteenth and Fifteenth Quartets, they made a fresh recording of the Fifteenth while wearing headphones that relayed the Fourteenth to them. They were thus able to achieve perfect synchronization.

While I was at Mills, Doris Monteux sent to me an excellent young virtuoso, the pianist Zadel Skolovsky, who wanted a new piece for piano and orchestra from me. I composed for him my Fourth Concerto. He played it many times and made a recording of it under my direction in Paris the following winter.

In France my health improved a little between 1949 and 1959, but was very unstable all the same. It was therefore only after much hesitation that I agreed to make myself available for a trip to Menton, where the National Radio had organized an evening to celebrate the 'Festival of the Lemons'. I had to be carried to the theatre by two of Menton's town firemen in order to attend my own *Barba Garribo*, in which a text by Armand Lunel was interspersed with popular songs and folk dances of the Menton area which I had adapted. The sets were by André Marchand. Several days later, some friends of ours took us by car to Aix-en-Provence. Along the way we came across many signs of carnival time: Nice was preparing for its Corso. During a brief stop in Vallauris, Picasso was kind enough to bring down to the car some of his enchanting ceramics, thus sparing me the trouble of getting out. We crossed Saint-Raphaël at the height of the Mimosa Festival, then finally arrived in Aix while it was still in the grip of Mardi Gras. For the first time since my youth, I saw once more the happy crowds thronging the Cours Mirabeau. The sight of so much health and happiness, the traditional fireworks and the beauty of the countryside at twilight awoke many happy memories within me. . . .

Ever since I finished work on my *Euménides* in 1922 I had always thought the score to be so difficult that I believed I would never get to hear it performed. Paul Collaer thought otherwise, however, and encouraged Brussels' Flemish Radio to do it. Franz André conducted the opera with great authority. I can never express to my two friends at Radio Belgium my gratitude at being proved so totally wrong by them. It was with the greatest pleasure that I saw for myself how well the singers had learned their parts — which I had always thought extremely difficult — with such speed and understanding. Twenty years before, while preparing the finale to *Les Euménides* for a single concert, I had been made aware of the great technical problems involved, which could only be overcome with a great deal of effort. . . . Here too, time had done its work. . . .

In May the Paris Opéra put on my *Bolivar* with superb sets by Fernand Léger. His contribution to the production was considerable: ten scene changes, three of which had to take place during the course of the action on stage. In the 'Earthquake' scene, whole village buildings collapsed to the ground, and in the 'Town Hall' the walls gave way to reveal the Main Square where the populace had gathered to welcome the victorious Bolívar's carriage; and finally in 'Crossing the Andes', the mountains appeared to rise up, revealing little by little the vast plateau upon which Bolívar's army spreads out in all directions. The production was also blessed by a thoughtful staging by Max de Rieux, the whole thing being brilliantly executed under the direction of André Clutyens. We got a divided press. Certain reviewers outdid themselves in hostility, going well past the legitimate boundaries of criticism. They hoped to have the opera withdrawn, but the public sided with me, and *Bolivar* played for two seasons. In 1950 I resumed contact with the world of film when Alain Resnais asked me to write the score for his documentary on Gauguin. Shortly afterwards, I did the music for *La vie commence demain* (*Life Begins Tomorrow*), a film by Nicole Vendrés, who was also responsible for *Paris 1900*. This time, Nicole wanted to put on the big screen some of the major figures of the twentieth century; André Gide, Sartre, Jean Rostand, Le Corbusier, Picasso, Prévert, etc. I did not have time to orchestrate my score before leaving for the United States, so I entrusted the task to Manuel Rosenthal.

For some years Madeleine had been director of the Maison Française at Mills College. She had engaged René Lenormand to give lectures there in the summer of 1951. We sailed with him and his wife, the actress Marie

Kalff. They were both surprised and delighted by campus life. Madeleine presented some scenes from René Lenorman's plays with her students at Mills, but she was a little timid about it. This was the first time Lenormand had seen his work performed by amateurs, and foreigners at that. But he was full of praise. I think this trip to America was one of his last pleasures, as he died shortly after returning to France.

The music critic Alfred Frankenstein had published an article in a San Francisco journal on General Lavine, who inspired Debussy to write the prelude *Le Général Lavine excentric*. Lavine was an American acrobat who had enjoyed a resounding success in Paris around 1910. One can't be sure whether Debussy actually wrote the music for him: one can only say that it was composed well after Lavine had left Paris. He went on to own a little workshop where he turned out pins which he had invented for attaching ribbons to army uniforms. He had lived at Twenty-Pine Palms, in Southern California. We rented a secluded little house there during the Christmas holidays. It was in a village situated on the edge of a national park overrun with a strange vegetation, which seemed to be made up partly from fleshy plants and partly from shrubbery. The unbelievable shapes of the Joshua trees gave the entire area a strange hallucinatory quality. I took advantage of the desert solitude there to write my Seventeenth Quartet which I dedicated to Daniel for his twenty-first birthday; then I immediately started work on my Eighteenth, the last in the series. In 1920 I had in fact stated in an issue of *Le Coq*, a journal published by Cocteau, that I wished to write eighteen quartets. This magazine often had a slightly pugnacious tone, at times even an impertinent one. If my declaration appeared to mean 'one more quartet than Beethoven', it was nevertheless not a young man's flippancy. I desired, in view of the aesthetic leanings of Cocteau — who was then busy glorifying 'music with a punch' — that is, of the circus and the music hall — to take up the defence (without seeming to do so) of chamber music, serious music; the music to which I have been faithful during my entire professional life. But the phrase haunted me. I often asked myself if I should ever complete my project. I started work on my Eighteenth Quartet with a sense of solemnity and melancholy, for it would complete a cycle on which I had laboured since 1912. I introduced in the final measures of this composition theme that appears near the end of my First Quartet.

A few weeks later, I accompanied Madeleine to New York. Mitropolous had asked her to take on the role of narrator in *Les Choëphores*. It seemed strange to me, who had grown so accustomed to having her by my side, to see Madeleine take the stage at Carnegie Hall. Mitropolous surpassed himself once again, with all his usual ardour and enthusiasm. Then we went on to Canada: one of my old students, Murray Adaskin, had organized a series of concerts for me in Toronto, where he lived. Two things impressed me in particular about my stay: one was the Toronto Museum which, specializing in Chinese art, has a unique collection of bronzes, porcelains and terracottas — all burial objects, removed from the ground. It is a magnificent museum, even if a museum of death. The other was, of course, the Niagara Falls; its huge cascades of water crowned with clouds of mist made me realize once again that natural phenomena, like great monuments, deserve their fame.

That year, the world of music was saddened by the death of Schoenberg. I had a deep respect and admiration for this man. He had an immense moral authority, refusing all compromise and keeping his ideals unremittingly high. I am happy that he lived long enough to see the tremendous influence of his twelve-tone theory established throughout the world.

The close proximity of San Francisco allowed us to get to the city easily, and hardly a week went by when there was not a concert or play that brought us there. Koussevitzky, although very ill, was touring with the Israel Orchestra. We were shocked by his appearance. He asked to see me the day after the concert, when he had taken to his bed. He proposed that I write a major new work for a forthcoming festival he was helping to organize in Israel to celebrate the three-thousandth anniversary of King David and the founding of Jerusalem. Composers through the ages have been urged to compose upon commission, and only the most perfect technique can withstand the imposition of such a discipline without constraint or loss of freedom. Normally, I use such occasions as an opportunity to concern myself with forms that I personally find interesting; but given the nature of this particular commission, I experienced a mixture of pride and anxiety at the thought of the responsibilities I was about to shoulder. Koussevitzky left the choice of textual collaborator to me. I thought of Armand Lunel. I liked working with him: we could discuss problems with the libretto together without fear of conflicts arising out of any unreasonable touchiness on either side, as is so often the case. Paul Claudel had made me accustomed to a wide and freehanded collaboration. He did once, however, ask me to write some incidental music which posed quite a problem for me. I'm thinking of the J.L. Barrault production of *Christophe Colomb*. I had already composed a whole opera to this text; I had, I believe, put the best of myself into it; and here I was, having to deal with the same material all over again, but in a way that would restrict my music, except in a few scattered moments, to the role of picturesque scene setting. But Claudel insisted in a friendly fashion, and I accepted and did it; although, of course, there was no resemblance between my opera and the incidental music.

We were invited to teach classes in August in Aspen, Colorado. This little town had enjoyed enormous prosperity around 1890. Duse and Patti had won applause in the quaint little theatre there, but when the money ran out, Aspen was transformed, like to many places in Colorado, into a virtual ghost village for most of the year, except during the winter. The Chicago industrialist Walter Paepcke thought it would make an admirable site for a summer festival and a music school. Thanks to his magic wand, this village of 990 souls was already bursting with students and music-lovers before we had even got there. Some old pupils of mine serenaded us outside our apartment from an old bandstand, which had lain abandoned since 1892. The concerts and excursions delighted us, and if we hadn't had to sail back to France at the beginning of September — that constant to-ing and fro-ing between two continents — we would have stayed much longer. While in New York, before embarkation, I spent a day out at West Point. The distinguished bandleader Captain Resta had asked me to write a piece to celebrate the 150th anniversary of the founding of the music school at the Academy. He also insisted that I hear the orchestra play. Imagine my surprise when I was welcomed by the traditional strains of 'Happy Birthday to You' played by this immense military ensemble. It was indeed September 4th, my sixtieth birthday.

Chapter Thirty-Six

1952–1956

M. Ezer, who instigated the *David* project, arranged for us to be invited by the Israeli government to visit Israel. This would enable me to steep myself in the atmosphere of the present-day state and see for myself what its musical resources were like.

What an exciting — and moving — trip that was! We visited the tombs of the Prophets, of Samuel, of Sarah; the wood of the Sycamores where the Philistines were beaten; the lake of Tiberius: everything filled us with the deepest emotion. Unfortunately modern Jerusalem is split in two, and the old part of the city belongs to the Jordanians, which means, paradoxically, that the Holy Places, the cradle of Christianity, have now become the responsibility of Islam rather than Israel!

However, the loss of the Wailing Wall means nothing to present-day Israelis, thanks to the rebirth of the State. Believers, orthodox Jews, monks, representatives of the Anglican, Greek and Russian churches are all fervent in their prayers; at the same time the enthusiasm of a young nation, filled with the desire to create and construct, turns. deserts into forests and orchards and gardens; tracks down King Solomon's mines; causes oil to spring forth from Negev, an area abandoned for centuries; and installs a vast irrigation system which will encourage the land of its fathers to blossom and bear fruit.

The Ministry of Education and culture put two young people in charge of showing us the country. They were just as keen for us to see places of Biblical interest as the ones they'd fought to defend four years previously. Hearing them talk about this conflict, waged with such magnificently headstrong determination, evoked so strong a bond between their heroism and their ancestors' that we determined to put it to dramatic use on the opera. I would have two choruses: one for the action, the other — present day Israelis — commenting and comparing their position with the ancestors'. For, just as David confronted Goliath totally unaided, the Israelis were completely on their own when they braved the might of five nations.

I used no popular tunes or quotations from the liturgy in my score, although I heard many of splendid quality. When the émigrés started arriving, recordings were made and carefully preserved in the Radio archives; for it could easily be foreseen that once those immigrants from Africa and Asia, with whose help Israel would grow into a great Mediterranean power, became assimilated into their adoptive country — something that would happen very quickly — all their cultural characteristics would disappear.

I started to compose *David* in the summer of 1952, in Aspen, and I finished this long work a few months later, at Mills. My music took shape just as rapidly as the libretto, and I made my unfortunate collaborator send it me by air mail, scene by scene. It reminded us of the time when we were both young, and I required him to deliver one scene of the *Malheurs d'Orphée* per day!

The *David* libretto was a tricky job. The protagonist was a man of very many parts, and we wanted to portray them all: singer, poet, Head-of-State, patriarch, lover ... we wanted to show Bathsheba without offending religious sensibilities. Lunel acquitted himself admirably. My music was not difficult to perform. My intention was for it to be interpreted by Israeli musicians, and when the opera was first performed, in Jerusalem in June 1954, all the singers with the exception of Hans Rehfuss (who sang the title role) were those whom I had auditioned myself at the house of the composer Marc Lavry.

It was Georges Singer who took on the job of conducting *David* and he needed all the patience he could muster. The orchestral parts, issued by Israeli Music Publications in Tel Aviv, took ages to complete and arrived in dribs and drabs. Rehfuss only arrived from Switzerland the day before the concert, and the other singers, who worked in various ministries, shops or kibbutzes, only attended rehearsals when they could. But in the end the singers, the Orchestra of the Jerusalem Radio reinforced by the brass from the Police Band, the Jerusalem Radio Chorus and the Students' Choir of the Conservatoire combined to form a remarkable group and they gave my work a rousingly ardent reading. It was, after all, *their* piece.

That evening will always count among the most moving of my life. The singers were transformed: they were singing their own history. The public sat watching its own national hero being glorified. When David, at the end of the third Act, decides to make Jerusalem the capital — just as the Israeli government had done a short time before — a kind of collective emotion seized the audience. During the 'Jerusalem! Jerusalem!' chorus we had the feeling they were all breathing at the same time.

When Victor de Sabaata was invited to conduct a concert in San Francisco, he came to see me at Mills to ask if he might give the European première of *David* at La Scala, Milan, where he was artistic director. What a great honour *that* was for me! And in January 1955 I was fortunate enough to be present at the great event.

The great La Scala tradition isn't just a matter of the exceptional quality of its singers and orchestra. There is an extraordinary respect and love for music apparent among all those who work there. I never saw anyone tired or impatient, even through long rehearsals which often lasted into the small hours. I never ceased to be astonished at the way the stagehands listened to the music in silence and were interested in the smallest details. This time, unlike Jerusalem, the public was a subscription audience for whom the subject had no special significance. It could, indeed, have been any old Biblical story. Nino Sanzogno's splendid conducting and Nicola Benois' adroitly-made sets allowed Margherita Wallmann's ambitious production to flow unimpeded and in record time. The numerous changes of scene seemed almost to take effect before our very eyes. David's role is very long, and the artistic administrators had realized that a star singer overburdened with tours and engagements would never have the time to learn it. So they entrusted it to a relatively little-known baritone, Anselmo Colzani, who studied it with fervent concentration. His performance brought him widespread acclaim and launched him on an international career.

I hope fate has something similar in store for the young baritone Harve Presnell, who created a sensation at the performacne of *David* in Hollywood on September 22nd 1956. This took place in the open air on the immense stage of the Hollywood Bowl, before an audience of 20,000 people. Izler Solomon conducted, and Harry Horner's production was truly spectacular. In such circumstances my opera took on the character of a great show for the people, just as I had tried to make it in Jerusalem. Unfortunately, I wasn't able to be present at the radio performance of *David* in Hamburg, nor at any of the productions in French — the libretto's original language — at the Théâtre Royal de la Monnaie in Brussels.

A friend of mine told me that the cab-driver taking her to the Hollywood Bowl had said to her, on seeing my name in lights, 'Quite a guy, that Milhaud! More than eighty years old and he works in three places at once!' Eighty was, perhaps, a slight exaggeration, but it is true that I divide my time between California, Colorado and France, and that alternating between the three, far from tiring me out, stimulates my enthusiasm for work. So central are all three to my present-day mode-of-existence that when the young film producer Ralph Swickart wanted to make a film about me I suggested he should shoot it in those three places, plus, of course, Aix-en-

Provence, my home town. The film was quite short, and we called it *A Visit to Darius Milhaud*; I composed a Sonatina for Violin and Cello to accompany it. We filmed it during the course of 1954, and great fun it was too. They shot one sequence at the Music Academy of the West at Santa Barbara in which students asked me what I thought of teaching. They turned to Mills to illustrate my daily life and the way in which I compose: also in that sequence there is a surprise 'jam-session' arranged by my old students Dick Collins, Jack Weeks, William Smith, Dave Kriedt and Dave Brubeck, most of whom have become well known in the world of jazz. At Aspen they filmed my outings in a jeep and an orchestral rehearsal during which I conducted a student orchestra. Lastly, they filmed a sequence in my flat in Paris, with my son and my musician friends: Auric, Poulenc, Sauguet and Jane Bathori, a marvellous singer who created all our vocal works and who, her great age notwithstanding, continued to devote herself to the music of young composers. At the very end was a sequence with Paul Claudel. Our final meeting — alas! — testifying to forty years of friendship and affectionate collaboration. He had just proved yet again with what a modest and easygoing attitude he would accept modifications in a vocal setting of one of his texts. I had often noted a lack of proportion in my opera *Christophe Colomb* between the first part — epic and visual — and the second — interior, mystical and abstract. After the transports that ended the first Act, the audience could only experience a certain weariness faced with a second Act that was so static. Madeleine thought that one could perhaps transpose the two acts, the role of the Narrator allowing the unfolding of the action to be understood. I suggested to Claudel that we begin the opera with Columbus's disappointments, the terrible injustice to which he was victim after the discovery of America, and to end it with Columbus disembarking in the New World to the sound of the *Te Deum*. Straightaway Claudel said: '*Christophe Colomb* is yours! Do what you want with it!'

This new version was performed under Manuel Rosenthal during the 1956 International Festival. Sadly, Claudel was no longer with us! But his family and my friends saw for themselves, as we did, that this change improved the unfolding of the work immensely. From now on my opera *Christophe Colomb* will be given in this form.

I had wanted for a long time to visit the Indian reservations, and in September 1954 I finally did so. Our friends Vronsky and Babin invited us to spend several days on their charming ranch at Santa Fe in New Mexico. We couldn't imagine better or more knowledgeable guides in Indian culture and civilisation! They took us to visit eleven Pueblo Indian reservations. This contact with a primitive and intact civilisation took us centuries back in time. The ceramics and pottery manufactured in each village are inspired by pre-Colombian forms; the dances, accompanied by chanting in unison and drum rhythms, seem never to have changed. . . . What contradictions and contrasts there are in Indian life, however! Their pagan rituals are held in the village square in front of an altar on which a statue of the Virgin Mary or of the village's patron saint has been placed, and during the week these enthusiastic dancers, with their vividly painted bodies, adorned with feathers and foxes' tails, become typical American workers, mostly employed at the large atomic centre at Los Alamos!

During the summer a Benedictine monk, Father Nicholson, had written to me asking me to compose a mass reviving the tradition — of which Victoria and Palestrina were such brilliant exponents — of alternating Gregorian chant with free polyphony. Not being a Catholic, I didn't feel able to write a mass, but as Father Nicholson was insistent, I decided to go to see him in Oregon. For three hundred kilometres the road from California to Oregon crosses an impressive forest sheltering a species of the rarest trees, the Redwoods. Some of them are more than two thousand years old and grow to more than 100 metres; their swarthy trunks are like the enormous plinths of gigantic columns.

The convent of Mount Angel looks over a delightful valley scattered with small farms. All these homes, as well as those in the village, are inhabited by the descendants of Swiss catholics who left their native land at the same time as the monks of the Benedictine convent and followed them all the way to Mount Angel in Oregon. The Benedictines are generous hosts; they put us up in a small apartment, and we took our meals in a private dining room with Father Nicholson. I explained my point of view to him. 'But', he said, 'Bach and Stravinsky weren't Roman Catholics, and they both composed a mass.' After a while we reached an agreement. Together we chose three Psalms and I set to work as soon as I reached Mills College. What I found especially interesting was to link a verse in Gregorian chant with a verse in free polyphony. This particularly delicate stylistic question gave me the idea of setting it as an exercise for my Conservatoire pupils.

Meanwhile I was continuing to compose symphonies: the Fifth was commissioned by the Italian Radio; the Sixth by Charles Münch, for the sixty-fourth anniversary of the Boston Symphony; and the Seventh was written for the Belgian Radio. The Belgian Radio Orchestra had been invited to perform in Venice, under Franz André, and wanted to play new works: a symphony by Sauguet and a Concerto for Orchestra by Tansman completed the programme.

I owe many satisfying artistic experiences to Italy, a country I have gone back to several times in recent years. The Rome Opera put on *Sagesse* and *Christophe Colomb*; *Bolivar* was staged at the San Carlo in Naples, *Les Malheurs d'Orphée* in Venice, and *Le Pauvre Matelot* and *David* at La Scala, Milan. I conducted the first performance of my Fifth Symphony for the Turin Radio; several musician friends came from Rome, Milan and Venice. I was seeing them for the first time since the war, and it was a great pleasure to make contact with them again. One of them, the eminent musicologist Luigi Rognoni, passed on to me some small notebooks that had belonged to one of his Sinigaglia forbears, containing tunes from the Piedmont region assembled by him after years of research. When Claude Delvincourt asked me to write a short cello piece for the winner of the prize that Piatigorsky bestows each year on an old pupil of the Conservatoire, I made use of some of these Piedmontese tunes, and called the piece *Suite cisalpine*.

Claude Delvincourt was an excellent director of the Conservatoire. He surrounded the students with care and affection, supporting them selflessly and courageously, trying to obtain for them scholarships, commissions and jobs. He died, sadly, in a car accident on his way back to Rome. The students and professors at the Conservatoire quickly realized the irreparable loss they had sustained.

If Italy forms part of the Mediterranean heritage that is so dear to me, it represents an essential element in my son's life through his many long visits there. What marvellous memories I have of Venice: going around, visiting concerts, museums and the theatre, one delightful pursuit after another. Unfortunately I fell ill some weeks later. Forced by a long attack of rheumatism to stay at home, I sensed for the first time the approach of old age, and, also for the first time, I did not have the strength to compose. I could not move except with the aid of two nurses and went out only in exceptional circumstances. I was carried to the Palais de Chaillot for the performance of my cantata *Le Château du feu*, which I insisted on conducting. I had set the magnificent text by Jean Cassou specially for this concert organized by the 'Réseau du Souvenir', an organization, founded by Mme Christian Lazard, whose aim was to keep alive the memory of those who had suffered deportation. Mme Lazard has already succeeded in having a national day in memory of the Deportation instituted by the government. The 'Réseau du Souvenir' also intends to commission paintings and sculptures inspired by this appalling subject.

Some weeks later, I had to be carried to the home of the oldest friend in my musical life. Arthur Honegger had just died, and I wanted to see him for the last time. I knew that his heart condition had threatened his existence for many years, but he displayed such energy that I thought he would keep this cruel illness at bay for a long time yet. He often came to see me. Three weeks before his death, we spent a long afternoon alone together, as so often before. As his voice was weak and his breathing laboured, I repeatedly had to draw close to him to make out what he was saying. His death was the first among Les Six, and a grievous blow to all of us. We were united by a friendship so strong and so fraternal that his death was heartbreaking for us all. But how intrusive and ruthless our mechanized civilization is! No sooner had Pascale Honegger told me of her father's death than the radio people invaded my apartment, placing a microphone by my bed so that I could make a statement; journalists rang to ask for my impressions and memories of him ... the television people begged me to introduce a documentary about Arthur, which went out on the very evening of his burial. I took every opportunity of talking about my wonderful friend. It was only some weeks later, when the shock of the news had receded, that I could collect myself to compose a piece of chamber music in his memory: my Fourth String Quintet (with two cellos), made up of four movements: 1, Lament on the death of a friend; 2, Memories of youth; 3, The beauty of a long friendship; 4, Hymn of praise. The first performance was given on Brussels Radio, as part of an evening devoted to Arthur. And before I went back to America, Andrée Honegger came to ask me if I would become President of the Académie du Disque français in succession to Arthur. I was profoundly touched and accepted.

In spite of grief and anxiety, 1955 was much brightened by Daniel's marriage to Nicole. The nearness of our two children was an extraordinary blessing for me. How good it is, on the threshold of old age, to feel life continuing!

Chapter Thirty-Seven

1956–1962

We continued to divide our time between France, California and Colorado, and I hope will do so for many more years.

When we came back to Europe, every other year, we spent the month of September with Daniel and Nicole. Their son David was born in February 1958 and the art of being a grandfather holds no more secrets for me. They were living at that time in Florence; as I particularly enjoyed driving, we packed ourselves into our children's 2CV enthusiastically. The wildest and most deserted Tuscan roads became familiar to us.

In 1957 we joined Daniel and his wife in Switzerland; they had rented a small place at Vex, beneath the Mayens-de-Sion where we had spent several summers before the war. Daniel had returned to a region familiar from his childhood, but above all to be close to his teacher, Oskar Kokoschka. Daniel had known him for a long time, and had often attended his summer schools in Salzburg. They drew students from all over the world, for the kindness and solicitude of this great artist were as legendary as the perfection of his teaching.

I was particularly happy to visit Kokoschka at his home at Villeneuve, where he was surrounded by his marvellous canvases. His huge *oeuvre*, so expressive, has left a deep impression on the art of our century, yet, by some inexplicable aberration, it is appreciated everywhere except in France, where it is more or less unknown and even, perhaps, wilfully misunderstood.

While we were exploring the area of Le Valais, between Lake Geneva and the sources of the Rhône, I became convinced that my Eighth Symphony should be called *La Rhodanienne*. It had been commissioned by the University of California, at Berkeley, for the inauguration of a new concert hall. I had no formal scheme for the symphony until I heard Smetana's

Vltava, which depicts picturesque and folk elements unfolding on the banks of that river, and it dawned on me that I too had a river to hymn: the Rhône. So it was that my Eighth Symphony came into being. First, amongst mist, clouds and wind, the stream is born in the high Alps; then the gentle crossing of Lake Geneva, which inspired me to write a calm, slow second movement; the sweep of the huge, impetuous river influenced the third, a rustic, violent scherzo, and the finale was clearly inspired by the Rhône meeting the Mediterranean, where the divided river enfolds my beloved Camargue in a delta.

Since that time I have composed four more symphonies: the Ninth at the request of a young conductor, Mario di Bonaventura, for the Fort Lauderdale Orchestra in Florida; and the Tenth in honour of the centenary of the State of Oregon. In the finale of the Tenth I introduced a seven-note theme corresponding to the letters of the word OREGON by way of a specific reference. It was conducted by Piero Bellugi.

My Eleventh Symphony, commissioned by the Dallas Symphony Orchestra and Public Library, was conducted by Paul Kletzki. This particular concert happened to coincide with a composers' conference at which I chaired the debates. As for the Twelfth, *La Rurale*, it crowned the efforts of a young composer called Jerome Rosen who, on his return from Paris, where he had spent two years as winner of the Prix de Paris, had been given the task of founding a department of music at Davis. This part of the University of California concentrated on rural economics, but such was Rosen's success that they had just inaugurated a 2,500-seat concert hall, in which Enrique Jorda conducted my new symphony, written for the occasion.

I have been very lucky in that all my symphonies have been premiered shortly after their composition. However, I have often found myself in situations that could have discouraged me, had not fifty years in music thickened my skin against knocks.

After much to-ing and fro-ing and meetings with Albert Vidalie, we wrote a ballet for Roland Petit, whose involvement throughout our discussions took in the minutest details. *La Rose des vents* included several songs that I composed in a deliberately very simple style for that exquisite dancer Zizi Jeanmaire. The show went on, but without any explanation the songs were cut. Roland Petit promised to reinstate them. This did not happen during the season in Paris. That left New York. . . . I was assured that Zizi would sing them in America. Needless to say, she did not.

Around the time of the centenary of *Mireille*, André Chamson offered me a marvellous libretto, based on Provençal folklore, which had depth and a dramatic quality and avoided the picturesque. Its title, *La Branche des oiseaux*, was taken from an old Provençal proverb which says: 'the highest branch of trees is only for birds and poets'. André Chamson was assured that the ballet would be staged at Orange in August 1959, and thereafter at the

Paris Opéra. I received letters and telegrams from the Ministry of Fine Arts asking me to expedite my work. The summer of 1959 came to an end without any performance of the ballet. We were still convinced that the Opéra would meet its obligations. Yves Brayer's designs were already being worked on, and so was the choreography, which had been entrusted to Georges Skibine; but Monsieur Julien, Director of the National Lyric Theatres, wrote to me every three months to inform me that the performance of the ballet had been postponed yet again. The result was that *La Branche des oiseaux*, without any rhyme or reason, never got staged at all.

Another infuriating experience: some years before, the director of the Opéra had encouraged me to compose *Vendanges*, a ballet by Philippe de Rothschild and Salvador Dalí, but never followed up his own suggestion!

Another experience brought me into contact with the theatrical jungle that is Broadway. Eric Bentley, who has translated many of Brecht's plays, had set up a production on an ostensibly serious basis. He wanted to present *Mother Courage* on Broadway with new songs. It was decided to draw up the contract before I left for New York. Some weeks later, in a hotel room (I would never have imagined that something so apparently simple would require so much negotiation), Eric Bentley's lawyer, the producer's and my own — my close friend Morton Miller, for whose tireless exertions on my behalf I was once more grateful — tried to define the terms of our collaboration. After a long day spent in whisperings, asides and conferrings, the contract was finally drawn up. All that remained was for me to write the songs. I enjoyed this huge job enormously but it ruined my holiday. I was bombarded with telegrams and new texts, as my collaborator frequently changed them . . . then the stage director David Brook begged me to send him a tape so that he could work out the exact movements. It was not easy to find a tape-recorder in Florence in high summer; fortunately an American institution run by nuns placed one at my disposal. Surrounded by the good sisters, in a husky voice, I recorded all my songs in an attempt to lighten my collaborators' burden, for I was well aware that in New York, the producer, the stage director, the scenic artists and performers were all fussing like mad over *Mother Courage*. At this point an unexpected intervention from Bertolt Brecht's son, a Harvard professor, put an end to the rehearsals! He was even going to begin a legal action that eventually fizzled out a year later. So much for *Mother Courage* on Broadway!

I ought to have forbidden the use of my music, or rather what was left of it, in the performances of Giradoux's *Judith* at the Théâtre de France, but I did not want to create problems for Jean-Louis Barrault, whom I like and admire. He had paid me the compliment of asking me to write incidental music. He had supplied me with an imposing list of musical cues which seemed to me somewhat disproportionate. In spite of my troubles — I had sustained some injuries in an accident in Naples, and my knees were extremely painful — I undertook this long and laborious but nevertheless interesting task. In line with Jean-Louis's wishes, it seemed to me necessary to write for two separate instrumental groups: one made up of musicians who would play at each performance, the other group pre-recorded on tape. I know that in the theatre one has to make changes to certain music cues to accord with the needs of the production: my long collaboration with Dullin had prepared me for that. So, when Jean-Louis came to see me to ask me to take out a substantial part of the music, I was not pleased, but I regarded it as normal procedure. So the live orchestra was scrapped and all the music was pre-recorded. I went to the dress rehearsal in an ambulance. Actors are always terrified of music! The person responsible for working the tape-recorder set the volume control almost at zero, and I could hear either nothing or next to nothing! I understood even less of what was going on than I had at a top-quality performance, under Pierre Boulez's direction, of Claudel's *Christophe Colomb* (with my incidental music), which was staged so wonderfully by Jean-Louis.

Over recent years I have been asked to compose four occasional contatas, but I have always been allowed to choose the form or the text myself.

The French government commissioned a work for the concert that took place in the Grand Place in Brussels for the inauguration of Expo 1958. I chose some fragments from the *Tragiques* by Agrippa d'Aubigné. The poetry of that period is sufficiently free to allow considerable rhythmic variety in the setting. The government sent the chorus and orchestra of the Opéra to Brussels to perform Florent Schmitt's *Psalm 47* and my *Tragédie humaine* under Louis Fourestier. Unfortunately, there is no way of avoiding the inherent problem of most open-air performances, and according to what my friends told me, one's aural impression was good or bad, or accompanied by a very disagreeable echo, depending on where one sat!

The department of music at the University of Iowa organized a four-day festival of my works and commissioned a cantata for chorus and orchestra, in English, for the occasion. I always feel somewhat inhibited when dealing with a poem written in a foreign language. In French, when I displace an accent for dramatic effect, I do so with an easy mind, but in a foreign language the smallest misaccentuation seems like a mistake. This seriously limits my freedom. I chose three fine poems by Chaucer and felt very much at ease with the superb English of the fifteenth century. I was very surprised, on arriving at the city of Iowa, to find a university with six thousand students, an orchestra, a marvellous choir, and an excellent opera school which put on my three tiny one-acters with enormous care.

The State of Israel organized a festival at the end of August 1961. I was asked to write a work for chorus and orchestra based on the Bible. I have written pieces of this sort so often that I did not know which scriptural episode to choose.

Then I had the good fortune to meet Rabbi Edouard Zerin at Aspen. He pointed out to me that 1961 was the thirteenth anniversary of the political resurrection of the State of Israel, with its religious majority. He suggested that I write a cantata inspired by this concept. Jewish boys have their religious initiation (barmitzvah) at the age of thirteen. During the ceremony, they are required to intone an extract from the Torah; in religious services, the reading from the Torah is always followed by a section (Haphtarah) made up of a fragment taken from the book of the prophets. I asked Rabbi Zerin to select a text in the Saturday morning service containing an allusion to the prophecy which foretells the reconstruction of the State of Israel. Quite by chance he suggested the very passages that I had read at my own barmitzvah, on September 16, 1905. This moving coincidence gave a genuine exaltation to my task. Unfortunately I knew no Hebrew, but my friend Dr Rinder marked the prosody of my text, making my job much easier.

If I tend to prefer setting liturgical or ancient texts, it is because I am so conscious of the difficulties faced by publishers of contemporary works when I ask an author to provide me with a specially-written text, the complications in such cases being very real.

Most radio stations celebrated the anniversary of the founding of the International Red Cross at the battle of Solferino on May 8, 1859. In 1959 France paid homage to this great institution, and I was asked to compose a cantata for this occasion. I turned to Loys Masson. He soon gave me a superb poetic text, overwhelming in its religious profundity. I scored the *Cantate de la croix de charité* for orchestra, tenor, bass, soprano, mixed chorus and children's chorus. I heard the broadcast in Brussels, at the home of Jeanne Collaer. The concert was preceded by a lengthy introduction in which announcers from various radio stations spoke in their own languages. It made a deeply moving impression, this chain linked by human charity bringing together radio stations from Africa, Asia, America . . . in fact from all over the world.

The Cork Festival in Ireland brings foreign choirs together every year. I composed for Cork an unaccompanied chorus on a poem by Verlaine, *Traversée*, of which I was especially fond. The poem had appeared in the Pléiade edition, but was almost unknown, as was frequently demonstrated when Madeleine used to amuse herself by reading it to various friends, writers or poets, and none of them guessed the author; they assumed it to be a contemporary poet. I had to pick my performers for Cork. I asked Yvonne Gouverné, who has always served the cause of choral music with so much talent and devotion, to assemble and rehearse the singers. She turned to the 'Madrigal' of the French Radio.

Shortly after this I wrote a violin concerto for the competition sponsored by Queen Elisabeth of the Belgians. In her honour I revived the title 'Concert royal', borrowing it from Couperin. I had been asked for a twenty-minute piece, but they forgot to tell me that the contestants had only a week to learn it. In my view a concerto *must* be very difficult so as to display fully the abilities of virtuoso players. This one was full of technical difficulties, and made the young violinists indignant — quite unnecessarily so, to judge from the excellent performance given by the winner, Jaime Larredo.

The many developments in technique and musical language in the postwar era have never affected me. Had I ever been tempted by the twelve-tone system, it would have been forty years ago, when Schoenberg started putting his theories into practice. Nevertheless, I accept the need for young people to study these developments. I was very glad to have in my class at the Conservatoire four highly talented young people: Betsy Jolas, Gilbert Amy, Claude Lefebvre and Jean-Claude Eloy. They express themselves naturally in every possible kind of serialism. If I take pleasure in naming them, it is because I sincerely hope that my confidence in them will prove to be well founded in the years to come.

If I have not followed fashion, I have instead drawn closer to some of my earlier works, those dating from the time of my polytonal experiments. I revived my style from the period of my six Chamber Symphonies when I wrote the *Aspen Serenade*, which I gave at the Aspen Festival in 1957.

In 1920 I composed some 'essays' that have never been published (apart from one brief exercise that appeared in the 1921 Cocagne Almanach). These consisted of phrases of varying lengths for four clarinets, repeated and played for however long was required. In the same way that the facets of a kalei-doscope show us a picture that changes with each turn, each instrumental reprise was different. I grafted onto these foundations a melodic line that the singer was free to begin *ad libitum*. When this melody had been completed, the clarinettists had merely to concentrate on the end of their melodic line, holding on to the last note until a final chord had been built up. I called these repeated and interwoven phrases 'cadenzas', because like cadenzas, they must be free and relaxed. Also at this time I wrote a setting of *Aérogyne femme volante* (a poem by Jean Cocteau), on the same principle, in which seven instruments launch into lively cadenzas, but I have mislaid the manuscript.

I took this expressive device up again in 1954, when I went to the Musique Concrète studio in Paris to create a musical montage, the *Etude poétique*. I constructed this piece using seven tapes (four cadenzas in different keys played by a small group of soloists: a song to words by Claude Roy for voice and two saxophones; a recording of the same song, unaccompanied; and a recording of the two saxophone parts on their own). My collaborator in these operations was Jean-Etienne Marie, and I derived much enjoyment from them. Unfortunately the studio was on the second floor and there was no lift, so I could only go there when my legs permitted — which did not always coincide with the availability of the studio! These complications eventually stopped me from making my own experimentations in real musique concrète.

For the five-hundredth anniversary of the printing of the Gutenberg Bible, the noted publisher Draeger wanted to give his customers a special set of records as a New Year's gift. I wrote a small, lightweight fantasy to a charming libretto by Max Gérard: *Le Mariage de la feuille et du cliché*. The performance, conducted by Pierre-Michel Le Comte, involved singers both from opera and music-hall, an actress, an orchestra and musique concrète. With considerable care I made a selection of the distinctive sounds of some of Draeger's printing machines (some of which even supplied a characteristic rhythm with which to begin a song), I measured the exact duration and asked Pierre Henry to give them the required sonority at the Musique Concrète studio.

Last summer, on the occasion of his sixtieth birthday, I sent the director of Universal Edition a piece based on a small Chinese poem called *Neige sur la fleuve*, in which I introduced two cadenzas for several instruments each playing to different metronome speeds. Quite recently, in developing my cadenza studies, I wrote a cantata, *Suite de quatrains*, on eighteen quatrains by Francis Jammes, for speaker and seven instruments. The latter must start playing on particular syllables of the text and continue to play freely in such a way that, as I hope, every performance will be unique. I am reserving the première for Mills College, which is organizing a festival in honour of my seventieth birthday in May 1963. In fact 1962 is the year of my seventieth birthday. This marks the end of my teaching career at the Conservatoire, but the appointment of my friend Jean Rivier, who has long acted as my deputy, assuming responsibility for my class every other year, will ensure continuity. He will direct the class in the same spirit as myself.

Teaching at the Conservatoire is wonderful. The young people who enrol for the composition class have generally achieved remarkable distinction in harmony, fugue and counterpoint. Teaching composition involves, I believe, allowing them to liberate themselves from all the conventional formulae inevitably acquired over seven or eight years of study. Their teacher's task seems to me to consist in helping them, by a sort of cleansing process, to realize their often sensitive and refined personalities, which many years of strict but necessary exercises have prevented from flowering.

Life is hard and one cannot prevent young people from imagining that a Conservatoire prize will ease their way in the future; one should not imagine, however, that conformity smooths the working path after leaving the Conservatoire. And I know from experience that most of my pupils have obtained, thanks to the personality and even originality of their own works, important commissions, jobs and performances.

I have reached my age-limit at Mills College as well, but Dr Rothwell, the College's President, and the administration too, have asked me to continue teaching as long as I like. I have accepted with pleasure and gratitude, as I realize that such a decision is altogether exceptional in the American academic world. I shall, of course, continue to go to Europe every other year. I am delighted that Luciano Berio, whose remarkable qualities of lyricism and imagination I admire, shares the work at Mills with me.

Chapter Thirty-Eight

Seventy

The year began badly. Last September, while being pushed by a porter at the station in Naples, my wheelchair hit a stone and I was hurled to the ground on my knees. My sufferings were eased by the concerned consideration of my friends, however, as well as by the loyalty and care of many well-known and also unknown musicians, who organized celebrations for my birthday everywhere.

In 1957 I was prevented from going to conduct at the Musica Viva festival in Munich by a bad attack of flu. As this would have been my first concert in Germany since the war, I was hugely disappointed, but what can one do about Asian flu? Manuel Rosenthal, with his usual devotion, took over the programme for me. Undeterred, the director of Musica Viva, Dr Karl Amadeus Hartmann, asked me to come to Munich in January 1962. I didn't want to disappoint him twice. In spite of the difficulties of this sort of journey (I was still unable to stand), I set off. Dr Hartmann placed two Red Cross nurses at my disposal, and they carried me onto the podium. The Hartmanns were even kind enough to bring me my meals in the artists' room, and when I had two rehearsals on the same day we picnicked together. Everything went well. The concert drew a large audience, including many young listeners.

Dr Hartmann had asked for a programme of early works: *Agamemnon* (1913); *L'Homme et son désir* (1917); *Protée* (1918) and *La Création du monde* (1923). Claude Rostand came especially from Paris. He knew none of these pieces other than *La Création du monde*. The critics paid a lot of attention to *L'Homme et son désir*. As I divide the orchestra into six independent groups, and the percussion has a vital role, they regarded this piece, dating from 1918, as a forerunner of today's fashion for spatial music!

The aesthetics of the 1920s, which people used to laugh at or mention ironically, now inspire essays and studies. Many theses are written on Cubism, Dadaism and Surrealism, and even the poor old Six were fêted at the Hôtel de Ville in Paris. The President of the City Council had the nice idea of reuniting us with Jean Cocteau, and of conferring on us, on the fortieth anniversary of *Les Mariés de la tour Eiffel*, the Medal of the City of Paris!

I had longed to set *Tristesses*, a series of twenty-four poems by Francis Jammes, ever since I was young; but I had hesitated, afraid of being unable to sustain a long work of this character. I put it off for ages, but eventually got down to work in 1956. I had the song-cycle performed during one of the concerts that the Ecole Normale de Musique was kind enough to put on for me.

The Vega company asked me to record my Third Symphony and my Concerto for Two Pianos, with Ina Marika and Geneviève Joy, so I put them down on the programme of the Société des Concerts du Conservatoire — the first time since the war that I had been engaged by one of the Sunday concert societies. I have always been asked to conduct my most recent works on the radio, however, and am pleased to acknowledge its loyal support. In 1962, especially, I was treated with quite exceptional generosity; a long-standing supporter, Charles Bruck, conducted my Twelfth Symphony for Radio Strasbourg. Maurice Le Roux conducted a Milhaud Festival; Marius Constant and Micheline Banzet put on ten concerts during 'Milhaud Week', with some recordings as well.

Most of my operas have been performed on the French radio. In May 1962 Manuel Rosenthal conducted *Maximilien*, a work loathed by every musician at the 1932 première, while the critics took an almost sadistic delight in vilifying it. Now it is enthusiastically acclaimed, and I myself heard them saying: 'But this is one of your best scores! How on earth, etc.'

For the twenty-fifth anniversary of the Maîtrise de la Radio, that wonderful boys' and girls' choir, I composed *L'Invocation à l'ange Raphaël*. The performance, under Pierre Dervaux, was a model of its kind: children's voices, fresh and astringent at the same time, have an especially moving effect. I had long wanted to set parts of Paul Claudel's *Livre de Tobie et de Sarah*, and it was an enormous pleasure for me, as I was composing *L'Invocation à l'ange Raphaël*, which forms a part of it, to re-experience the sensation of being caught up in Claudel's characteristic poetic and rhythmic richness, which had become so familiar to me during our long collaboration.[1] Since Claudel's death I had kept in touch with Mme Claudel, his

[1] A collaboration that can be traced in our correspondence (*Cahiers de Paul Claudel*, vol. 3, Gallimard, Paris, 1961).

children and also his grandchildren. This year, in a friendly gesture, they organized a concert of some of my Claudel settings at Royaumont Abbey, in the presence of Her Majesty Queen Elisabeth of the Belgians.

I cannot draw up a balance sheet of all the celebrations marking my birthday. I can only say how much I appreciated them. . . . Léon Algazi invited me to conduct the first performance of my *Service sacré* and the *Cantate de l'initiation* at the synagogue in the rue de la Victoire. I had the pleasure of conducting two concerts in Brussels — a city where my music has been constantly played. At the start of the first concert Paul Collaer spoke a few words, with tact and feeling, touching me deeply. And each day brought further proofs: Marcel Mihalovici presented a concert on Radio Basle; Radio Frankfurt organized three discussions, with Claude Rostand as chairman; Radio Hamburg broadcast *David*; Radio Jerusalem devoted a programme to me, as did Radio Helsinki and the Vancouver Festival! The New York Philharmonic commissioned an overture to commemorate my birthday and the inauguration of their new concert hall at the Lincoln Center; three acts of *David* were performed by the San Francisco Symphony; *Médée* and *'adame Miroir* at Mills College; and the Paris Opéra, now happily entrusted to the care of Georges Auric, revived *Bolivar*. The Aix-en-Provence Festival puts on *Les Malheurs d'Orphée* this summer. I went there at Easter, as Monsieur Bigonnet's guest at the Hôtel du Roi René, to settle various details relating to the performance.

I had grown used to not having a house in Aix, but it was depressing to see for myself the changes inevitably wrought by the development of a rapidly expanding town and the needs of urbanization. There is nothing left of L'Enclos apart from a few trees. It is a new district altogether. I was surprised to discover that the council have named an avenue after me, a reminder that I had spent a good part of my life in the vicinity.

I was unable to attend the production of *Les Malheurs d'Orphée*, due to a longstanding commitment to the Aspen Festival. In Aspen itself the Mayor declared that July 14 (Bastille Day, as the Americans call it) would be designated a holiday in my honour. Inspired by Thérèse David, one of its most active citizens, the whole town took part in this friendly celebration. They organized a flea market, with stalls, fairground booths and tombola. They had their photographs taken with their heads in cardboard guillotines, made by the local doctor, and they sold just about everything; crêpes, records, French books, hot dogs. There were pony rides for the small children, while the bigger ones rode in the majestic fire engine . . . and the profits from all this were set aside to endow an international scholarship in my name at the Aspen Music School. In the evening, the Mayor presented me with the keys of Aspen, while a little girl festooned me with a large crown of aspen leaves. A group of young dancers performed a charming ballet and presented me with pictures which they had made themselves. A huge farandole and fireworks brought this memorable day to a close. The dancing continued for some time to the strains of an accordian band, for which Henri Sauguet (who had arrived the night before) had been more than happy to compose some of 'our sort' of tunes.

I was very grateful to the director of the Aspen Festival, Norman Singer, as well as the public relations people, for having invited Yvonne Loriod, Messiaen and Sauguet, the two polar opposites of French music. Their huge success added to the brilliance of the Festival which this summer honoured the old patriarch I had become!

Chapter Thirty-Nine

Friends and Nuisances

How hard it is to avoid the constant intrusion of nuisances who waste your time and stop you working! Like most composers I receive endless requests for photographs, autographs, envelopes with stamps showing composers, and whoever they might be, I am asked to put my name on the stamps. There are Americans who copy the final lines of various chapters of *Notes without Music* and ask me to sign them. And the questions! I have decided not to answer them any more. What I do on Sundays, whether I have a hobby or why I like Beethoven are of no concern to anyone! And then there are the unexpected visitors whom one hasn't seen for years. They never phone to announce their arrival: they just arrive. Sometimes they ask: 'Am I disturbing you?', and if I reply 'I'm working!', it doesn't stop them from making themselves at home and, very frequently, inflicting interminable compositions on me — for they almost always have records or tapes with them. It's like being at a performance of Molière's *Les Fâcheux*!

I love to see friends or my old pupils, however. I am always curious about their work. In Paris, visits give me even more pleasure since, living on the mezzanine floor, I rarely go out. Besides, where would I go? It's difficult to park the car and even to move about. At Mills it's completely different: the car comes right up to the door, I feel totally free and take full advantage of it! We go regularly to the theatre, the cinema, to restaurants — above all Chinese restaurants. Chinatown, even though it has lost some of its character, is always of interest to visiting friends. San Francisco attracts many artists, performers and actors, and many of them come to see us at Mills College. When Monsignor Maillet returned from his tour of Japan, he brought his Petits Chanteurs to dine with us. We gathered tea-chests and boxes for them to sit on, and the meal was very jolly. It ended with a concert, the children singing beneath our windows. Monsignor Maillet told me that crossing the time zone on the voyage made him 'lose' Good Friday, and he had been very worried about the children. 'But Monsignor', I said to console him, 'if you had gone in the other direction, you would have had two!'

Neighbouring universities would often invite foreign composers to teach and take part in concerts of their works. We were happy to take advantage of their proximity. It was in this way that we got to know Earle Brown, whom I had invariably missed in Paris and of whom Betsy Jolas had spoken with affection. Dallapiccola taught at Berkeley for a term and often came to see us. One day I mentioned an article by him that had appeared in an Italian review, in which he described having discovered features in Mozart which were taken up at the beginning of this century by the Expressionists, especially in Austria: for example the use of very large intervals, sometimes even a tenth in the vocal line. I amused myself by asking him if he knew the twelve-note row in the second scene with the Commendatore in *Don Giovanni* — I had quoted it in *David* because of the dramatic similarity (when, after the Bathsheba episode, David hears from the prophet Nathan what his punishment is to be). Dallapiccola was pretty sceptical until I showed him the score, then he had to accept the evidence: the melody here has a quite unexpected curve forming a nine-note series that can be completed by taking three notes from the bass. Dallapiccola then asked me to write an open letter to the review in which his article had appeared. Reading my letter inspired Roman Vlad to write variations on this twelve-note row by Mozart.

The English composer Humphrey Searle and his charming wife often came to see us. An ex-pupil of Webern working at Stanford, Searle was a rigorous exponent of the twelve-note system. Madeleine put on his opera *The Diary of a Madman* at Aspen. Based on Gogol, it was a work of great dramatic momentum, much enhanced and intensified, in the purest Expressionist tradition, by the use of taped electronic music.

Even though a considerable distance separates my works from today's avant-garde, I like to broaden my knowledge of the swiftly changing language of contemporary music. . . . After the war, the young were completely besotted with serialism; forty years later, it appeared to take root, with its limitations and technical amenities, without harming the imaginative faculty. Returning to France in 1948 I had mentioned this growing dodecaphonic influence to Schoenberg: 'Ach so! so!' he replied thoughtfully, 'but do these young composers put music into it?' Now, thanks to the conquering strength of Xenakis, serial musicians feel themselves pushed to one side. The development of musique concrète and electronic music opens new possibilities and attracts the young in particular. There are many centres for electronic music in the United States, and I myself insisted that there should be one at Mills College. Before using this means of expression, however, students should acquire a strong technique. Technique does not inhibit, it liberates. When Jean-Claude Eloy visited the Centre at the College, he admitted that even though he had never been drawn towards electronic music, he had spent at least four years studying it. Unfortunately our young fanatics press buttons at random, creating sounds without knowing why, and the unforeseeable results satisfy and enchant only them.

Luciano Berio, who founded the Studio in Milan, has worked in it for years. When he composes a purely electronic work, or one with voices (such as *Visage*), or if he mixes electronic elements with an orchestra, singers and speaker (as in *Laborintus II*), his complete mastery allows him to realize fully what he has set out to achieve. In my opinion, Berio is one of the finest composers of his generation, the only one with a sense of lyricism. Moreover — and this is rare — he has a generous spirit. He dedicated his opera *Passaggio* to me because he admires certain works of mine — such as *Les Choëphores* or *La Mort du tyran* — that influenced his own early experiments.

I don't think Stockhausen has such a generous spirit. I had the pleasure of having him in my class at the Conservatoire for a few months in 1952, as a listening student. I didn't meet him subsequently, until he taught in California, at Davis, when I had occasion to see him several times; I even introduced him in a concert of his works at Mills. Stockhausen is charming, pleasant, seductive. He amused me greatly when he leafed through the score of my Piano Quartet, which I had just received from my publisher, for in spite of his politeness he couldn't help saying: 'How odd that people still write like this!'

Many young musicians either repudiate or do not know — or claim not to know — music written before their own. They make exceptions: Debussy's *Jeux* alone among his works is not taboo. For myself, who adore the whole of Debussy, I have never been able to account for this particular choice. There are, however, young composers who are less sectarian. . . . I was extremely pleased to get to know Theodore Antoniou, who taught successfully at Stanford. He played me most of his compositions and showed a keen interest in mine. This young Greek has a lot of talent; he employs the most up-to-date means of expression deriving from graphic or aleatoric notation using tape.

My first ventures into the field of aleatoric music date from 1920. For some years I have tended to revive the style of some of my early works, bringing to it, I hope, greater maturity. I blended aleatoric with fixed elements in the second part of my String Septet. Then I took these experiments a bit further, giving different metronome markings to the fixed and aleatoric elements in the third part of *Musique pour Graz*. When Marius Constant asked me for a piece for the wonderful group he directs so imaginatively and with such total mastery, I wrote *Musique pour Ars Nova*. In each movement there are always certain instruments forming a separate aleatoric group; in each piece also, the metronome markings are always different for the contrasting groups.

I would be tempted to agree with Picasso's statement: 'Fashion is what I make unfashionable', and have gone on working without any concern as to what may be 'in' one day and 'out' the next. I am grieved to detect a real anxiety among composers of about 35 or 40 when they find that those younger than themselves label them as having moved from the avant-garde to the arrière-garde! I am no more pleased when a composer wants to please the public at any price. Benjamin Britten came to Aspen to receive an award, a considerable sum made available to him by a Maecenas who felt that there were artists who did not qualify for a Nobel Prize who should nevertheless be rewarded. Britten made a speech before a large assembly, and I was shocked to hear him say that he composed in accordance with the taste of his audiences. A composer of his stature ought not to make concessions to win 'the people's vote'. In any case the public is often very ungrateful and quickly forgets what it was that it has been enthusiastic about. To make amends, it sometimes discovers something unknown or misunderstood during an artist's lifetime. This is true of Satie, who died in poverty, and is now played non-stop, snippets of his music being used constantly in the cinema or on the radio. They write theses on him in England and the United States. It is also true of Charles Koechlin, most of whose compositions are still unpublished. All it needed was for Dorati to record *Les Bandar-Log* between a piece by Boulez and one by Messiaen to intrigue those musicians in England who bombarded me with questions about him: 'What sort of man was he?' I was happy to recall this modest, gentle soul who never made any concessions. It was the same with Charles Ives, discovered after so many years of neglect. And Varèse too! And Paul Claudel. Pleasantly surprised by the recent success of one of his plays, he wrote to me: 'I think I have a good future.' He had just celebrated his seventy-seventh birthday!

Chapter Forty

Ecumenical Matters

At the age of 71 I had the pleasure of seeing the whole of the *Orestie* performed! I was afraid I never would. *Agamemnon, Les Choëphores*[1] and *Les Euménides* had been given in concert and on the radio (especially *Les Choëphores*), but the trilogy had never been staged in its entirety until the Berlin Opera took the initiative. So as to keep the performance to a reasonable length, the text between the musical sections of *Agamemnon* and *Les Choëphores* was cut. *Les Euménides*, of course, remained in the form in which I had conceived it, as a three-act opera. The action was perfectly clear and comprehensible, the whole logically drawn together by the director Zellner and the painter Raffaelli. He had conceived a vertical décor, so that the action could unfold on several planes while remaining firmly unified from a stylistic point of view. Hermann Scherchen was suggested as the conductor, which delighted me since this old friend had shown a good understanding of my music over many years. But he wanted me to make changes (such as the unwelcome addition of electronic music) as well as cuts. I had no objection to cuts provided that I could approve them or, better, that I made them myself, but I couldn't allow any changes. Scherchen dug his heels in. For him there was no alternative: all or nothing. I refused, he withdrew. But he didn't hold it against me. When I met him again in Milan some weeks later, we fell into each other's arms, and he remained loyal to my music until his death. Hollreiser conducted the *Orestie* instead, with fire and precision, respecting all my intentions.

I owe a debt of true gratitude to the Berlin Opera, for the performances of *Christophe Colomb* in 1930, and those of the *Orestie* count among the most

[1] *Les Choëphores* was staged at the Monnaie in Brussels in 1935.

satisfying of my entire career, the more so as I knew that it would be impossible to mount these two works in France. During the intervals of the *Orestie*, some members of the audience came up to me and recalled *Christophe Colomb*, which seems to have particularly impressed them. A stagehand who had been in charge of the lighting brought me a programme: how had these few pages managed to escape the wholesale destruction of Berlin? This good fellow was undergoing hospital treatment and had obtained permission to come out that afternoon to be present at the performance of the *Orestie*.

On returning to Paris I was visited by Michel de Bry, the Secretary and presiding spirit of the Académie du Disque français. He spoke with enthusiasm of the encyclical of Pope John XXIII, which had just appeared, and tried to convince me to draw inspiration from it for a choral work. His idea seemed idiotic. Collaborating with a pope! What insurmountable difficulties that might involve! Michel de Bry was unimpressed by my arguments and made me promise to read the encyclical forthwith. It made a profound impression on me, laying bare the injustice of our society and upholding all my most cherished beliefs. I began to think seriously about De Bry's project, but it seemed to me unrealizable, and moreover I knew that it was forbidden to shorten a papal of liturgical text. De Bry, always dedicated and dynamic, offered to make the necessary approaches to Rome. He obtained all the appropriate authorizations from the Vatican: the right to select extracts from the encyclical for a choral symphony, to edit them and express them in my own way. The only stipulation, made in order to underline the ecumenical character of this event, was that the Vatican wanted the first performance to be conducted by a Protestant.[2] There was nothing left but for me to set to work.

Inspired by the sentiments of this great patriarch, who fiercely attacked discrimination, racism, injustice, the threat to liberty and atomic weapons, and expressed a fervent desire for world peace, I wrote *Pacem in Terris* between July 7 and August 6.

Henri Barraud had often commissioned me to write for the radio station of which he was a director and requested that *Pacem in Terris* be performed at the inauguration of the ORTF concert hall. Münch conducted the first performance, as well as one given several weeks later at Notre-Dame, which was celebrating its eight-hundredth anniversary. The presence of the papal legate, cardinals and archbishops, the beauty of the church, the audience's concentration, the purity of the voices, all gave this performance a deep intensity and the true sense of its meaning.

After a brief visit to Florence to make the acquaintance of my grand-

[2] My publisher, Mme Salabert, is Orthodox Jewish, and the recording of *Pacem in Terris* was conducted by Maurice Abravanel in the Mormon Tabernacle, Salt Lake City.

daughter, Solange, who had the charming notion of being born on March 22, like Madeleine, I returned to Berlin to conduct some of my works with the Philharmonic. I had asked the orchestra's director, Monsieur Streseman, if I could share the programme with Serge Baudo, because I no longer had the strength to undertake an entire concert. To our great astonishment, we learned that the orchestra's principal players had the contractual right to refuse to play except under their designated conductor, Herr von Karajan; we were, therefore, incredibly, deprived of the best musicians in the orchestra!

The end of my visit was saddened by the announcement on the radio of the death of Jean Cocteau. Jean, friend and witness of those mad years of our youth! Jean, that heart of gold, shining with intelligence and spirit! Together with Henri Sauguet we went to gather around his tomb. A mixed crowd of young and old, peasants and workers, filed silently in front of the little church at Milly which Jean had decorated himself. In the physic garden, individual flowers were placed alongside a multitude of small posies and enormous bouquets sent by associations of every sort. Jean's kindness, unselfishness and generosity were legendary. He was loved by everyone!

What a sad autumn it was! On November 23 President Kennedy was assassinated. The conductor of the Oakland Symphony, Gerhardt Samuel, sent a telegram asking me to write something in homage that could be played at the next concert, on December 2. I wrote *Meurtre d'un grand chef d'Etat* on November 25. I sent it straight off to Samuel, who prepared the orchestral material. The piece was played as planned on December 2, then repeated.

Monsieur Valcarenghi, director of the house of Ricordi, had been asking me to write an opera for a long time. I thought of Beaumarchais's *La Mère coupable*, the play that completes the cycle which begins with *Le Barbier de Séville* and continues with *Le Mariage de Figaro*. It concerns the same characters, now older, wiser and perhaps more human. Its subtitle is '*Le Nouveau Tartuffe*', because in it Beaumarchais introduces a treacherous character, Begaers, who tries to ruin Count Almaviva for his own ends: Figaro alone manages to thwart his wicked schemes. Valcarenghi asked Madeleine for a synopsis of the play, and after acquainting himself with it he asked her to provide the libretto. She reduced the five long acts to three, speeded up the action, arranged the effects — the 'suspense' — employing nothing but Beaumarchais's actual text. *La Mère coupable* was staged at the Grand Théâtre in Geneva. Dr Herbert Graf showed perfect understanding during the preparation of the production and was always ready to accept my suggestions. The production was in the hands of Louis Ducreux and the scenery by Malclès. Serge Baudo conducted. Up to their eyes in previous engagements, two very famous singers did not have time to learn their roles.

We were very worried, but fortunately a last-minute miracle happened. Our singers' beautiful voices, and their great talent, made me forget my anxiety. An ORTF television team came all the way to Geneva (they had followed my every move that summer, to Aix and to Basle, where I had attended an excellent performance of *Les Malheurs d'Orphée*). Pierre Vozlinski and Jacques Trebouta were making a film for the series '*L'Homme et sa musique*'. They had begun it in Paris while I was rehearsing *Ode pour les morts des guerres* and had every intention of going to Aspen.

Ode pour les morts des guerres was commissioned by André Malraux, Minister of Cultural Affairs, in a spirit of ecumenicism. He had also approached a Catholic composer, Messiaen, and a Protestant, Migot. The titles of the movements of my Ode are: 1, Lament on the massacred civil populations; 2, Prayer for those who died in captivity and deportation; 3, Funeral hymn for those killed in battle.

I had been back at Mills College for some weeks when the New York representative of Italian radio telephoned me. He had been asked to invite me to be present at a concert at the Vatican during which my music would be played. I politely declined the invitation. The next day I received a very long telegram from the director of the Rome Radio Station asking me to reconsider my decision because Paul VI 'was absolutely counting' on my presence. He added that I would be seated near to His Holiness. Unable to discover any more information, I left for Rome without really knowing why, and it was only after I arrived that my friend Rieti told me that this was to be the first ecumenical concert. Stravinsky would represent the Russian Orthodox faith, Malipiero the Roman Catholic. As for the Protestants, a piece by Sibelius was to be played, as it was also his centenary. It was a memorable and very moving afternoon! We were in fact seated near the Pope, who rose after each piece to talk to the composer. Simply, and in a kindly manner, he thanked me for having come, as he knew that the journey was tiring for me. His demeanour — so different from the one I knew from photographs — impressed me very much, with its pentrating sweetness, full of promise and hope.

We were invited to dinner with Malipiero and Stravinsky by the director of the radio station. I hadn't met Igor for a very long time. I had been tempted to visit him on many occasions, but I would be told: 'He's going to conduct a concert at. . . .' or else 'We're leaving tomorrow for. . . .' I found him terribly changed, walking painfully and unsteadily. During the meal he felt unwell, and I shuddered to think that he was flying back to New York first thing in the morning.

I could never forget the affection he showed towards us and the feeling of anguish we felt on leaving him.

Chapter Forty-One

Music for . . .

To date I have composed over 430 works. Most of them are published, but by several firms, naturally, some of which must accept more responsibility than others. When I had just completed my Twelfth Symphony, one of these publishers, whose catalogue contained a large number of my works, said to me, 'Now that's enough!' I understood that he wanted to concentrate his efforts on avant-garde music, and didn't hold it against him.[1] Fortunately Monsieur Marietti, director of Maison Eschig, was willing to consider bringing out everything I offered him.

I did not stop writing symphonies, but a minor incident prompted me to give them other titles. Some years ago, after I had just conducted the Boston Symphony, one of my students entered my box with his grandmother. Once the usual compliments were over the grandmother said to me: 'All that is very nice but it is not music for Boston!' This comment amused me so much that in 1965, when Roman Totenberg commissioned me to write a piece for Boston University, I called it *Music for Boston*. And since then I have named certain pieces after the town or country that commissioned them. Thus there are: *Musique pour l'Indiana, Musique pour la Nouvelle-Orleans, Musique pour Prague, Musique pour Lisbonne*, etc. These titles are not related to memories or picturesque impressions, they are totally abstract. Anyway, do I not have an illustrious precedent?[2]

I had not been back to Prague since 1933. I retained an extraordinary impression of the city and was impressed anew, thirty years later, when I

---

[1] He nevertheless subsequently published two chamber pieces of mine.
[2] Perhaps the 'Prague' Symphony of Mozart is intended (Translators' note).

was invited to conduct *Musique pour Prague*, commissioned by the Spring Festival.

This organization's artistic efforts defeat the imagination: three concerts a day, recitals, opera performances, shows of various kinds, all without any political restriction or constraint.[3] Artists of every nationality — many Americans among them — follow one another over a period of several weeks. Czech journalists were intrigued when I confided to them that I was going to write a contata on a text by Comenius. It was, it must be said, purely by chance. Julien Cain had asked me for a piece to celebrate twenty-five years of UNESCO. The ideas of the seventeenth-century philosopher seemed to me absolutely in line with UNESCO: he was a supporter of universal education, without racial or financial barriers. He also predicted an audio-visual system, something which was to fascinate Kokoschka. I had no luck locating a text by Comenius in French; the Bibliothèque Nationale possessed his books in Latin only, which meant that I had to have a translation made. I turned to the charmingly obliging Corie Siohan, who discovered — not without some difficulty — extracts from Comenius published by UNESCO.

The Gulbenkian Festival in Lisbon is quite different in character from that of Prague. It generally features two composers from different periods, so in 1968 they chose Purcell and myself. The Gulbenkian Foundation commissioned me to write a piece for the Festival's Chamber Orchestra. I was asked to attend the first performance of *Musique pour Lisbonne*, as well as the opening of an exhibition, organized by Lesure from the Bibliothèque Nationale, which brought together manuscripts, photos and personal souvenirs. I wondered how I was going to get to Lisbon, because this was in May 1968. . . . No planes, no trains and no cars, because there was no petrol! I followed events very closely. At the Conservatoire, some agitators demanded the suppression of Beethoven, Chopin and Schumann and their replacement by Berio, Xenakis and Stockhausen (Boulez was not mentioned!). During a debate at the Chatillon Festival, a woman called vehemently for loudspeakers to be placed in the streets to transmit Xenakis non-stop!

After several days waiting and expecting first one thing, then the other, I ended up taking — not without difficulty — a coach to Brussels, and thence a plane to Lisbon, where I arrived just in time to see a performance of *Les Malheurs d'Orphée* nicely staged by Erlo, and one of *Salade* with new choreography by Lifar, bursting with life and spirit. The concerts and operas were given in a huge auditorium. The tickets were very reasonably priced, and the hall was packed to capacity. The Festival put the same shows on in various provincial Portuguese towns. I would have loved to stay much

[3] This was in 1966.

longer in Portugal, a truly engaging country, but I had to go to Graz, where the Opera was mounting a new version of *Christophe Colomb*. It had already been successfully performed in concert, but I was anxious to judge its effect on stage, especially as my publishers seemed sceptical about it. After the performance they had to admit that the new version was more effective than the old. The staging was totally successful. The company was a true company, without stars, and with a chorus that had rehearsed for over nine months. . . . I could not help being reminded of the revival of *Médée* at the Paris Opéra some weeks previously. It was postponed several times because of union action, and when it finally did reach the stage leaflets were handed out at the entrance to the theatre. Before the performance a representative of the musician's union came out to explain to the audience that the Services Culturels had accepted certain concessions which the Services Financiers had refused, and that as a protest the performance would begin half an hour late. To precede *Médée* they performed Dallapiccola's superb opera *Il prigionero*, a work of a highly poignant tragic lyricism. Before the curtain rose, someone came out to read a letter from the composer informing the audience that he disapproved of the producer's unfortunate idea of having the character of the Prisoner constantly doubled by a dancer. All of this should have had a disastrous effect on the audience, but to my great astonishment they accepted these incidents without demur.

Personally I have nothing but praise for the Paris Opéra, where three operas and one ballet of mine have been staged with care and taste; but I fear that the spirit of discord that currently reigns there compromises the future of our Parisian lyric theatres. I do not sense this insecurity at Nice, where, on the initiative of Monsieur Lattès, who is responsible to the municipality for fine arts, the opera house staged *David* in December 1967 — a difficult piece to bring off on stage, but a success thanks to the goodwill and keen enthusiasm of everyone involved.

Before proceeding to Nice, I stopped off at Aix, because the mayor, Monsieur Ciccolini, had arranged for a plaque to be placed on the wall of Le Bras d'Or, the house where I spent my childhood. It was a joyous ceremony, for the custom is to pay this sort of homage to the dead; yet I myself was present, alive and well and among my Aixois friends — these are rare, alas! — and my wife and son, both very happy. In Aix, the entire week was dedicated to me. I conducted a concert in tandem with Monsieur Villette, the director of the Aix Conservatoire, before a large audience who for the most part were setting eyes on me for the first time! The Bibliothèque Méjanes had a part of the Lisbon exhibition on show, and I was received into the Académie d'Aix. Dr Charpin, who cared for my parents so devotedly until they died, made an extremely moving speech, in which he recalled them with affection, as well as his brother-in-law, my friend Léo Latil.

Sadly, most of the Jews living in Aix vanished during the war; the synagogue was sold and became a Protestant church. During a time when numerous Algerians were settling in Aix, the need for a synagogue became strongly felt. . . . Monsieur Maza, the director of the American Institute, set the project in motion in spite of the various difficulties involved in constructing one. He found a site, obtained the necessary authorizations, and in May 1970 the Rabbi of Aix asked me to cut the first tranch on the site of the future synagogue, which would also be a cultural centre. It was for me a great honour and an emotional moment, for it had been my great-grandfather, Joseph Milhaud, who had inaugurated the old synagogue in 1840.

Even though I no longer have a home there, I love going back to my native city. It is a little unfriendly towards me, to be sure, with its bad paving stones, narrow pavements and excessive traffic, but I'm always glad to be back.

Chapter Forty-Two

From California to Geneva

Monsieur Michelet, the Minister of Cultural Affairs, asked me for a work for the seven-hundredth anniversary of St Louis. Henri Doublier, who was responsible for the realization of this project, made a skilful selection from thirteenth-century texts for the dramatic sections. For the sung sections I took some extracts from two poems on St Louis by Paul Claudel. I composed an opera-oratorio for four characters: an austere work, without any picturesque touches. The entire action is entrusted to the solo singers and small chorus, made up of sixteen singers who take the smaller roles. They are accompanied by a group of thirty instrumentalists playing in the corner of the stage who are drawn from the full orchestra, so as to avoid additional expense. The full orchestra and large chorus are in the pit, and take part only in the interludes between the scenes and at the ends of acts. Happily, in spite of a fairly long interruption for reasons of health, I was able to complete my opera *Saint-Louis, Roi de France* before leaving for the United States in February 1971.

I had decided that this would be my last visit to Mills College, and had already given up Aspen, but not without regret. Together with Madeleine we had done real pioneer work there, and kept it up every summer for twenty years; but the altitude was affecting my health. As for Mills, it kept me too far apart from Daniel and his children. His wife and he had just separated by mutual agreement, and we felt an even greater need to be close to him again.

The announcement of my departure was greeted with sadness, and what I believe to be sincere regret was expressed. I had taught at Mills for more than thirty years! I had been very happy there and used to work well in the calm atmosphere, surrounded by quiet neighbours and good friends, but my age and delicate health made it necessary to make what seemed to everyone a rational decision. This last visit was somewhat unrestful. We had to divest ourselves of furniture, knick-knacks, books and music, and give away our old car — a legend on the campus and in the neighbourhood — which we had had for more than fifteen years.

Shortly before his death, Frank Lloyd Wright had been commissioned to plan the construction of administrative buildings for Marin County, a few kilometres from San Francisco; school, library, town-hall, courthouse, prison and a concert hall. We were deeply impressed by this brilliant architect's ideas. Blue and maroon buildings backed onto the hill and seemed to blend into it. Trees grew along the walkways, and one would constantly come across flowery courtyards. Everything formed part of a natural environment while being perfectly conceived for its particular purpose. Unfortunately the concert hall was not yet finished. I had hoped to be present at its inauguration, when they were to play my *Suite en sol*, composed especially for the occasion; but continual strikes had held the work up.

Several times a year the San Francisco Symphony organizes concerts for primary school children who are brought in by bus, sometimes from a good distance. It is fascinating to watch hundreds of black and white youngsters listening attentively to a programme designed for them and introduced intelligently by the conductor. They play works from every period and concertos with very young soloists. It was thus that I heard my Percussion Concerto, admirably performed by a fourteen-year-old boy. I was asked to compose a piece for these concerts and did so with great pleasure. . . . I introduced clapping, stamping and whistling into my score; specific sounds that the young audience had to make at certain moments. The music department at Mills College put on a concert in my honour. I suggested works of widely varying periods to show that there was no stylistic break between them. The department's director, Dr Margaret Lyon, had the charming idea of inviting all 420 students who had worked with me; not all of them came, but a large number gathered from all over the United States. Mme Agnès Albert commissioned Daniel to paint my portrait, and donated it to the college, where it was hung at the entrance to the concert hall. I said with a smile, 'So you will never see the back of me.' We were pleased to see this painting by Daniel since his entire output had been destroyed by fire in 1970, and he had needed great courage to resume work.

But I had to organize our life in Europe. I could not imagine living the whole year in Paris. There were too many disruptions there: it was difficult to work, to get about and to relax. However, I needed to live in a city with doctors and hospitals. I like city life but cannot be overwhelmed by it. Geneva seemed to have all the qualities required to substitute for California — except, of course, for the climate! I took a small apartment there and I can compose in peace, just like at Mills.

This winter (1971) I wrote a choral work, *Promesse de Dieu*, for the 200th anniversary of Dickinson College, selecting extracts from Isaiah and Ezekiel predicting the restoration of Jerusalem.

Some years ago, at the request of the radio station at Graz, I wrote *Musique pour Graz* for small orchestra. They asked me to nominate one of my former students to be commissioned to write a piece for the same programme. The station also wanted me to write an unaccompanied choral piece, allowing me to realize a project I had been thinking about for a very long time: to create a comedy for unaccompanied choir like Vecchi's *L'Amfiparnaso* or Banchieri's *Festino*. I drew on a little comedy by Regnard, one of the ones they used to perform at the fair at Saint-Germain: *Les Momies d'Egypte*. The text was elegant, amusing and lively.

And so I embark upon my eightieth year! Celebrations are already under way. In Rome I conducted *Les Choëphores* in a concert of my works at the Accademia Santa Cecilia. A few weeks earlier, I had the pleasure of hearing the first performance of *Saint-Louis* on Italian Radio. This opera has had a curious history up till now. Commissioned by the French government, it was turned down by French Radio, premièred in Rome and staged at the Rio de Janeiro Opera.

Thanks to the loyal attentions of Monsieur Lattès, the Nice Opera put on *Fiesta, Le Pauvre Matelot* and *Vendanges*, a ballet that had lain on my shelves for over twenty years. At Aix-en-Provence the Festival will restage *Les Malheurs d'Orphée*, and a young people's cultural group under the direction of Monsieur Nugues will put on two of my quartets in the Place d'Albertas and *Le Pauvre Matelot* in the Parc Jourdan. Marius Constant, to whom I am indebted for an excellent concert at the Espace Cardin — the first actual celebration in my honour this year — is going to conduct a concert of my works at the synagogue in Carpentras. In February 1973, J.S. Bereau conducts a concert performance of *Saint-Louis* in Rouen.

And then there is Brussels, which has so often been linked to my music through the work of Paul Collaer. Next December the Brussels Philharmonic will devote an entire week to my music, and I will be officially received into the Belgian Royal Academy. Other honours have been bestowed on me: this year, it was the Grand Prix National de la Musique et l'Institut. I had been asked to apply for it many times but I turned each entreaty down. But when Emmanuel Bondeville, permanent secretary of the Institute, asked me: 'If you didn't have to write a letter, or attend, and if you were nominated, would you accept or not?', I found it impossible to reject such a friendly offer. I was unanimously elected to Marcel Dupré's seat.

I hope to be present at most of these ceremonies, as well as at the inauguration of the Aix Conservatoire, which will be named after me, but I am never certain of fulfilling my plans. Much as I am used to disappointments of this sort, they are none the less painful to me. However, if I were to draw up a balance-sheet for the past eighty-four years, I couldn't complain. In spite of my miserable physical state, I have had a marvellous life.

In 1962 I was asked to talk about myself at an American college. I recalled my parents, who were so understanding, my wife, my son and his children, who have brought me nothing but joy. In short, I said that I was a happy man. At that moment I sensed general consternation — almost panic — in the hall. Some students came to talk to me after the conference: how had I been able to create in these conditions? An artist *needs* to suffer! I replied that I had managed to arrange things differently.

How pleasant it is to end these memoirs by repeating that I have had a happy life, and if God permits, I hope to continue to work and to enjoy the company of my wife and my children for a few more years. . . .

June 1972

Darius Milhaud died in Geneva, June 22, 1974.

Catalogue of Works by
Darius Milhaud

1909

Désespoir, for voice and piano
(unpublished)

1910–12

Poèmes de Francis Jammes, Vols 1 and
2, for voice and piano, Op. 1
(unpublished)

1910–14

La Brebis égarée, opera, Op. 4

1910–16

Trois Poèmes de Léo Latil, for voice
and piano, Op. 2 (unpublished)

1911

Violin Sonata No. 1, Op. 3

A la Toussaint, for voice and piano
(unpublished)

1912

String Quartet No. 1, Op. 5

1912–13

Poèmes de Francis Jammes, Vol. 3, for
voice and piano, Op. 6
(unpublished)

*Sept Poèmes de la connaissance de
l'est*, for voice and piano, Op. 7

1913

Suite, for piano solo, Op. 8

Alissa, for voice and piano, Op. 9
(revised 1931)

*Trois Poèmes en prose de Lucile de
Chateaubriand*, for voice and piano,
Op. 10

Poème sur un cantique de Camargue,
for piano and orchestra, Op. 13
(unpublished)

Agamemnon, opera (1st of the trilogy
'*L'Orestie*'), Op. 14

1913–14

Trois Poèmes romantiques, Set 1, for
voice and piano, Op. 11 (unpublished)

*Symphonic Suite No. 1, 'La Brebis
égarée'*, Op. 12

1913–19

Protée, incidental music, Op. 17

1914

Sonata, for piano and two violins, Op.
15

Le Printemps, for violin and piano, Op.
18

Trois Poèmes romantiques, Set 2, for
voice and piano, Op. 19 (unpublished)

Quatre Poèmes de Léo Latil, for voice
and piano, Op. 20

Le Château, for voice and piano, Op. 21
(unpublished)

Poème du Gitanjali, for voice and
piano, Op. 22

Mazurka, for piano solo, in '*Album des
Six*'

1914–15
String Quartet No. 2, Op. 16

1915
Variations on a theme by Cliquet, for piano solo, Op. 23 (unpublished)
D'un Cahier inédit du journal d'Eugénie de Guérin, for voice and piano, Op. 27
L'Arbre exotique, for voice and piano, Op. 28 (unpublished)
Notre Dame de Sarrance, for solo voice, Op. 29 (unpublished)
Deux Poèmes d'amour, for voice and piano, Op. 30
Deux Poèmes de Coventry Patmore, for voice and piano, Op. 31

1915–16
Les Choëphores, opera (2nd of the trilogy '*L'Orestie*'), Op. 24

1915–17
Quatre Poèmes de Paul Claudel, for baritone and piano, Op. 26

1915–19
Printemps, Vol. 1, for piano solo, Op. 25

1916
String Quartet No. 3 (with soprano), Op. 32

Piano Sonata, Op. 33
Poèmes juifs, for voice and piano, Op. 34
Child Poems, for voice and piano, Op. 36
Trois Poèmes, for voice and piano/chamber ensemble, Op. 37 (unpublished)
No. 34 de l'église habillée de feuilles, for vocal quartet and piano (six hands), Op. 38 (unpublished)

1916–17
Deux Poèmes du Gardener, for two voices and piano, Op. 35 (unpublished)

1916–19
Deux Poèmes, for unaccompanied voices, Op. 39

1917
Violin Sonata No. 2, Op. 40
Le Retour de l'enfant prodigue, for mezzo-soprano, tenor, three baritones and orchestra, Op. 42
Chamber Symphony No. 1 '*Le Printemps*', Op. 43
Chansons bas, for voice and piano, Op. 44
Verso Carioca, for voice and piano, Op. 44b (unpublished)
Deux Poèmes de Rimbaud, for voice and piano, Op. 45 (unpublished)

1917–22
Les Euménides, opera (3rd of the trilogy '*L'Orestie*'), Op. 41

1918
String Quartet No. 4, Op. 46
Sonata, for piano, flute, oboe and clarinet, Op. 47
L'Homme et son désir, ballet, Op. 48
Chamber Symphony No. 2 'Pastorale', Op. 49
Poèmes de Francis Jammes, Vol. 4, for voice and piano, Op. 50 (unpublished)
Deux petits airs, for voice and piano, Op. 51
Deux Poèmes Tupis, for four women's voices and handclapping, Op. 52 (unpublished)
Psalm 136, for solo voices, men's chorus and orchestra, Op. 53
L'Ours et la lune, incidental music

1919
Psalm 129, for voice and orchestra, Op. 53b
Poèmes de Frances Thompson, for voice and piano, Op. 54 (unpublished)
Les Soirées de Petrograde, for voice and piano, Op. 55
Machines agricoles, for voice and chamber ensemble, Op. 56
Symphonic Suite No. 2 '*Protée*', Op. 57
Le Boeuf sur le toit, ballet, Op. 58

Cinéma-fantaisie, for violin and piano/
orchestra, Op. 58b

Tango des Fratellini, for piano solo,
Op. 58c

1919–20

Printemps, Vol. 2, for piano solo, Op.
66

1920

Trois Poèmes de Jean Cocteau, for
voice and piano, Op. 59

Catalogue de fleurs, for voice and
piano/chamber ensemble, Op. 60

Cinq Etudes, for piano and orchestra,
Op. 63

String Quartet No. 5, Op. 64

Feuilles de température, for voice and
piano, Op. 65 (unpublished)

Saudades do Brazil, for piano solo, Op.
67

Caramel mou, for piano solo, or
clarinet, trumpet, trombone, piano and
voice/saxophone, Op. 68

Cocktail, for voice and three clarinets,
Op. 69

1920–21

Sérénade, for orchestra, Op. 62

Saudades do Brazil, for orchestra, Op.
67b

1920–23

Ballade, for piano and orchestra, Op. 61

1921

Les Mariés de la Tour Eiffel, ballet, Op.
70

Chamber Symphony No. 3 'Sérénade',
Op. 71

Psalm 126, for unaccompanied men's
chorus, Op. 72

Poème du Journal intime de Léo Latil,
for voice and piano, Op. 73

Chamber Symphony No. 4, Op. 74

1922

Chamber Symphony No. 5, Op. 75

Sonatine, for flute and piano, Op. 76

String Quartet No. 6, Op. 77

Trois Rag caprices, for piano solo or
chamber ensemble, Op. 78

1923

Chamber Symphony No. 6, Op. 79

Quatre Poèmes de Catulle, for voice
and violin, Op. 80

La Création du monde, ballet, Op. 81

*Recitatives for Chabrier's 'Une
éducation manquée'*, Op. 82

1924

Salade, ballet, Op. 83

Le Train bleu, ballet, Op. 84

Les Malheurs d'Orphée, opera, Op. 85

1925

Six Chants populaires hébraïques, for
voice and piano/orchestra, Op. 86

String Quartet No. 7, Op. 87

*Deux Hymnes 'Hymne de Sion' and
'Israel est vivant'*, for voice and piano,
Op. 88

Deux Hymnes, for orchestra, Op. 88b

1925–27

Esther de Carpentras, opera, Op. 89

1926

La Création du monde, arranged for
string quintet, Op. 81b

Le Carnaval d'Aix, for piano and
orchestra, Op. 83b

Pièce de circonstance, for voice and
piano, Op. 90 (unpublished)

Impromptu, for violin and piano, Op. 91
(unpublished)

Le Pauvre Matelot, opera, Op. 92

1927

Violin Concerto No. 1, Op. 93

L'Enlèvement d'Europe, opéra-minute,
Op. 94

Polka, for orchestra or piano solo, Op.
95, in 'L'Eventail de Jeanne'

*Prières journalières à l'usage des juifs
du Comtat Venaissin*, for voice and
piano, Op. 96

Trois Caprices de Paganini, for violin and piano, Op. 97

L'Abandon d'Ariane, opéra-minute, Op. 98

La Délivrance de Thésée, opéra-minute, Op. 99

Sonatine, for clarinet and piano, Op. 100

1928

La Bien-aimée, ballet, Op. 101

Christophe Colomb, opera, Op. 102

Cantate pour louer le Seigneur, for chorus, children's chorus and orchestra, Op. 103

Actualités, film score, Op. 104

Vocalise, for unaccompanied voice, Op. 105

1929

Quatrain, for voice and piano, Op.106

La P'tite Lilie, film score, Op. 107

Viola Concerto No. 1, Op. 108

1929–30

Percussion Concerto, Op. 109

1930

Maximilien, opera, Op. 110

Suite from 'Maximilien', for orchestra, Op. 110b

Choral, for piano, Op. 111 (unpublished)

A Flower Given to My Child, for voice and piano (unpublished)

1931

Organ Sonata, Op. 112

1932

Deux Poèmes de Cendrars, for unaccompanied voices, Op. 113

Deux Elégies romaines, for unaccompanied women's voices, Op. 114

L'Automne, for piano solo, Op. 115

La Mort du tyran, for chorus and chamber ensemble, Op. 116

L'Annonce faite à Marie, incidental music, for vocal quartet and chamber ensemble, Op. 117

A propos de bottes, for voices and piano or chamber ensemble, Op. 118

Un petit peu de musique, for voices and piano or chamber ensemble, Op. 119

Le Château des papes, incidental music, Op. 120 (unpublished)

Adages, for vocal quartet and chamber ensemble, Op. 120b

Suite, for ondes martenot and piano, Op. 120c

String Quartet No. 8, Op. 121

1933

Devant sa main nue, for unaccompanied women's voices, Op. 122

Le Funeste retour, for voice, Op. 123 (unpublished)

Les Songes, ballet, Op. 124

Liturgie comtadine, for voice and piano/orchestra, Op. 125

Hallo Everybody, film score, Op. 126 (unpublished)

Piano Concerto No. 1, Op. 127

Madame Bovary, film score, Op. 128

L'Album de Madame Bovary, for piano solo, Op. 128b

Trois Valses, for piano solo, Op. 128c

Deux Chansons, for voice and piano, Op. 128d

Quatre Romances sans paroles, for piano solo, Op. 129

Le Tour de l'Exposition, for piano solo, Op. 162 (revised 1937), in 'A L'Exposition'

1934

Pan et Syrinx, for vocal sextet and chamber ensemble, Op. 130

Se plaire sur la même fleur, incidental music, Op. 131 (unpublished)

Les Amours de Ronsard, for vocal quartet or chorus and chamber ensemble, Op. 132

Un petit peu d'exercice, for voices and piano or chamber ensemble, Op. 133

Exercice musical, for pipes and piano, Op. 134

Concertino de printemps, for violin and orchestra, Op. 135

Cello Concerto No. 1, Op. 136

L'Hippocampe, film score, Op. 137 (unpublished)

Tartarin de Tarascon, film score, Op. 138 (unpublished)

Le Cycle de la création, incidental music, Op. 139 (unpublished)

1935

String Quartet No. 9, Op. 140

La Sagesse, for narrator, soloists, chorus and orchestra, Op. 141

Le Cygne I & II, for voice and piano, Op. 142 (unpublished)

Quatrain, for voice and piano, Op. 143 (unpublished)

Dixième sonate de Baptiste Anet (1729), free adaptation, for violin and piano, Op. 144

Le Faiseur, incidental music, Op. 145 (unpublished)

Voix d'enfants, film score, Op. 146 (unpublished)

Pastorale, for oboe, clarinet and bassoon, Op. 147

1935–36

Bolivar, incidental music, Op. 148 (unpublished)

Trois Chansons de négresse, for voice and piano, Op. 148b

1936

La Folle du ciel, incidental music, Op. 149 (unpublished)

The Beloved Vagabond, film score, Op. 150 (unpublished)

Tu ne m'échapperas jamais, incidental music, Op. 151 (unpublished)

Six Chansons de théâtre, for voice and piano, Op. 151b

Bertran de Born, Moyen Age fleuri, Trois Chansons de troubadour, Op. 152

Suite provençale, Op. 152b

Le Trompeur de Séville, Op. 152c

Le Quatorze Juillet, incidental music, Op. 153 (unpublished)

Introduction et marche funèbre, for orchestra or wind band, Op. 153b

Le Conquérant, incidental music, Op. 154 (unpublished)

Fragments dramatiques, for orchestra, Op. 154b (unpublished)

Cantique du Rhône, for unaccompanied voices, Op. 155

Amal, ou La Lettre du roi, incidental music, Op. 156 (unpublished)

Le Voyageur sans bagages, incidental music, Op. 157 (unpublished)

Suite, for violin, clarinet and piano, Op. 157b

Jules César, incidental music, Op. 158 (unpublished)

1936–37

Trois Chansons de négresse, for voice and orchestra, Op. 148c

La Fête de la lumière, for voice and chamber ensemble, Op. 159 (unpublished)

1937

La Duchesse d'Amalfi, incidental music, Op. 160 (unpublished)

Roméo et Juliette, incidental music, Op. 161 (unpublished)

Suite d'après Corrette, for oboe, clarinet and bassoon, Op. 161b

Le Tour de l'exposition, for piano, Op. 162

Liberté, incidental music, Op. 163 (unpublished)

Cantate pour l'inauguration du musée de l'Homme, for vocal quartet, speaker and chamber ensemble, Op. 164

Le Médecin volant, incidental music, Op. 165 (unpublished)

Cantate de la paix, for unaccompanied chorus, Op. 166

Scaramouche, for two pianos, Op. 165b

Cinq Chansons, for voice and piano, Op. 167

Cantate nuptiale, for voice and orchestra, Op. 168

Main tendue à tous, for unaccompanied chorus, Op. 169

Les Deux Cités, for unaccompanied chorus, Op. 170

Chansons de l'opéra du gueux, incidental music, Op. 171

Chansons du carnaval de Londres, for voice and piano/orchestra, Op. 171b

Le Carnaval de Londres, for chamber ensemble, Op. 172

Naissance d'une cité, incidental music, Op. 173

Chanson du capitaine; La Java de la femme, for voice and piano, Op. 173b

Mollenard, film score, Op. 174 (unpublished)

Macbeth, incidental music, Op. 175 (unpublished)

La Citadelle du silence, film score, Op. 176 (unpublished)

Hécube, incidental music, Op. 177 (unpublished)

Rondeau, for voice and piano, Op. 178 (unpublished)

Holem tsaudi — Gam hayom (harmonization of a Palestinian tune), for voice and piano, Op. 179

Quatrain, for voice and piano, Op. 180 (unpublished)

L'Oiseau, for orchestra, Op. 181 (unpublished)

Grands feux, film score, Op. 182 (unpublished)

Prends cette rose, for two voices and orchestra, Op. 183

La Conquête du ciel, film score, Op. 184 (unpublished)

1938

Cantate de l'enfant et de la mère, for narrator and chamber ensemble, Op. 185

Plutus, incidental music, Op. 186 (unpublished)

La Tragédie impériale, Raspoutine, film score, Op. 187 (unpublished)

Fantaisie pastorale, for piano and orchestra, Op. 188

Les quatre éléments, for two voices and orchestra, Op. 189 (not extant)

Tricolore, incidental music, Op. 190 (unpublished)

Médée, opera, Op. 191

Le Bal des voleurs, incidental music, Op. 192

La Première Famille, incidental music, Op. 193 (unpublished)

Magali, for chorus and orchestra, Op. 194

Récréation, for solo voice, Op. 195

Les Otages, film score, Op. 196 (unpublished)

Agamemnon, radio score (unpublished)

1938–39

Concerto for flute, violin and orchestra, Op. 197

1939

Scaramouche, for saxophone and orchestra, Op. 165c

Islands, film score, Op. 198 (unpublished)

Trois Elégies, for two voices and strings, Op. 199

Hamlet, incidental music, Op. 200 (unpublished)

Incantations, for unaccompanied men's chorus, Op. 201

Espoir, film score, Op. 202 (unpublished)

Cortège funèbre, for orchestra, Op. 202b

Voyage au pays du rêve, radio score, Op. 203 (unpublished)

Cavalcade d'amour, film score, Op. 204 (unpublished)

La Cheminée du roi René, for wind quintet, Op. 205

Quatrains valaisans, for unaccompanied chorus, Op. 206

La Reine de Saba (harmonization of a Palestinian tune), for string quartet, Op. 207 (unpublished)

Gulf Stream, film score, Op. 208 (unpublished)

Fanfare, for orchestra, Op. 209 (unpublished)

Symphony No. 1, Op. 210

1940

Couronne de gloire, for voice and chamber ensemble, Op. 211

Indicatif et marche pour les bons d'armement, for brass and percussion, Op. 212 (unpublished)

Cantate de la guerre, for unaccompanied chorus, Op. 213

Sornettes, for children's voices, Op. 214 (unpublished)

Un petit ange de rien du tout, incidental music, Op. 215 (unpublished)

Le Voyage d'été, for voice and piano, Op. 216

Cours de solfège; Papillon, papillon-ette, for children's voices and piano, Op. 217 (unpublished)

String Quartet No. 10 (Birthday Quartet), Op. 218

Moïse, ballet, Op. 219

Opus Americanum No. 2, for chamber ensemble or orchestra, Op. 219b

Introduction and Allegro (orchestration of music by François Couperin), for orchestra, Op. 220

Sonatine, for two violins, Op. 221

Sonatine à trois, for violin, viola and cello, Op. 221b

1940–41

Quatre chansons de Ronsard, for voice and piano/orchestra, Op. 223

1941

Black Keys (Touches noires): White Keys (Touches blanches), for piano solo, Op. 222

La Bien-aimée, ballet (new orchestration), Op. 101b

Scaramouche, for clarinet and orchestra, Op. 165d

Mills Fanfare, for strings, Op. 224 (unpublished)

Piano Concerto No. 2, Op. 225

Sonatine, for violin and viola, Op. 226

Four Sketches (Esquisses), for piano solo or chamber ensemble, Op. 227

Madrigal — Pastoral (originally *Eclogue*), for clarinet and piano, or wind quintet, Op. 227b

First Concerto for two pianos and orchestra, Op. 228

Pastorale, for organ, Op. 229

Clarinet Concerto, Op. 230

Choral, for piano solo, in 'Hommage à Paderewski'

1942

L'Annonce faite à Marie, incidental music (second version), Op. 231 (unpublished)

Nine Preludes, for organ, Op. 231b

Cinq Prières, for voice and organ/piano, Op. 231c

String Quartet No. 11, Op. 232

Rêves, for voice and piano, Op. 233

Suite anglaise, for violin (or harmonica) and orchestra, Op. 234

Fanfare de la liberté, for orchestra, Op. 235

1942–43

Quatre Visages, for viola and piano, Op. 238

1943

Bolivar, opera, Op. 236

La Libertadora, for two pianos, Op. 236b

Les Songes, for two pianos, Op. 237

1944

Borechou; Schema Israël, for cantor, chorus and organ, Op. 239

Viola Sonata No. 1, Op. 240

Caïn et Abel, for narrator and orchestra, Op. 241 (unpublished)

Air, for viola and orchestra, Op. 242 (unpublished)

Jeux de printemps, for chamber ensemble or orchestra, Op. 243

Viola Sonata No. 2, Op. 244

La Muse ménagère, for piano solo or chamber ensemble, Op. 245

La Libération des Antilles, for voice and piano, Op. 246

Symphony No. 2, Op. 247

Suite française, for orchestra or wind band, Op. 248

Sailor Song, from '*Suite anglaise*', for violin and piano

1944–45

Le Bal martiniquais, for two pianos, or orchestra, Op. 249

1944–47

Accueil amical, for piano solo, Op. 326

1945

Kaddisch, for cantor, chorus (ad. lib.) and organ, Op. 250

Elégie, for cello and piano, Op. 251

String Quartet No. 12, Op. 252

Printemps lointain, for voice and piano, Op. 253 (unpublished)

Introduction; Marche; Fête de la victoire, additional movements for a ballet version of '*Suite française*', Op. 254

Cello Concerto No. 2, Op. 255

Danses de Jacarémirim, for violin and piano, Op. 256

Sonata for violin and harpsichord, Op. 257

Duo, for two violins, Op. 258

Les Cloches (based on Edgar Allan Poe's 'The Bells'), ballet, Op. 259

Deux Marches, for orchestra or wind band, Op. 260

1946

Les Cloches, suite for orchestra, Op. 259b

Pledge to Mills, student song, Op. 261 (unpublished)

Farandoleurs, for violin and piano, Op. 262

Violin Concerto No. 2, Op. 263

Lidoire, incidental music, Op. 264 (unpublished)

Chants de misère, for voice and piano, Op. 265

Six Sonnets composés au secret, for unaccompanied voices, Op. 266

String Quartet No. 13, Op. 268

Une journée, for piano solo, Op. 269

Piano Concerto No. 3, Op. 270

Symphony No. 3 'Te Deum', for chorus and orchestra, Op. 271

The Private Affairs of Bel-Ami, film score, Op. 272 (unpublished)

1946–47

Sept Danses sur des airs palestiniens, for chamber ensemble, Op. 267 (unpublished)

1947

Dreams That Money Can Buy, film score, Op. 273 (unpublished)

String Trio, Op. 274

Carnaval à la Nouvelle-Orléans, for two pianos, Op. 275

Trois Poèmes, for voice and piano, Op. 276

Méditation, for piano solo, Op. 277 (unpublished)

Concerto for marimba, vibraphone and orchestra, Op. 278

Service sacré, for baritone, narrator, chorus and organ (or orchestra), Op. 279

La Maison de Bernarda Alba, incidental music, Op. 280 (unpublished)

Symphony No. 4 '1848', Op. 281

1948

Le Grand testament, radio score, Op. 282 (unpublished)

'Adame miroir, ballet, Op. 283

Paris, for four pianos, Op. 284

Sheherazade, incidental music, Op. 285 (unpublished)

L'Apothéose de Molière (based on music by Baptiste Anet), for chamber ensemble, Op. 286

Kentuckiana, for two pianos or orchestra, Op. 287

Le Jeu de Robin et de Marion, incidental music, Op. 288

L'Enfant aimé, for piano solo, Op. 289

L'choh dodi, for cantor, chorus and organ, Op. 290 (unpublished)

1948–49

String Quartets Nos 14 & 15, also *String Octet*, Op. 291

1949

Naissance de Vénus, for unaccompanied chorus, Op. 292

Piano Sonata No. 2, Op. 293

Les Rêves de Jacob, for wind quintet, Op. 294

Piano Concerto No. 4, Op. 295

Ballade nocturne, for voice and piano, Op. 296

La Fin du monde, radio score, Op. 297 (unpublished)

1949–50

Barba Garibo, for chorus and orchestra, Op. 298

La Cueillette des citrons, ballet, Op. 298b

1950

Gauguin, film score, Op. 299 (unpublished)

Suite opus 300, for two pianos and orchestra, Op. 300

Le Repos du septième jour, radio score, Op. 301 (unpublished)

Jeu, for piano solo, Op. 302

String Quartet No. 16, Op. 303

La Vie commence demain, film score, Op. 304 (unpublished)

Les Temps faciles, for voice and piano, Op. 305 (unpublished)

Le Conte d'hiver, incidental music, Op. 306 (unpublished)

String Quartet No. 17, Op. 307

1950–51

String Quartet No. 18, Op. 308

1951

Concertino d'automne, for two pianos and chamber ensemble, Op. 309

Cantata from Proverbs, for women's chorus and chamber ensemble, Op. 310

Concertino d'été, for viola and orchestra, Op. 311

String Quintet No. 1, Op. 312

West Point Suite, for wind band, Op. 313

Les Miracles de la foi, for narrator, tenor, chorus and orchestra, Op. 314

Le Candélabre à sept branches, for piano solo, Op. 315

1952

Suite concertante, for piano and orchestra, Op. 278b

String Quintet No. 2, Op. 316

Vendanges, ballet, Op. 317

Christophe Colomb, incidental music, Op. 318

Petites légendes, for voice and piano, Op. 319

1952–53

David, opera, Op. 320

1953

Samaël, radio score, Op. 321 (unpublished)

Symphony No. 5, Op. 322

Harp Concerto, Op. 323

Sonatine, for violin and cello, Op. 324

String Quintet No. 3, Op. 325

Concertino d'hiver, for trombone and chamber ensemble, Op. 327

Le Dibbouk, radio score, Op. 328 (unpublished)

Suite campagnarde, for orchestra, Op. 329

Ouverture méditerranéenne, for orchestra, Op. 330

1953–54

Hymne de glorification, for piano solo, Op. 331

1954

Suite cisalpine, for cello and orchestra, Op. 332

Etude poétique, radio score, Op. 333 (unpublished)

Saül, incidental music, Op. 334 (unpublished)

Caprice, for clarinet and piano, Op. 335

Danse, for saxophone and piano, Op. 335b

Eglogue, for flute and piano, Op. 335c (unpublished)

Ils étaient tous des volontaires, film score, Op. 336 (unpublished)

Sonatine, for oboe and piano, Op. 337

Le Château du feu, for chorus and orchestra, Op. 338

Trois Psaumes de David, for unaccompanied chorus, Op. 339

1954–55

Viola Concerto No. 2, Op. 340

1955

Protée, incidental music (second version), Op. 341

Pensée amicale, for strings, Op. 342 (unpublished)

Symphony No. 6, Op. 343

Symphony No. 7, Op. 344

Service pour la veille du Sabbat, for children's chorus and organ, Op. 345

Piano Concerto No. 5, Op. 346

Deux Poèmes, for unaccompanied voices, Op. 347

Petite suite, for organ, Op. 348

Juanito, incidental music, Op. 349 (unpublished)

1956

Les quatre éléments, for voice and orchestra, Op. 189b

String Quintet No. 4, Op. 350

Duo concertant, for clarinet and piano, Op. 351

Fontaines et sources, for voice and piano/orchestra, Op. 352

La Couronne de Marguerite; Valse en forme de rondo, for piano solo, in 'Variations sur le nom de M Long', Op. 353

Valse en forme de rondo (La Couronne de Marguerite), for orchestra, Op. 353b

Sonatine, for piano solo, Op. 354

Tristesses, for voice and piano, Op. 355

Le Chat, for voice and piano, Op. 356 (unpublished)

Le Mariage de la feuille et du cliché, for speaker, vocal quartet, chorus and orchestra, Op. 357

1956–57

Le Globe trotter, for piano solo or chamber ensemble, Op. 358

Ecoutez mes enfants, for voice and organ, Op. 359 (unpublished)

1957

Les Charmes de la vie, for piano solo, Op. 360

Les Charmes de la vie, for chamber ensemble, Op. 360b

Aspen Serenade, for chamber ensemble, Op. 361

Symphony No. 8, 'Rhodanienne', Op. 362

Symphoniette, for strings, Op. 363

Celle qui n'était plus, film score, Op. 364 (unpublished)

Oboe Concerto, Op. 365

Segoviana, for guitar, Op. 366

La Rose des vents, ballet, Op. 367

1958

Divertissement, for wind quintet, Op. 299b

String Sextet, Op. 368

La Tragédie humaine, for chorus and orchestra, Op. 369

Fiesta, opera, Op. 370

Huit Poèmes de Jorge Guillen, for unaccompanied chorus, Op. 371

Péron et Evita, television score, Op. 372 (unpublished)

Concert royal (Violin Concerto No. 3), for violin and orchestra, Op. 373

1958–59

La Branche des oiseaux, ballet, Op. 374

1959

Paris, suite for orchestra, Op. 284b

Burma Road, television score, Op. 375 (unpublished)

Symphonie concertante, for trumpet, horn, bassoon, double bass and orchestra, Op. 376

Cello Sonata, Op. 377

Sonatine, for viola and cello, Op. 378

Mother Courage, incidental music, Op. 379 (unpublished)

Symphony No. 9, Op. 380

1959–60

Cantate de la croix de charité, for soprano, tenor, bass, chorus, children's chorus and orchestra, Op. 381

Symphony No. 10, Op. 382

1960

Sonatine pastorale, for solo violin, Op. 383

Symphony No. 11 'Romantique', Op. 384

Les Funérailles de Phocion (Hommage à Nicolas Poussin), for orchestra, Op. 385

Cantate sur des poèmes de Chaucer, for chorus and orchestra, Op. 386

Aubade, for orchestra, Op. 387

Cantate de l'initiation (Bar mitzvah Israël 1948–1961), for chorus and orchestra, Op. 388

1961

Chamber Concerto, Op. 389

Symphony No. 12 'Rurale', Op. 390

Neige sur la fleuve, for chamber ensemble, Op. 391 (unpublished)

Judith, incidental music, Op. 392 (unpublished)

Traversée, for unaccompanied chorus, Op. 393

Second Concerto for two pianos and chamber ensemble, Op. 394

1962

L'Invocation à l'ange Raphaël, for women's chorus and orchestra, Op. 395

Fanfare, for wind, Op. 396 (unpublished)

Ouverture philharmonique, for orchestra, Op. 397

Suite de quatrains, for narrator and chamber ensemble, Op. 398

A Frenchman in New York, for orchestra, Op. 399

Fanfare, for two trumpets and trombone, Op. 400

1963

Suite de sonnets, for vocal quartet and chamber ensemble, Op. 401

Caroles, for chorus and chamber ensemble, Op. 402

Préparatif à la mort en allégorie maritime, for voice and piano, Op. 403 (unpublished)

Pacem in Terris, for contralto, baritone, chorus and orchestra, Op. 404

Meurtre d'un grand chef d'Etat, for orchestra, Op. 405

Ode pour les morts des guerres, for orchestra, Op. 406

1964

Harpsichord Concerto, Op. 407

String Septet, Op. 408

L'Amour chante, for voice and piano, Op. 409

Adieu, for voice, flute, viola and harp, Op. 410

Adam, for unaccompanied voices, Op. 411 (unpublished)

1964–65

La Mère coupable, opera, Op. 412

1965

Music for Boston, for violin and orchestra, Op. 414

Musique pour Prague, for orchestra, Op. 415

Elégie pour Pierre, for viola and percussion, Op. 416 (unpublished)

1965–66

Cantata from Job, for baritone, chorus and organ, Op. 413

1966

Piano Quartet, Op. 417

Musique pour l'Indiana, for orchestra, Op. 418

Jerusalem à Carpentras, incidental music, Op. 419 (unpublished)

Musique pour Lisbonne, for chamber ensemble, Op. 420

Hommage à Comenius, for two voices and orchestra, Op. 421

Musique pour la Nouvelle-Orleans, for orchestra, Op. 422

1967

Vezelay 'La colline éternelle', for voice and orchestra, Op. 423 (unpublished)

Promenade Concert, for orchestra, Op. 424

Cantate de Psaumes, for voice and orchestra, Op. 425

L'Histoire de Tobie et Sara, incidental music, Op. 426 (unpublished)

1968

Paul Claudel, film score, Op. 427

Symphonie pour l'univers Claudelien, for orchestra, Op. 427b

Piano Trio, Op. 428

1968–69

Musique pour Graz, for chamber ensemble, Op. 429

1969

Stanford Serenade, for oboe and chamber ensemble, Op. 430

Suite en sol, for orchestra, Op. 431

Musique pour Ars Nova, for chamber ensemble, Op. 432

1969–70

Six danses en trois mouvements, for piano solo/two pianos, Op. 433

1970

Musique de théâtre, for wind band, Op. 334b

Saint-Louis, Roi de France, opera-oratorio, Op. 434

1971

Hommage à Igor Stravinsky, for string quartet, Op. 435

Musique pour San Francisco, for orchestra (with audience participation), Op. 436

Harp Sonata, Op. 437

Fugue du massacre, second version of a lost movement of the ballet '*Les Mariés de la Tour Eiffel*', Op. 70b

1971–72

Promesse de Dieu, for unaccompanied chorus, Op. 438

1972

Les Momies d'Egypte, for unaccompanied chorus, Op. 439

Ode pour Jérusalem, for orchestra, Op. 440

Ani maamin, un chant perdu et retrouvé, for four narrators, soprano, chorus and orchestra, Op. 441

1973

Etudes, for string quartet, Op. 442

Wind Quintet, Op. 443

Index of Names

Index of Milhaud's Compositions

Opus numbers given in square brackets [ ]